A WING AND A PRAYER

Rev Malcolm Weisman OBE, MA (Oxon) Barrister at Law; Recorder SE Circuit; Chaplain to her Majesty's Forces; to universities; and to the Lord Mayor of Westminster (1992-3) and several other Mayors; Chairman and Gen Sec of Allied Air Force Chaplains' Committee; Member Chief Rabbi's Cabinet; and Minister for Small Communities. Ambassador, Trustee or Patron of many educational, cultural and interfaith organisations country and worldwide.

A WING AND A PRAYER
My Life and Times

MALCOLM WEISMAN

VALLENTINE MITCHELL
LONDON • CHICAGO

First published in 2024 by Vallentine Mitchell

Catalyst House,	814 N. Franklin Street,
720 Centennial Court,	Chicago, Illinois,
Centennial Park, Elstree WD6 3SY, UK	IL 60610 USA

www.vmbooks.com

Copyright © 2024 Malcolm Weisman

British Library Cataloguing in Publication Data:
An entry can be found on request

ISBN 978 1 80371 051 8 (Paper)
ISBN 978 1 80371 052 5 (Ebook)
ISBN 978 1 80371 053 2 (Kindle)

Library of Congress Cataloging in Publication Data:
An entry can be found on request

All rights reserved. No part of this publication may be reproduced in any form or by any means, electronic, mechanical, photocopying, reading or otherwise, without the prior permission of Vallentine Mitchell & Co. Ltd.

I dedicate this book to my late wife Rosalie and our two sons Brian and Daniel for their steadfast support and encouragement for what has been an unusual lifestyle for them and an incredibly satisfying career for me.

Acknowledgements

I have long wanted to highlight the significant sector of Anglo-Jewry living across the country outside of the mainstream, as well as my adventures in the legal profession and in military chaplaincy.

I would like to thank Geraldine Auerbach for encouraging me to do this and for initiating and steering this book over many years, from its inception to completion. I thank her for finding David Cohen with whom I spent many happy hours. He was an exceptional interviewer familiar with many of my friends and associates, who gave me much pleasure to tell my tales in his company. Geraldine invited writer, Lawrence Joffe to help her to bring my story to life. I am very happy that my sons Brian and Daniel have also helped with refining the script, finding the pictures, and avoiding any *faux pas*. Geraldine also enlisted the help of her husband Ronnie Auerbach, for polishing, proofreading, and fact-checking the first drafts. Without Geraldine, with her quiet insistence and smooth narrative, there would be no book.

I gratefully acknowledge the patience and support of my family for my strange lifestyle. I would like again to record my thanks to my late wife Rosalie and our sons, Brian with Lucille, and Daniel with Sybil, and our grandchildren Shoshana, Peri and Saul, for their constant encouragement and love.

I salute my military colleagues who have made me so welcome at our bases and at our chaplaincy meetings and conferences. I also would like to thank my legal colleagues in Chambers and on the Bench for making my legal work so enjoyable.

I give my thanks to the succession of Chief Rabbis who have all warmly supported my role as their Minister for Small Communities, starting with Chief Rabbi Israel Brodie (1948-1965) followed by Chief Rabbi Immanuel Jakobovits (1966-1991). Next was Chief Rabbi Lord Jonathan Sacks (1991-2013) with whom I had a particularly productive relationship. I have been delighted to work with the current Chief Rabbi, Sir Ephriam Mirvis since 2013, whom I warmly thank for his kind message in this book. I am also immensely grateful to the Jewish Memorial Council, the Hillel Foundation and several other institutions and individuals who have generously supported my work in this field over the decades.

We are all enormously grateful to the donor in Jersey who has supported this book project over the years, in recognition and appreciation of my services to the Jersey Jewish Community. I am touched by all those who have contributed their thoughts and stories for this book.

I extend special thanks to the leaders and members of all the small communities across the country, who have so warmly welcomed me into their homes, their synagogues, and their hearts.

List of Illustrations

1. Our house, 61 Clissold Crescent, Stoke Newington 1930s — 1
2. My mother and father, with my brother and I, 1940 — 8
3. Oxford Synagogue buildings — 25
4. Being presented with the cake with my Rover car on it, Oxford 2013: — 29
5. In full RAF uniform at one of our RAF bases, 1957 — 36
6. Meeting with Pope John Paul II, outside the Vatican, 1990s — 43
7. Legal regalia, the gown and wig — 50
8. Gray's Inn Square — 52
9. Climbing stairs to our interfaith event in Clifford's Tower, York 1990 — 67
10. My Council of Christians and Jews colleagues, 2008 — 75
11. Moses Montefiore Memorial Synagogue, Grimsby, consecrated 1888 — 83
12. Montefiore synagogue interior, reconsecrated 100 years later — 94
13. Exeter Synagogue, exterior — 100
14. Norwich Synagogue, with Chief Rabbi Immanuel Jakobovits, 1969 — 105
15. Cheltenham Synagogue, exterior. — 107
16. Medieval synagogue, Guildford. — 113
17. New synagogue, Guildford — 115
18. Chatham Memorial Synagogue, 150th anniversary, 2015 — 122
19. Campus synagogue, Lancaster University, with Queen Elizabeth, 1969 — 128
20. Sunderland Synagogue in Ryhope Road — 137
21. Sunderland Synagogue, stained-glass window — 137
22. Merthyr Tydfil Synagogue, South Wales — 150
23. Aberdeen Synagogue, Chief Rabbi Ephraim Mirvis visit, 2015 — 153
24. Jersey Synagogue, St Brelade, 1972 — 162
25. Jersey Synagogue, consecration, 1972 — 163
26. Jersey, an early High Holydays Service — 166
27. The 'Admor' of Malta — 169
28. Karachi Synagogue, street entrance — 181
29. Chesed El Synagogue Singapore, exterior — 183
30. Chesed El Synagogue Singapore, interior — 184
31. Lancaster University, greeting the Queen, 1969 — 190
32. Lancaster University, group when I was made an Honorary Fellow — 193
33. Buckingham Palace courtyard, with my family, 1997 — 194
34. Receiving my OBE from the then Prince of Wales, 1997 — 195
35. St Paul's Cathedral, concert collage, 1995 — 197
36. Rosalie and my wedding, 1958 — 203
37. Cotswold Cottage, a quiet moment with Rosalie, 2000 — 205
38. Robin and Nitza Spiro — 210
39. Chiefs of Army Chaplains Conference — 215
40. Ed Horwich of the Small Communities Network visiting me, 2022 — 219

Contents

Preface   xi

1. Early Days – My Family.   1
2. My Jewish Education   12
3. Oxford Days   20
4. The Military – From National Service to NATO   33
5. The Law – Barrister and Recorder SE Circuit   48
6. Interfaith   64
7. Out on a Limb – Small Communities: Origins and Issues   80
8. Old Communities in Modern Times   96
9. Smaller Communities – an Internal Diaspora   118
10. Seaside Communities, Wales, Scotland and Geographical Quests   141
11. Jersey, Malta and the Commonwealth Jewish Council   159
12. The Long Haul – Journeys East   175
13. Meetings with Royalty and Concerts in St Paul's Cathedral, Canterbury Cathedral and Westminster Abbey   189
14. My Wife Rosalie and her Family, the Spiros   202
15. Conclusions   213

Glossary   223

Index   230

Office of The
CHIEF RABBI

July 2023
מנחם אב תשפ"ג

**MESSAGE FROM THE CHIEF RABBI
IN HONOUR OF THE REV MALCOLM WEISMAN OBE**

The Reverend Malcolm Weisman OBE has given an unrivalled, multi-faceted contribution to the British Jewish community. He has worn his many hats with distinction, providing exceptionally devoted service to students, the military, numerous communities in the UK and Commonwealth, together with significant interfaith activity, not to mention his outstanding legal career.

It is a privilege for me to know Reverend Weisman and, like so many others, I am inspired by his indefatigable devotion, his selfless commitment to people and communities and his natural love of his fellow Jews, whoever they are and wherever they might be.

In the Ethics of the Fathers, our great sage, Hillel, teaches that we must not separate ourselves from the community. The feeling of connectedness to something larger than ourselves is a very significant lifeline which Reverend Weisman's work in communities and as a chaplain to students and the armed forces has helped to provide for so many.

Small communities operate in a unique local environment. Each one has a distinctive set of challenges and opportunities and, as such, it takes a special kind of person, with great patience, vision and enthusiasm to provide effective leadership and guidance. In this very spirit, Reverend Weisman has been at the heart of so many small communities, which have been indebted to him for their vitality and development.

Few people can claim to have had the impact on Jewish life in regional communities that Reverend Weisman has had. His warm and endearing personality has touched the hearts of many. His life's work has been an ongoing *Kiddush Hashem* – sanctification of the name of God.

This project promises to be a fascinating overview, not only of the life and work of Reverend Weisman, but also of the changing landscape of the Jewish community over the last seventy years.

With every best wish,

Chief Rabbi Sir Ephraim Mirvis KBE

Preface

When my dear late wife Rosalie and I became engaged in 1957, I was in the Royal Air Force on three years' National Service, and about to go to the Bar. Little did we realise, quite how our lives would pan out. She had no inkling, that between my work for the Armed Services and in Legal Chambers, I would, for over 60 years, whisk her from one end of the country – and the Commonwealth – to the other. This was not only in pursuit of my main professional duties, but also in search of sustaining Jewish life and heritage in tiny communities, in universities and in interfaith settings, wherever I discovered the need.

I sometimes think I must have a split personality. Until recently, I was still running, concurrently, what other people might consider three full time careers, working as a Military Chaplain, a Barrister at Law and a Minister to Small Communities. Did I ever mix them up? Well on one occasion, when I was sending someone down for a long period in jail, I was told that the prisoner felt the sentence was fair, but that the summing up had sounded like I was giving him a sermon. A couple of weeks later, when officiating at a wedding at the Grand Hotel in Eastbourne, the couple said to me, 'When you addressed us under the wedding canopy, it sounded as if you were sentencing us to life imprisonment!'

There was also an occasion when I left home at 6:00am, got into the car and drove down the A40 towards the M40 heading northwest for Cheltenham in Gloucestershire. When I got to the junction with the M25, I suddenly realised I was not meant to be going to Cheltenham but to Chelmsford in Essex, in the opposite direction! Just in time, I managed to get onto the slip road to go east. That was the one occasion that I nearly made a mistake.

Many people have suggested that I write a book about my experiences. No one has been as insistent as Geraldine Auerbach MBE, the Founder and former Director of the Jewish Music Institute, with whom I have worked, as religious advisor, on major interfaith concerts at Canterbury Cathedral, York Minster and St Paul's Cathedral. Over decades, Geraldine not only persisted, but also provided practical solutions. It was she who sat down with me to write a synopsis and insisted that I get a tape recorder. Geraldine also found help from the oral historian David Cohen of London. I spent many happy hours with him, between 2015 and 2018, recalling the exploits over several decades of my life. I am very grateful to David for spending this time with me and to Lola Majekodunmi who transcribed the interviews.

I give special thanks to Geraldine, who has so greatly helped me to compile this book of my memories and to describe what has clearly been a very meaningful way of life for me. She has been assisted by journalist and writer Lawrence Joffe (who first encountered me when I visited his community in Bristol and then when he was a student at Oxford University). I am also grateful to my sons Brian and Daniel for their help with the book as well as to all those who have supported this project with their comments and contributions.

The number of people who have come up to me to say, 'You probably don't remember me, but you made such an impact on my life' is what has sustained us in our travels. The recognition of my effect on the Jewish journeys of hundreds if not thousands of people, between 1957 and 2022, who had little or no other support to help them maintain a Jewish life, is what kept Rosalie and I and often our two sons, continually on the move. We have found great satisfaction in visiting small places where our friends find our visits so stimulating. I would like to express my profound appreciation to the late Rosalie and to our sons Brian and Daniel for being so exceptionally supportive and accommodating of this strange lifestyle. I am glad to know that the places they have visited, people that they have met and events we were able to attend together through my work, have given them great pleasure too.

I hope that this story of my activities, as I recall them also gives you an insight into the vicissitudes of the Jewish Community in Britain in earlier times, and in the latter half of the twentieth century going into the twenty first. I also hope that my travels and adventures will be as interesting to you, as undertaking them, has been to me.

Malcolm Weisman OBE, London, 2023

1
Early Days – My Family

My parents and grandparents and my secular education

I was born at home at 61 Clissold Crescent, Stoke Newington on 11 December 1930. The area had first attracted a few Jewish residents in the

1. Our house, 61 Clissold Crescent, Stoke Newington.

late 18th century. These included Sephardi Jews who worshiped at Bevis Marks Synagogue. One of them was Isaac Disraeli, who lived at 7 Church Row around 1798. He was the father of Benjamin Disraeli. He had resigned from the synagogue after being elected warden (without his consent) rather than pay the forty-pound fine for refusing the honour. He subsequently had his four children, including the future British Prime Minister, baptised in the Church of England in 1817!

Clissold Crescent was originally called 'Park Lane' as it bordered a huge private estate planted with trees and shrubs. By 1894 two terraces of fine houses were built along the Crescent. The idea was to encourage London's expanding population of newly rich merchants and bankers to come to live in in an attractive setting within easy reach of the commercial hub of London.

The Crescent borders Clissold Park, a beautiful open space which is part of the original estate. The parkland had been saved from development by a passionate local campaign in the 1880s and is still the jewel at the heart of Stoke Newington.

By the end of the 19th Century, the Jewish demography was changing dramatically as Eastern European Jews fleeing severe circumstances began flocking into the area. From their point of entry at London's Docks in the East End, they were moving northwards. By the end of the First World War, many thousands of deeply religious Jews had settled in Stoke Newington and increasingly in its neighbouring suburb to the northeast, Stamford Hill. To this day the N16 postcode in the London Borough of Hackney is home to the largest concentration of Hassidic and other ultra-orthodox Jews in Europe.

Let us spend a minute considering this miraculous migration to the free world of nearly three million Jews out of the restricted area of the Russian Empire called the Pale of Settlement. This is an area very much in the spotlight right now in early 2022 because of Russia's invasion of Ukraine. It falls mostly within the boundaries of today's Poland, Russia, Ukraine, Lithuania, Latvia, Belarus, and Moldova. Russia's Catherine II had first decreed this a 'restricted area' for Jews in 1791 and the later Russian rulers between 1835 and 1917, compelled Jews to live there in small towns and villages, known in Yiddish as '*shtetlach*'.

In most of these villages the majority of the population was Jewish. Although impoverished because of severe restrictions and the lack of economic opportunity, Jews nevertheless were able to live an intense and rich Jewish life, according to their own laws and customs. Life revolved around Jewish ritual, their rabbis and their synagogues. They created their own educational establishments, the *Cheder* for small children, the *Talmud*

Torah as the boys got older and the *Yeshiva* for intense Torah study for young men as their 'University'.

Tsar Alexander II, who ruled from 1855 made some liberating decrees like abolishing serfdom. When he was assassinated in 1881, Russia was plunged into turmoil. It was rumoured that Jews were behind his death and that spelled extra trouble for them. They lived in fear of physical attacks, theft and even harsher restrictions. But they were permitted to leave Russia – and leave they did!

In this miraculous migration, between 1881 and about 1920, more than two and a half million impoverished and mostly pious, Yiddish-speaking Jews, made the difficult journey to start a new life in the free world. Men who had never been far from the surrounding area of their *shtetlach*, undertook the immense and difficult journeys on trains and boats across borders, countries and oceans, seeking a better life for their families. Young men, barely out of their teens, set forth. Older men left their intended or their wives and small children behind, in the hope that they could earn enough money to send for them. Thank goodness they did so.

Although I seem to have managed to appear to be a regular Englishman, addressing the Oxford Union in reply to a motion on 'Englishness', or summing up as a Crown Court Recorder and Deputy Circuit Judge, the fact is that all four of my grandparents were born in Eastern Europe. They arrived in Britain at the turn of the 20th Century with Yiddish as their mother tongue. Delving into my own family history reveals much about the course of Jewish history – of immigration, survival, and reinvention in new lands, yet maintaining the heritage that nurtured and inspired us.

My father's family – the Weismans

My father, David Weisman, was born into a large family of *Biala Hasidim* in 1905. His hometown of Mezrich in Poland was famous throughout the *Hasidic* world of Eastern Europe as the seat of Dov Ber ben Avraham, who was the chief disciple of the founder of *Hasidism* and was known over a wide area as the *Maggid* (the Guide).

Hasidism

The Hebrew word '*Hasidut*', means piety or saintliness. The movement known as *Hasidism* began with Rabbi Yisroel Ben Eliezer who was born in Western Ukraine in c1700 and lived until 1760. He was revered throughout a wide area of Eastern Europe becoming known as the *Baal Shem Tov* (Master of the Good Name) – or *Besht* for short. He and his associates, encouraged singing and dancing, infusing worship with a joyful dimension.

Hasidism focused far more on an individual's personal relationship with God and with his fellowman rather than on the intricacies of Jewish law. They abhorred fasting and asceticism. They taught that physical pleasure can also give rise to spiritual pleasure. This was in contrast to the more scholarly religious Jews.

Such teachings were regarded with deep suspicion, or even as heresy, by the traditional rabbinic establishment trained in the religious colleges, the *Yeshivot*. Nevertheless, the *Besht*'s ideas and philosophies spread to thousands of Jewish communities across the Ukraine, Poland and Lithuania helped by a group of outstanding disciples (the *Tzaddikim* - especially righteous and saintly persons by Jewish religious standards) who became leaders of the movement.

Each locality had its own *Tzaddik* who was referred to as 'The *Rebbe*' and who was revered over and above the ordinary religious leaders. Each *Tzaddik* or *Rebbe* had his own court of followers who travelled to be with him on festive occasions.

Rebbes founded their own dynasties where the son or son in-law followed as leader after the death of the *Rebbe*. Dynasties were often named after the locality. Many *Hassidic* dynasties survive to the present day in Brooklyn, Switzerland, Jerusalem, and in Manchester and London's Stamford Hill. The best-known *Hasidic* dynasty today is the *Lubavitch*, or *Chabad*, based in Brooklyn, New York, because of the movement's vigorous outreach programmes across the world and of the worldwide fame of the wisdom of their charismatic *Rebbe,* Menachem Mendel Schneerson who died in 1994.

The *Besht* died in 1760, leaving as his successor the energetic Dov Baer of Mezrich – the town from which my Weisman family of *Hasidim* hailed. Dov Ber founded the Biala Dynasty of *Rebbes* – all descendants of the Rabinowitz family.

The swift rise of the *Hasidim* troubled the traditional rabbis in these same areas. They and their followers constituted the opposing movement, called the *Mitnagdim* – literally the 'opposers'. They were equally pious and very learned in their *Torah* study. The two powerful groups lived side by side in the towns and villages of Eastern Europe with their own synagogues and with much friction and mistrust between them. Much of the antipathy towards Hasidim came from the *yeshivot* (Talmudic colleges) and the supposedly more learned, legalistic, austere and Talmud-trained Jews of

Lithuania. The famous Ponevezh Yeshiva was pre-eminent, in its objections to *Hasidism*.

Both of my grandfathers had achieved rabbinic status in Eastern Europe, but each from the opposing movement. My paternal grandfather Jacob Weisman, affectionately known as Reb Yankel, grew up in Poland, within the dynamic atmosphere of *Biala Hasidism*, where joy in religious fervour was expressed. My maternal grandfather Bernard Lewis Segal was born in Lithuania and received his rabbinical ordination at the more austere Ponevezh Yeshiva.

By the late 19th century, the once intense *Hasidic-Mitnagid* battle had tempered. Both groups of very religious Jews now faced common enemies such as assimilationists, Reform Jews, the enlightened *Haskalah* modernising movement, and socialist or Marxist revolutionaries. *Hasidim* had also lost their probably unfair reputation as drunken revellers and had won respect as scholars in their own right.

I had 'both sides' of the orthodox-religious debate living harmoniously within my own family. Both my grandfathers arrived safely in Great Britain, in the late 19th century and once they were part of the same family, they got on very well together.

Although my grandfather Reb Yankel Weisman was so steeped in Jewish learning that he could have worked as a rabbi, he chose rather to become a businessman. By 1910 Reb Yankel and his parents, brothers and sisters and his children all left Poland for Antwerp where there were better business opportunities. I do not recall what kind of business he was involved with. However, being in Antwerp I wonder if they were involved in the diamond trade, as were many religious Jews in that 'Flemish diamond' city.

When the Germans invaded Belgium at the start of the First World War, my Weisman grandparents and all their children were very fortunate to escape, with their funds, to London. Their getaway was not easy, but it was certainly fortuitous. The citizens of Antwerp suffered greatly when German forces bombarded and besieged the city in the autumn of 1914. A number of my uncles, my father's brothers, had remained there. Other members of my family had moved back to Belgium in the interwar years, but sadly their fate in the Second World War was much worse and several members of my family were murdered in Auschwitz.

When they arrived in Britain, my Weisman grandparents first stayed in Portland Place, between Regents Park and Oxford Street, near the current site of the BBC. Soon they moved to a very large house, number at 52 Pyrland Road in Highbury New Park, Islington.

Some of my earliest memories of my grandfather Reb Yankel, were of his prodigious *Talmudic* knowledge. He was well served by a famously photographic memory (which I am glad to say I have somewhat inherited). He knew all of the Hebrew *Talmud* and commentaries by heart – yet Yiddish was his main language and he never fully mastered English.

When we were teenagers, I sometimes invited my friend Leonard Gerber, later to be a renowned circuit judge and a best man at my wedding, to join me on a visit to Reb Yankel on a Sunday. It was a treat for Leonard and a rare chance to leave the East End for the leafier environs of Islington. As a dare, I bet Leonard that my grandfather could remember any page of the six tractates of the *Mishna* or the *Gemara* which make up the *Talmud*.

The *Talmud* is a record of the rabbinic debates in the 2nd to the 5th century on the laws and teachings of the *Torah*. It presents actual cases being brought to judgement along with the debate on the matter, the judgement that was given, and often the minority opinion, as well as the spirit of the Torah that guided that judgement.

The *Talmud* comprises the *Mishna* and the *Gemara*. The *Mishna* is divided into six sections by subject matter each section dealing with laws about various practical matters. The first is called 'Seeds' and deals with laws pertaining to agriculture. The second section is called 'Seasons' and deals with laws pertaining to sabbaths and festivals. The third section deals with 'Women' and discusses laws regarding vows, marriage and divorce. The fourth section 'Damages' deals with laws concerning civil and criminal matters. The fifth part deals with 'Sacred or Holy' things and the last section deals with 'Purity'. Commentaries on the *Mishna* compiled by learned Rabbis over the next four centuries in the land of Israel and in Babylonia, are known as the *Gemara* and also form part of the Talmud.

The future jurist would shout out, *Gemara, Baba Metzia,* chapter 23, page four – and my granddad would trot out the right answer each time – earning in the process a delighted grandson 10p each time! Undaunted, Leonard would try his luck on successive Sundays, and on each occasion, I emerged enriched.

My mother's family – the Segals and Rifkinds

My mother was Jeannie Pearl Segal. Her father, Bernard Lewis Segal, was raised in Lithuania, and as a young man had studied at the renowned Ponevezh *Yeshiva* (*Talmudic* Academy). Just before the First World War, he received his *smicha* (rabbinical ordination) and then left Europe to settle in Edinburgh. At the turn of the last century, between 1880 and the 1920s, once a Jewish immigrant from a particular Eastern European shtetl had arrived in a city or town and could see his way to making a good living, he encouraged and helped many friends and relatives from the same or neighbouring villages to follow suit.

My mother's mother Sarah was a Rifkind. Many of the Rifkind family had arrived in Scotland in about 1886, from Mysad in the Kovno province of Lithuania. At one stage it seemed as if much of the Jewish community of Edinburgh was part of my mother's family! Even now, a good proportion of what remains of the Edinburgh community is probably related to my mother. The Rifkind family held a reunion in 2005 attended by more than 200 people, all direct descendants of my maternal great grandparents.

Two notable family members were the leading British Conservative politicians Malcolm Rifkind and Leon Brittan. Sir Malcolm Rifkind KCMG QC was the Member of Parliament for Edinburgh Pentlands from 1974 to 1997. He served in the cabinets of Margaret Thatcher and John Major from 1986 to 1997, and most recently was chair of the Intelligence and Security Committee of Parliament from 2010 to 2015. Barrister Leon Brittan was a Member of Parliament from 1974 to 1988. He was a cabinet minister, and Home Secretary in Margaret Thatcher's government, and served as a European Commissioner from 1989 to 1999. He was created a life peer in 2000 and took the title Baron Brittan of Spennithorne. He died in 2015.

My maternal grandfather Rev Bernard Lewis Segal, with my grandmother Sarah (née Rifkind) left Edinburgh in 1921, to take up the prestigious post of *chazzan* (cantor) and *shochet*, (ritual slaughterer) for the Jewish community of the fashionable spa town of Harrogate, North Yorkshire. They stayed there for the next forty years until his death in the mid-1960s.

Harrogate is often described as one of the happiest and most romantic places in the world in which to live. It has a dry mild climate and special 'healing' waters attracting aristocratic tourists travelling on the newly opened railway lines. In the early 1900s several Jewish families ran hotels and boarding houses in the town and opened amenity shops catering for such visitors coming to sample the waters. The community grew gradually and was officially established with twenty-two families in 1918. Synagogue services began in a room over an antique shop. In 1925 the premises of a church school became available and remained in use as a synagogue for over forty years until the new synagogue was built in 1968 on the same site.

My grandfather Reverend Segal was considered a *Ba'al Chesed* (a righteous man) and a *Talmid Chacham* (great Torah and Talmud scholar). I remember him very clearly, because, as evacuees from wartime London, my mother, younger brother and I (from the age nine to fourteen) had spent nearly five years, with him and my grandmother in Harrogate.

My parents

In 1928 my father, David Weisman, married their daughter Jeannie Pearl Segal who was a young schoolteacher. She was born in Edinburgh in 1905, but by the time they met, she was living in Harrogate where her father Bernard Lewis Segal was the cantor to the Jewish community from 1921 for over 40 years.

The young couple, David and Jeannie Pearl Weisman, came to London and settled in Stamford Hill in the midst of the ultra-orthodox community of London, before moving to Clissold Crescent in nearby, but leafier, Stoke Newington where I, and four years later, my brother Maurice, were born.

My Childhood

2. My mother and father, Pearl and David Weisman with their two sons, my brother Maurice aged 6 and me aged 10 in 1940.

I remember my early years as a period of some upheaval, because of the dislocation caused by the Second World War.

In 1934, aged four, I attended a kindergarten in the neighbouring district of Stamford Hill. It had been established by the ground-breaking

1. Early Days – My Family

Jewish educator, Rabbi Dr Victor Schonfeld. My earliest memory of school days was on my very first day, finding myself standing quite alone in the street outside the school, feeling somewhat bewildered. For some reason I seem to have been abandoned. A policeman came along and asked me what I was doing. Fortunately, I remembered my address, so he took me home. It is quite a long way on foot from Stamford Hill to Stoke Newington. I don't know what had happened. Apparently, we were meant to go home at lunch time. Either my parents were not aware of that, or I might have missed the taxi. Anyway, thanks to the kind British 'Bobby' I was safely delivered home and my schooldays proceeded without hitch henceforth.

Following kindergarten, I went to the local Clissold Primary School. When war came, I was separated from my parents and evacuated from London together with other children from my school. I was sent to a village called Bampton in Devon, where I was accommodated with the family of a man who controlled the local level crossing. It was very exciting for me to help him ring the bells, change the signals for the trains and close the gates.

My hosts did not understand anything about Judaism. They insisted that I and my co-evacuee, the son of a Jewish neighbour, accompany them to church on Sunday mornings. Unwittingly, their speciality on the menu was roast rabbit – which obviously I knew was not kosher and that I could not eat it. When my parents heard about all this, they immediately fetched me back to London! (My co-evacuee, had no problems in this respect and was happy to stay there.)

Once the Blitz started though, it was clear we should move again to avoid the bombs. We witnessed V1 rockets descending over London. I remember seeing Spitfires flying overhead and once our house was damaged to such an extent that the ceilings came down. We had to spend time in shelters. At the height of the Blitz, I remember a house 200 yards away being destroyed, killing the Jewish family who lived there.

As my mother's parents, Bernard and Sarah Segal, were well established in Harrogate in Yorkshire, my mother, my younger brother Maurice, and I moved in with our grandparents between 1940 and 1945. I went to the local primary school there, and later started my secondary schooling at Harrogate Grammar School.

My father David Weisman had remained in London to look after the business. After the Blitz had ended, we returned to London for short periods. In one of those intervals, I celebrated my Bar Mitzvah at the Adas Yisroel Synagogue in London. I remember that after the service, while we are all enjoying some wine and some kosher delights, that were still available at the time (1943) the air raid sirens went off and we all had to scamper for the shelters.

My father had joined a relative in a small firm in Shoreditch, called Kaufmanns, that specialised in the manufacture of fashionable handbags. The frames came from another relative who owned a metal firm near Birmingham.

During the war this metal firm manufactured parts for military aeroplanes – maybe the very ones we saw flying overhead. After the war they reverted to making the frames for my father's handbag business.

My father was suddenly called up for army service – but as he had omitted to renounce his Polish nationality, he was called up to serve in the Polish Army! That was the last thing he wanted, not least because he could not speak a word of Polish. My mother also had a Polish passport, even though she had been born in Edinburgh. They both quickly relinquished their Polish citizenship, and my father went into the British Army instead. He served in the Royal Pioneer Corps for three years, doing light engineering and guard duties.

After the war when we had returned to London and the family was reunited, I entered Parmiters School. This excellent grammar school based in Bethnal Green had benefitted from the largess of the wealthy silk merchant Thomas Parmiter who died in 1681. It had an outstanding reputation as a high performing government school.

My younger brother went to Hackney Downs, a very distinguished Grocers' Company School. Many famous Jewish people whose families lived in the area attended that school. They included the Nobel Prize-winning playwright and poet, Harold Pinter, who later married historical biography writer, Antonia Fraser (Lord Longford's daughter). Amongst other famous alumni were the eminent lawyer and master of University College, Oxford, Lord Goodman, the playwright and actor, Steven Berkoff, one former head of Mossad, Efraim Halevy, Frank Cass the publisher, Leon Kossoff the painter, and the innovative graphic designer, Abram Games. Other 'Old Boys' were two current peers of the realm: Lord Michael Levy, ally of former Prime Minister Tony Blair, and Baron Stanley Clinton-Davis. In fact, I was to have interesting dealings with the latter many decades later, when I was an electoral boundaries adjudicator. But that is another story!

Schooling in Northeast London later became problematical. The local authority wanted to take over these remarkable schools which often meant downgrading them. In 1977 my old school Parmiters relocated to Garston in Hertfordshire and is now flourishing there as an Academy. (In later years,

I became a Trustee of Parmiters.) Hackney Downs, on the other hand, deteriorated, and sadly has now closed.

Although I participated enthusiastically in secular school life and excelled at my studies and also at games, I was aware that I was part of a family steeped in orthodox Judaism. Therefore, there was the serious matter of my Jewish religious education, which I describe in the next chapter.

2
My Jewish Education

As we have seen, both my grandfathers, were very knowledgeable and pious. Both had received rabbinical training and ordination, and both were firmly entrenched in the ultra-orthodox Jewish religious tradition and way of life, though from opposite ends of the spectrum. Grandfather Rev Bernard Lewis Segal had received his training in the learned Lithuanian tradition at the famous Ponevezh *Yeshiva* (Talmudic College) which was opposed to *Hasidism*; and Grandpa Reb Yankel Weisman was a Polish *Hasid*. My grandfathers, however, were not the only religious influences in my life. My own father, while not quite as religious in practice as his parents, had nevertheless insisted that I should have a thorough Jewish education and many memorable teachers were highly influential in my Jewish religious instruction.

When I was just three years old, even before I was fluent in English (we spoke Yiddish at home) my father hired a Hebrew teacher to teach me about Judaism. This was Mr Rockman, a very well-informed man whose own son became a rabbi. Being a widower with nothing much to do, my father decided that he would be an ideal person to teach me.

What can you teach a three-year-old? I used to have a short lesson on a Sunday morning. Then as I reached six or seven, he came in every evening. After school, I used to have an hour with him on Monday, Tuesday, Wednesday and Thursday. As he was living on his own, when it came to the Sabbath, my parents very often took pity on him, and invited him to come for Friday night dinner or to have lunch with us on a Saturday after synagogue. If he did, he would say 'Look, while I'm here, for, no charge, I'll give your son an extra lesson'. So, not only did I have intense lessons with him every weekday, but I used to get bonus sessions with him on the Sabbath as well – whether I liked it or not!

Mr Rockman was a superb teacher and we got on very well. He remained my mentor and main teacher, all the way through my schooldays. From the age of eight or nine I started learning *Talmud* with him – the collections of rabbinical discussions pertaining to Jewish law biblical interpretation, ethics, customs, and history. Mr Rockman also taught me to *leyen* – to chant from the *Torah* (the scrolls of the Law) for my *Barmitzvah* (my coming-of-age ceremony at age 13). He continued to teach me throughout my teenage years.

Nor did it end there. When I was at Oxford University, he used to wait for me to come back. During the vacations, I would continue the one-on-one lessons with him every weekday, and, if I was unfortunate, on a Friday night too, and a Saturday afternoon. Even though I was an eager and willing student – it got a bit too much. He was still around when I joined the Royal Air Force. At that stage my father said to me, it is your turn to pay him. So, I kept him on as a teacher as I embarked on my military chaplaincy career. I studied with him until he passed away when I was 35 years old.

Another teacher I studied with was Dr Skidelsky (1907 – 2005). He was a most interesting character. His father had been a millionaire sugar tycoon in pre-Communist Russia, but everything had been confiscated by the Communists. Dr Skidelsky had fled the revolution and landed up living in a flat in Islington, a few doors from my grandparents. When I was in my teens, both my grandfather, Reb Yankel, and also Chief Rabbi Brodie, born in Newcastle, whom we knew very well, suggested that it might be a good idea for me to go and have some lessons with this learned Rabbi. I used to meet Dr Skidelsky weekly at my grandparents' house. The money that he earned from my lessons kept him going. Life was really that tough for him.

Wherever I moved, I could not escape from my teachers. I had to carry on learning with them. I did not always appreciate it at that time, but in retrospect it was a remarkably good grounding for my future.

When I was 15 or 16, the Etz Chayim Yeshiva of the East End, opened a branch in Stoke Newington High Street. I was persuaded to also go along there for further study. Here I met Rabbi Bendish, who was the assistant head of the college. I did not last too long in that atmosphere. Being accustomed to intensive individual lessons, going at my pace – which I believe was quite fast – suddenly to find myself in a class with others was not stimulating for me. One afternoon, I was sitting at the back of the class, holding one of those huge tomes of the *Gemara* (the *Talmud* commentaries) but actually reading the hidden Dandy and Beano comics inside. Suddenly Rabbi Bendish, walked right up. I did not see him – but I definitely felt his hand – *klup, klup*, bash, bash. I was in utter disgrace.

Synagogues

At first, my parents and grandparents became members of the Dalston Synagogue. This was one of the leading and grandest synagogues in London at that time. Curiously enough, despite its name, the synagogue was not in Dalston but in Poets Road, Islington, close to my grandparents' home. It was a magnificent Victorian building, similar in style to the ornate cathedral-like New West End Synagogue in St Petersburg Place, Bayswater, and the Princes Road Synagogue in Liverpool.

It was part of the mainstream orthodox 'United Synagogue' organisation, headed by the Chief Rabbi. The congregation had been founded in 1874. In July 1885, the crowning stone of the holy ark was laid by Mr Samuel Montague, an observant Jew who was elected Liberal MP for Whitechapel that same year and was later ennobled as Lord Swaything. This was part of a special service conducted by the Chief Rabbi elect, Dr Herman Adler together with the Chief Cantor, Rev Marcus Hast, of the Great Synagogue, in Dukes Place, Aldgate. There was an enormous choir made up of members of several synagogues.

At the time that my family joined, after arriving in this country in 1914, the congregants were mainly German speaking Jews who had come from Europe a few decades earlier. By 1914, they had become somewhat anglicised.

Dalston Synagogue had a fine musical tradition. In 1936 Jacob Koussevitzky – one of the four famous brother cantors – was appointed Cantor there, and there was also a magnificent choir. One of its choristers was Rev Reuben Turner MBE who himself became a cantor and who worked tirelessly all his life to make Jewish music better known, understood, and loved. In the 1960s and 70s, he created and chaired a 'Jewish Music Council' and presented annual 'Jewish Music Months' in synagogues around the country. Reuben Turner was the inspiration for the later Bnai Brith biennial Jewish Music Festivals, organised by my friend Geraldine Auerbach MBE from 1984 to 2000. I was pleased when Geraldine called on me to be religious advisor for some special interfaith events in British cathedrals (which I have written about in the chapter on my Interfaith work). Arising from these month-long festivals in 1999, Geraldine also founded the Jewish Music Institute which is now based at the School of Oriental and African Studies, University of London and of which I am proud to be a Trustee.

Adath Yisroel Synagogue

Despite Dalston Synagogue's grandeur (or maybe because of it) my grandparents preferred to pray in the more intensely religious atmosphere of the smaller *Beit Hamidrash* (House of study) that was housed within the

Dalston Synagogue complex. Here the services were run in the more familiar traditional Eastern European style.

Dalston Synagogue in Islington was a bit too far from Stoke Newington for my parents and my brother and I to walk to every Sabbath. Therefore, in the 1930s, we began attending the nearby Adath Yisroel Synagogue, which at that time was in Burma Road N16, just around the corner from our house.

The Adath Yisroel Synagogue was established by Rabbi Dr Victor Schonfeld a pivotal figure in orthodox Jewish religious life and education in England. He was born in Hungary in 1880. He first studied medicine but felt called to the rabbinate. To prepare himself he studied philosophy at the Universities of Vienna and Giessen. Schonfeld was clearly interested in Britain as he wrote his doctoral thesis on the philosophy of Anthony Ashley Cooper, the third Earl of Shaftesbury. He then spent six years studying at the famous rabbinical college of Pressburg from which he received his Rabbinic ordination. He distinguished himself there as a speaker and thinker and was elected the President of the elite study group there, the *Chevra Tiferes Bachurim*.

Schonfeld's rabbinic career started at the prestigious Montefiore Society in Vienna where his oratory was highly valued. In 1909 he was appointed Rabbi of the North London *Beit Hamidrash*. Though this was as yet small and insignificant, he saw the potential and the need for organising orthodox Jewish life in Anglo-Jewry. He adapted himself to English conditions very quickly and spent his first years in London building up and consolidating the religious elements in the north of London. Two years later, in 1911, he established the *Adath Yisroel* (Assembly of Israel) Synagogue, the parent synagogue of what was to become the Union of Orthodox Hebrew Congregations (UOHC) which he established in 1926.

I had started to go regularly to Adath with my father David Weisman (and sometimes with my grandfather Reb Yankel Weisman) in 1938 or '39 from the age of eight or nine, when this congregation was still ninety percent German-speaking. Many worshippers had come from Austria, so I learnt to speak the language fluently – with an Austrian twang.

When I took my O-level German oral examinations years later, the examiner said, 'You have passed with distinction, well of course you were born in Germany, weren't you?' I said, 'No I was not. I attended a synagogue whose members were German speaking, and nobody there spoke English. These days my German is a little rusty.'

What was remarkable about that *Adath* community was that although the rabbis and congregants were steeped in Jewish teachings, they, like

Rabbi Schonfeld, also had a broad cultural outlook and could speak several languages. Right up to the late 1960s, you would find *Adath Yisroel* congregants from the Anglo-German background who, whilst they were very familiar with and knowledgeable about their Jewish background and religious texts, you could also talk to them about Beethoven, Goethe, Schiller and Shakespeare. They knew them just as well and could converse about all the great writers. They enjoyed going to the opera, the theatre and symphony concerts. That was a very significant influence on my early life.

Members of the community followed the concept of '*Torah Im Derech Eretz*', meaning that you combine the best of Jewish learning with the best of secular culture. They believed in the importance of understanding the host society, while having a deep respect for their Jewish heritage. That concept came to me from the synagogue, even more than from my parents. This duality appealed to me very much and has been a guiding principle of my life. This ethos or attitude is not seen nowadays amongst the ultra-orthodox.

The Rabbis Schonfeld father and son

Rabbi Dr Victor Schonfeld was an outstanding preacher and teacher, wielding great influence well beyond the confines of his own congregation. When he had arrived in England in 1909, he was shocked to find that Orthodox Judaism was totally disorganised and therefore weak and powerless. He determined to put this right and set himself the task of consolidating it on a firm basis.

By 1926, he had founded the Union of Orthodox Hebrew Congregations (UOHC) in England. This was an umbrella organisation of Orthodox and Ultra-Orthodox Jewish congregations, primarily in London. The stated mission was 'to protect traditional Judaism'. At one stage it had an affiliation of nearly 90 synagogues, as well as a number of educational institutions, which, while retaining their independence, accepted the authority of its rabbinate. Most of these affiliated congregations were in the London suburbs of Stamford Hill, Golders Green, Hendon and Edgware.

In 1929 Victor Schonfeld finally founded the Jewish Secondary Schools Movement, having worked hard all his life to establish sound Jewish education for children of religious families. But sadly, he died suddenly the following year in 1930, aged just 50.

His son Solomon, born in London in 1912, was all set to become a lawyer, but the community decided that they needed continuity with another Schonfeld. (In true *Hasidic* tradition, the dynasty was paramount).

They persuaded Solomon to give up his legal studies, sent him off to *Yeshiva*, in Lithuania, and he came back three years later with the required rabbinical ordination.

In 1933 Solomon Schonfeld at just 21, succeeded his father by becoming Rabbi of the Adath Yisroel Synagogue. He also became the Presiding Rabbi of the Union of Orthodox Hebrew Congregations and President of the National Council for Jewish Religious Day Schools in Great Britain. He was certainly well equipped, mentally and spiritually for the job.

When I met him in the early 1940s round about my barmitzvah time, I found Solomon Schonfeld now 31, to be one of the most charismatic people I have ever come across. He was a total eccentric, completely mad at times. If you never met him, you missed a great privilege. Quite a remarkable man with whom I spent a lot of time in my youth and who was a tremendous influence on my life.

He was also the motivating Executive Director of the Chief Rabbi's Religious Emergency Council, set up in 1938 until 1946, under the auspices of his father-in-law, Chief Rabbi J H Hertz. Its main purpose was to rescue Jews from Central and Eastern Europe whose lives were in jeopardy from the ascendent Nazis. Solomon was personally involved in travelling to Europe and saving hundreds of Jewish children from the ghettos of Poland and bringing them to Great Britain.

The Schonfelds were not only noted rabbis. One of Victor's brothers became a great pillar of Bnai Brith, another became the knighted philosopher and economist, Sir Andrew Schonfeld.

Shabbat activities for our young crowd

My teenage years were very richly imbued with Jewish study and closely associated with Rabbi Solomon Schonfeld. There was a whole group of young teenagers that would do the rounds together. On Friday nights we might have attended services at different synagogues, but after going home for dinner we would assemble at Rabbi Schonfeld's little cottage, in Lordship Road, not far from the Adath Yisroel Synagogue. The atmosphere was electric. Between our discussion on the *Torah* portion of the week there were many jokes and tasty refreshments. It was intensely enjoyable for us youngsters to be in Rabbi Schonfeld's company.

Rabbi Solomon Schonfeld had married the daughter of Chief Rabbi Hertz, a very suitable match for him. She was a very nice lady but took no part at all in her husband's public life. As a young girl before her marriage, after her mother had died, she had had to stand in and conduct the duties of the wife of a Chief Rabbi and be the hostess at all his official functions. When she married Solomon Schonfeld, she made it clear to him that she did not want to participate in his public life. She used to stay in their house in Shepherd's Hill in Highgate with their children and we hardly ever saw her in shul except occasionally on a Yom Kippur, or a Rosh Hashanah. Rabbi Schonfeld kept a cottage in Lordship Road, to be near his synagogue for *Shabbat* and this is where we used to go to be with him on Friday nights and Saturday afternoons.

On Saturday mornings, if we wanted to hear some great cantorial singing, we went to Dalston Synagogue in Poets Road to listen to Jacob Koussevitzky. Otherwise, we attended our nearest shul, the *Adath Yisroel*, where Schonfeld was the Rabbi.

After *shul*, we would again congregate with Rabbi Schonfeld in Lordship Road for a *shiur* (a study session on the weekly portion of the Law). He was a such remarkable character. He was not only passionate about our spiritual development, but he was very keen that we should exercise ourselves physically as well. There were twelve of us and we created a club called the Bnei Yaakov, the (12) 'Sons of Jacob'. Schonfeld said, 'Now you've got 12, we will have a cricket team'. The Adath Yisroel Cricket team turned out 11 players and one reserve. Occasionally, Rabbi Schonfeld himself would join in to play as well.

Having won our very first cricket match against some other shul (I myself having scored most of the runs) I wrote a glowing report saying that 'Malcolm Weisman's magnificent captain's innings was fierce and ferocious'. Although appreciated, as was my innings, it was felt that I had overstepped the mark in praising myself so profusely.

Rabbi Tarsis was one of the rescued rabbis that Rabbi Schonfeld had brought over from Eastern Europe. He started a *shtiebel* (a small home-based prayer hall) in Highbury New Park, Islington, that I would also attend at times. Rabbi Tarsis was another example of that remarkable blend of Judaism and general culture. He could discuss *Midrash* and recite *Torah* fluently; and then, in the breaks, he would give me his thoughts on Trollope or Jane Austen and Shakespeare! You do not see such broad culture amongst orthodox rabbis these days. It was quite remarkable, and I like to follow in that direction.

There was another shtiebel, Goldblum's, just round the corner from our home. My friends and I used to go there sometimes on a *Shabbat* afternoon, after having attended a service in the morning and been home for lunch. We had a learning session there with Rabbi Tarsis or Rabbi Schonfeld before *Mincha* (the afternoon service). Then I would chant from the *Sefer Torah*

(Scrolls of the Law) at *Mincha*. We enjoyed being there, exchanging witticisms, and imbibing some nice cake and tea. It was good fun. I used to do a lot of *leyening* (chanting from the Torah scrolls) at the time, I do it now only when I have to, for instance during the services on the High Holydays.

My group of friends were not only cricketers, but also keen football fans. Some Saturday afternoons we would join a learned shulgoer, Mr Graham for a study session at his home. We used to study the Talmud for about an hour, and then his wife would give us a really delicious tea. The most interesting aspect of going to study with Graham was that his house was about a ten-minute walk from the Arsenal football ground. In those days they used to open the gates at half-time and you could get in for nothing. When Arsenal was playing at home, we made a point of going to the Graham family. We arranged to have the study session early followed by the sumptuous tea. Then at about five minutes to half time we would all rush round to Arsenal to see the second half of the match.

I thoroughly enjoyed my teenage years in the company of like-minded friends and particularly of Rabbi Schonfeld. I did not realise how useful, nay essential, my thorough Jewish learning in those years would be in all my future activities – in the military, the ministry and even the law.

3

Oxford Days – as a Student, Chaplain, Visiting Minister and Trustee of the Community

Oxford as a Student 1951 - 1954

I had a particularly strong desire to study law at Oxford University. My school, Parmiters, had told me that it was too difficult to get in. So, I applied to and was accepted at the London School of Economics (LSE). I passed the first year of Law studies having spent most of my time editing the LSE's student newspaper, *The Beaver,* which is a substantial magazine. When I tell people now, they say it is a prestigious thing to do. But I knew jolly well that I wasn't going to stay there. I still had my heart set on Oxford.

I applied directly to St Catherine's Society (later to become a college) – and was rejected. I wrote back to the Censor, the college head, saying: 'I object to your decision. You were not fair.' He agreed to discuss it. I went up to Oxford and found him looking grumpy. He sighed and said: 'Now that you are here, do you play cricket?' Clearly there was a key vacancy waiting to be filled. I said 'yes'. He said: 'You're in.'

I have found that chutzpah often pays. Had I taken 'no' for an answer, a huge element of my life would be missing: my seventy years' love affair with Oxford – as a student, as the Chaplain to the Jewish students and as a visiting rabbi and trustee of the Oxford community and most recently as a patron of *OxfordShir*, the Jewish community choir.

I had already surmounted one other hurdle. I had realised that to read Law at Oxford I had to have A-level Latin. I had studied Latin at school, but not to A-level. So, in the middle of my sixth form, I had to go through the course from scratch to exam, in just six months. Thank goodness I got through, otherwise I would not have been given the place at Oxford. It probably doesn't apply now, but in those days, you needed Latin for Law.

Once at Oxford, there were further obstacles: I had no money. Because I had received a grant for the first year at LSE, I was not eligible for another

3. Oxford Days

first-year state subsidy. Luckily my school was very kind. The Governors gave me an award to cover the costs for my first year at Oxford. And then a generous uncle in America helped me out too. I was able to have a very comfortable first year at Oxford after all.

I did all the right things during my sojourn there from 1951 to 1954. I joined the JSoc (the Students' Jewish Society) and ate kosher meals at George Silver's popular restaurant, Long Johns. I went to shul on *Shabbat* and on Saturday afternoons I used to join in with the 'bun-fights' at the Roths. This was a discussion group that met at Cecil Roth's house. Cecil has been described as one of the greatest Jewish historians of the 20th century. As well as being an esteemed historian and educator he was also an expert on Jewish art and Hebrew book publishing. I remember our discussions being illuminating. At the time he was Reader in Post-Biblical Jewish Studies at Merton College, a position he held from 1938 until 1964. Cecil's wife Irene Roth used to get girl students to make a pile of sandwiches at the beginning of term, which then went into her freezer for the Saturday seminars.

I was also active in the Oxford Union. I was proud to be an honorary officer. I remember how nervous I was when I made my maiden speech. When you are an ordinary member speaking from the floor, you have just three minutes to state your case. After that, the secretary sitting at the desk rings the bell and flashes a card. If you go over the three minutes you have to stop. Now how did I do it? I made my three-minutes speech, but it took me about six weeks to prepare it, writing it, trying it out in the mirror, re-writing it. You are not allowed to read your speech, though you can have your notes in front of you. I think I needed a shower afterwards because I was in a bath of sweat. But after that I began to find that speaking for any length of time, short or long became no problem. A useful skill both for a barrister – and for a rabbi (but that came later – I was all set to qualify in law!)

I enjoyed what seemed to me the drama and theatre of the Oxford Union. To mark the ascension to the throne of Queen Elizabeth II, in 1952, a debate was held on whether the second Elizabethan reign would be as brilliant as the first.

I suddenly burst through the door wearing full Elizabethan regalia (courtesy of Moss Bros in London).

I'm not sure what I said, acting as an agent of the first Elizabeth, but my entrance caused a sensation. It was received with shouts and cheers. It brought the house down. This happened to be the first televised full debate at the Union and as they would say these days, it 'went viral' around the country. The film probably still exists in the archives, as it has been shown in decades since.

My friends along the corridor and I seemed to be full of practical jokes like this. Once we were chatting over coffee about what we would do if we were each left a million pounds. Somehow a rumour emerged that my American uncle had actually bequeathed me a fortune. Suddenly, I began to get dozens of begging letters. The more I denied I was wealthy, the more they persisted. What began as a joke, was picked up and exaggerated. The Daily Mail, Daily Telegraph and local papers got hold of the story and before long I was being invited to endow fellowships and scholarships. People who had never spoken to me before, now wanted to be my close friend. It was very interesting and amusing at first, but quite aggravating in the end. Our family home in London was surrounded by reporters on a daily basis. My parents were furious. My mother threatened to break my neck when I got home!

The JSoc was also a lively place, though locations were a challenge. In those days we students would hold meetings in members' rooms in colleges, or in the tiny synagogue on Richmond Road, Jericho, in central Oxford near Worcester College. The Society, which these days has a membership of around 500 people, was the first of its kind when it was founded in 1904. The initiative had come from the then Chief Rabbi, Dr Hermann Adler, who encouraged the founding of an intellectual society for Oxford's Jewish students who were first admitted to the university in 1856. (College fellowships were only opened to all in 1871.) It was called the Adler Society in his honour. The following year, the Zionist Society was founded and, in 1933, the two groups merged to form the Jewish Society.

While I was there as an undergraduate from 1951 to 1954, we founded another Judaic Institution – the rather tongue-in-cheek 'Cholent Society'. There were all kinds of dining and drinking clubs created by students at Oxford. We felt we should start one with a particularly Jewish flavour. We chose 'Cholent' the slow cooking bean stew that people made the day before the Sabbath and kept warm during the day of rest.

As did other such clubs, we used to hold a black-tie dinner every term, at which we served the notoriously stodgy dish in special pots. We invited internationally renowned speakers who all had to refer to cholent in some way in their after-dinner speeches. In the spring term, we used to dine on kosher haggis as well as cholent. The Alka-Seltzer company donated unlimited antacids to take after the feast. And there must have been a lot of hot air, one way or another! The Cholent Society ran for several decades going bankrupt about 20 years ago. In fact, it still owes me about £100. That was a lot of money back then. (I had better thank my 'rich uncle in America'.)

One of the really active JSoc people, with whom I have stayed in touch for decades, was the property developer Fred Barschak. He was at The Queen's College. Over the years Fred used to hold regular reunion tea parties for our contemporary Jewish students at Oxford, like the Hoffbrands, Anna Landau, who was married to the late distinguished composer Joseph Horovitz; Eddie Mirzoeff, one of Britain's most distinguished and respected TV film and documentary makers, who has perhaps received more awards than any other documentary maker including a CBE for his services for British broadcasting, a CVO for his documentary, 'Elizabeth R', and four Baftas. Another TV documentary maker in our group is Jeremy Isaacs, producer of ITV's 'The World at War' and later general director of the Royal Opera House, and winner of Emmy, BFI and BAFTA fellowships.

Visiting Chaplain

I have maintained and enjoyed a special relationship with Oxford ever since. I returned as visiting chaplain to the students and in time became the honorary rabbi and a director of the Oxford Synagogue and Jewish Centre (OSJC) Ltd (the company responsible for replacing the old building in Jericho in 1974). Funnily enough, the same George Silver who fed me as a hungry student, now worked with me on OSJC matters, together with his wife Frieda, George was a key fundraiser for the new synagogue building and became the synagogue president. True to form, their son Andrew Silver took on that role in subsequent years.

As visiting chaplain, I have clearly made a deep impression on several generations of students. It is very gratifying when leaders of communities up and down the country come up to me at various functions and say how I influenced them in their Jewish journeys and have ultimately changed their lives. Often, I can't remember their names – but they remember me.

One was Daniel Taub. To be honest, when I saw the name, it didn't ring a bell. He was an undergraduate at Oxford in the early 1980s, about to go to Israel. He was subsequently appointed Israel's Ambassador to London from 2016 to 2020. At a chief rabbi's conference, he saw me and threw his arms around me, saying we must get together again. He invited my family and I to spend a very pleasant *Shabbat* with him and his family at the Israeli Ambassador's official residence in St John's Wood.

In the course of my travels, I naturally encounter many who have an Oxford background. In the small Cheltenham community, I met someone who was applying to be the community's Hebrew teacher. In fact, he was a former Oxford academic and was very good at language teaching. But he was also a confirmed atheist. He offered to teach the children Hebrew but under no conditions any of the blessings! He would share general ideas on ethics but make no mention of God. That can be difficult with six-year-olds at a religion class! His offer was politely declined. I last met this same gentleman in Oxford in 2013 at the celebration honouring my many years of service. Two months later he was back reciting Kaddish at the local Holocaust Memorial service at Keble College. I wonder what happened.

Honorary Minister to the Community

The resident Oxford Jewish community of today, is an exemplary and a unique model of open-minded coexistence. The majority of members are Orthodox – but they also want freedom for the other groups. The main sanctuary in their building is normally used by the Orthodox; but they have a smaller room, a *beit hamedrash* at the back. Here non-Orthodox congregants can have services whenever they want them.

Everybody belongs to the same community. The synagogue chairperson could be Liberal, Reform or Orthodox. The same ethos applies to Hebrew classes, which are quite big and are always mixed. The whole arrangement works very well. Having one collective congregation means there is no poaching of members from one group to the other – as happens in a few other places where I have worked!

The secret of their success, I think is the fact that they do not have a resident rabbi. They keep me as their visiting minister as they know that I am fine with parallel services taking place at the same time and in the same building. As well as Orthodox, there could be a Masorti, Liberal or Reform service going on, depending on the group that wants to run it. It is a true multi-denominational community. If needed, say for a Barmitzvah, the Reform congregation will borrow the main shul. The Orthodox are fine to hold their service in the small room if they do not have a special event themselves!

The only stipulation is that the two services should finish at same time so that they can have a joint, unified *kiddush* (blessings over wine and bread and a social get-together sharing delicious refreshments) all together. That is particularly so on High Holy Days. Naturally, part of the deal is that all food is kosher. We are very strict about this.

3. The Oxford Synagogue Buildings

It was a great honour when the community invited me, the Jewish chaplain to the university and their honorary visiting minister, to officiate at the inauguration of the redeveloped building in 1974.

Membership of the Congregation is open to 'all persons of the Jewish faith', albeit with the crucial rider that any individual's access to religious rites (including bar/batmitzvah, marriage, burial etc) depends on his/her *halachic* status.

Halacha – literally means 'the way'. In Judaism it means the totality of the oral law and ordinances that have evolved since bible times to regulate the daily life and conduct of the Jewish people. From time to time these oral traditions were codified into laws according to the interpretations of the rabbis involved. The main issues that concerned my strictly orthodox parishioners were that to be considered 'halachically' Jewish, and so be eligible for various roles, rituals and honours, such as being called to read from the *Torah*, the person concerned, would have to have had an orthodox Jewish mother, and his parents (women are not allowed to read from the *Torah* in the orthodox world) had to have been married according to orthodox Jewish law.

At Oxford, unlike most orthodox congregations, both men and women are counted as full members, with non-Jewish spouses/partners of members offered non-voting associate status. There is no animosity or hostility amongst the members, because you are all equal parts of the same community, and all the cultural activities are unified. What a great example this is. I wish that this extreme and unusual tolerance would take off in other centres.

Having said that, I cannot deny that problems can arise from time to time – sometimes the result of new stringency, coming ironically from certain young students. And often it involves the *mechitza*, the barrier of some sort, to separate male from female worshipers – actually to hide the women so that the men are not distracted from their prayers.

I remember that this was a real issue in Aberdeen, Scotland, where some mental flexibility got us out of a fix. Someone complained that there wasn't a proper screening barrier. There was a simple horizontal railing that we put in place to demarcate the areas. After close examination, and discussion and correspondence with, and sanction from, the then Chief Rabbi, Jonathan Sacks, the community was eventually satisfied. The railing has now become the yardstick. When we have this problem every year at Oxford, of strictly observant students arriving from Golders Green or North Manchester, or having been part of a religious youth group like *Bnei Akiva*, who are horrified at the lack of an obvious complete barrier, I show them the letter from Rabbi Sacks in 1993 saying that for the purposes of this congregation, this sort of railing is valid as a mechitza. And that is the end of the argument.

Jewish history of Oxford

The resident Oxford Jewish community these days is about 300 member households – a considerable increase after a period of decline in the postwar years. There is the repeated interplay of Town and Gown, of settled Oxford folk with bright undergraduates and graduates 'passing through' – and present for only 24 weeks per year.

What we see today, and for the last two hundred years or so is the 'second coming' of the Jews to Oxford. A lively if small community existed before the expulsion of 1290. In fact, Jews were recorded as having settled in Oxford as early as 1075, shortly after the Norman invasion. It is said that Dead Man's Walk, near the Christ Church Meadows, was so named because of Jewish funeral processions. And Carfax, the medieval clock tower at the heart of modern Oxford, was rumoured to have been the Oxford Jewish Quarter. (Its name is derived from Quadrifurcus, where the four roads from the four city gates meet.) In fact, the old rumour was apparently true –

recent archaeological findings among the remains of Aaron the Jew's Hall, show that the owner kept a kosher diet some eight centuries ago. Or at least, it showed that he did not eat pork.

Oxford Botanic Gardens put up a memorial within their grounds in 2012, marking the spot where Oxford's first Jewish cemetery used to be. The burial ground was built on water meadows by the Cherwell River that medieval Jews bought shortly after 1177.

To their credit, Oxford City Council erected a plaque nearby in 1931. This newer memorial is much grander and features both English and Hebrew text – a fitting tribute to a long buried (if you will pardon the pun) facet of Oxford's extraordinary history. Across the road from the gardens stands Magdalen College, and during construction work on college land in 2016 builders discovered human bones, which turned out to be those of long-dead Jews of the 12th century. Those remains were respectfully reburied; and in 2019 the college put up their own marker to their memory.

After the friendly rule of the first two English Norman kings, William and his son Rufus, matters got more challenging for Oxford's Jews. Following a nineteen-year-long war between brother and sister royals in the 12th century, the two nobles pressurised local Jewish moneylenders to cover their battlefield costs. In 1231 the Hospital of St John was allowed to appropriate most of the Jewish-owned land around Magdalen, north of the High Street.

After the Ascension Day riot of 1268 the whole community was temporarily imprisoned and only released after the King got them to pay for a gold and marble crucifix in Merton College. In 1290, all Jews were banished from England.

It is said Jews seldom return to places where they had bad prior experiences, even many centuries before. But a small group of Jews re-established themselves near the city's East Gate in the 1730s. They were mostly pedlars and traders. In the 1930s there was a sizeable influx of Central European Jewish refugee academics to Oxford. Famous names included the visiting Albert Einstein. Sir Isaiah Berlin became only the fifth Jewish staff academic in Oxford when he took up his All Souls College post in 1932.

An aspect of Oxford life that I particularly cherish is the chance to share Jewish customs and concerns with the broader community. In my capacity as University Jewish Chaplain and also as Her Majesty's Armed Forces Jewish Chaplain I have been honoured to speak at many different colleges – for instance, on one Remembrance Sunday I lectured at Lady Margaret

Hall (LMH) where I talked about 'journeys' which was quite fitting for me I suppose.

Holocaust Memorial Day events

Throughout my work as military and university chaplain, and through interfaith activity, I have created, attended and officiated at many Holocaust Memorial events. Few instances can give greater satisfaction than seeing a one-off experimental event turn into a well-attended yearly occurrence. Such is the case with the annual Oxford University Holocaust Memorial service at Keble College

The story begins in the early 2000s, when the Chaplain of Keble College, a Christian prelate of Chinese origin, who became a good friend of mine, contacted me to talk about the Holocaust. I suggested that they might like to hold an interfaith service in their chapel, to commemorate those dark events. Keble chapel is particularly beautiful and offers a sympathetic setting for readings from Holocaust literature as well as hymns and prayers. Since then, the event has become an annual event for the whole university. The Oxford Jewish Community Choir, *OxfordShir* sings alternately with the Keble Chapel Choir. Each year Keble College finds a distinguished national speaker to enrich the occasion and make it more memorable.

The last such event that I attended was in January 2020, just before lockdown. The guest was Dame Stephanie Shirley, who had been a Kindertransport child refugee and who rose to become a pioneering businesswoman, champion of computing and of women in the workplace, as well as an irrepressible philanthropist. In 2010, the speaker at the chapel service had been Gillian Walnes MBE, who, with Anne's father, had set up the Anne Frank Trust. This organisation puts on travelling exhibitions of the story of Anne Frank so that her powerful and tragic story can help young people understand and challenge prejudice and hatred, and to embrace positive attitudes, responsibility, and respect for others.

Celebration of my 50 years on the Road

I was really touched when in 2013 the Oxford Jewish Community hosted a big celebration of my 'first fifty years' as minister for small communities. It was an extraordinary event to which my wife, children and other close family and friends had been invited.

One guest was the current Israeli ambassador, Daniel Taub. He, as we have seen, remembered me fondly as Chaplain from his student days at

Oxford in the 1980s. He paid me a glowing tribute, which I greatly appreciated. Another speaker was David Gifford, then Chief Executive of the Council of Christians and Jews, and many letters of commendation from all sorts of VIPs, Jewish and non-Jewish, from around the country were read out.

My son Brian went to great lengths, to arrange the viewing of the Bergerac television episode recorded at the synagogue in Jersey in which I had 'acted' as the rabbi in the synagogue (see the Jersey chapter). And I can never forget the gigantic cake they prepared, crested with a miniature model of my Rover 75, complete with its number plate – KC54 LTK.

It was very moving to me, to see how guests made such tremendous efforts to be there from so many of my small communities. The president of our tiny Canterbury group and his wife came by train, on a Sunday, all the way to St Pancras in London, then crossing over to Paddington, to get the train to Oxford, and returning home the same evening.

It was John Dunston, a member of the Oxford Jewish Congregation, and Music Director of the Choir, who orchestrated the event. He was kind

4. Professor Raymond Dwek is presenting me with the special 50th anniversary cake with my Rover car iced on it, at the Oxford celebration of my *first* 50 years on the road.

enough to say: 'Rev Weisman deserved no less. We wouldn't survive without him.' Brian Fidler Supernumerary Fellow and former Principal of Harris Manchester College, Oxford, added: 'He has been a beacon of light — sharing warmth, encouragement and a sense of belonging to towns where the Jewish community is measured in dozens, not hundreds or thousands.'

I replied that it has always been sad to me that mainstream Jewry does not appreciate that you can have a positive Jewish life in a small community with only 10 people. I shall keep going until I drop. The Oxford Community choir that John conducted sang a specially written song about my life on the road — it was fantastic.

This is the song they wrote and sang to me:

The song is based on 'Joseph's coat of many colours,' from the musical: 'Joseph and his Technicolour Dreamcoat.'

> *Malcolm Weisman is a very special guy,*
> *Peripatetic, he really can't deny,*
> *Ten thousand miles behind the wheel,*
> *To reach us all is no big deal,*
> *Contact with small groups really is his domain*
> *Anti-isolationist he will remain!*
> *And that is why, we can't deny*
> *He shows how much he cares,*
> *Communications begin to flow,*
> *'Get-togethers' start to grow,*
> *How we love his wise administrations,*
> *He's the best in skilled negotiations,*
> *He's a mensch above the rest,*
> *We wish him all the very best,*
> *Fifty years and Malcolm's not retiring*
> *He will keep the Jewish flag a-flying in:*

Oxford, Basildon, Bedford, Bognor, Bradford, Cambridge, Canterbury, Chatham, Chelmsford, Cheltenham, Chesham, Chester, Colchester, Cornwall, Coventry, Darlington, East Grinstead, Grimsby, Eastbourne, Exeter, Guildford, Harlow, Harrogate, Hastings, Hemel Hempstead, Hereford, High Wycombe, Lincoln, Luton, Maidstone, Margate, Northampton, Norwich, Nottingham, Peterborough, Plymouth, Reigate, Southampton, Staines, Stoke-on-Trent, Sunderland, Swindon, Totnes, Wallasey, Worthing, York, Llandudno, Newport, Swansea, Aberdeen, Dundee, Isle of Man, Jersey, Cork,
AND WE HOPE WE HAVEN'T LEFT ANYONE OUT!!

And they played Adon Olam in the style of Bach — my favourite composer.

This is how José Patterson of the Oxford Centre described the idea and preparations for the event which she said was such a wonderful and unforgettable occasion – a labour of love:

John Dunston, our cherished choir leader, always had something up in his 'musical' sleeve. On one such occasion he suggested that we should celebrate Malcolm Weisman's amazing achievement of 50 years in his role as peripatetic Rabbi to small Jewish communities throughout the UK.

'Malcolm was no stranger to Oxford – probably the largest of the small 'Rabbiless' communities – and being an Oxford man himself and a devotee of Oxfordshire Choir was assured of a warm welcome whenever he 'popped in' to our rehearsals. Malcolm was 'tickled pink' to be asked for a guestlist and set about inviting 'the world and his wife' with alacrity.

Then – shock horror – John and I discovered that Malcolm owned neither a computer nor a laptop! We could not understand how this wonderful energetic man kept in touch so successfully with 75 plus towns without any digital connection. In addition, Malcolm would phone with a list of additional VIP guests and vague instructions to phone Whitehall, House of Lords, the Archbishop's office and the like. When I had reached saturation point, I sent a one-word email to John – HELP! He arrived with his own portfolio of Malcolm's handwritten list of invitees together with an up-to-date Jewish Yearbook for essential clues for addressees. This took time and effort but later we were both rewarded and inundated with eager invitees from all over the UK keen to come to pay tribute to Malcolm.

Thanks to John's hard work and masterly organisation the celebration was an outstanding success. The synagogue hall was packed to bursting, the choir was in fine voice, and Malcolm's son, Brian produced a clip from the TV series Bergerac, filmed in Jersey, in which Malcolm had been asked to stage himself leading a typical Shabbat service in the synagogue. Delicious refreshments were served which included a superb cake topped with icing in the form of Malcolm's treasured Rover car! It was the creation of Sandra's sister, a baker extraordinaire!

Malcolm was truly moved when he was presented with a book of tributes from those who were unable to attend. The celebration ended when John led the choir with a song dedicated to Malcolm!

Brian Weisman sent the choir a heartfelt letter of thanks to John and the choir which he wrote on behalf of his father. He stated that although Malcolm was not short of accolades from his many walks of life, the Oxford Jewish

Centre together with Oxfordshire's 50th anniversary celebration for Malcolm, was by far the one which Malcolm would treasure all his life.

Lifelong connections to Oxford.

Every now and then, I get an invitation to lunch with the president of my old Oxford college, St Catherine's (Catz). Also, the college law alumni meet every three or four years. Being the Jewish Chaplain to the University of Oxford, I also had many invitations to address various events at other colleges. And of course, to round up my Oxford days, I was pleased to play cricket for my college.

4

The Military – From National Service to NATO

In 1957, having recently graduated from Oxford, I had begun to read for the Bar. Then compulsory National Service caught up with me. Under the National Service Act, introduced in 1947, healthy British males aged over 18 were obliged to serve in the Armed Forces, in my time for two years. This meant that all men born between 1927 and 1939, whose childhoods had already been clouded by economic depression, wartime bombing and evacuation, now had to be rounded up and forced into military service.

I was called up for the army. However, I felt a strong preference to be in the Royal Air Force (RAF) instead. I went round to the Air Ministry, which was in Theobalds Road at the time, and asked to see someone official. They told me that they really could not help me. But when they saw that I was not going to leave the building, they said, 'Hold on – there's a group captain upstairs who will see you.' There I met the officer in question who asked me: 'Your name is 'Weisman, are you related to a Group Captain Wiseman?' I replied, 'I've got a big family, could well be'. He said, 'Ok, we'll take you.'

I learned that during the Second World War, Group Captain Donald Wiseman had been the personal assistant to Air Vice Marshall Sir Keith Park, and in this role, he frequently conversed with Churchill when he rang to enquire about the current situation. Interestingly, it turned out that after the war, Donald Wiseman took a degree at Oxford in Hebrew and *Akkadian* (Assyrian and Babylonian) languages and became a biblical archaeologist and lecturer. He was appointed Keeper of Egyptian and Assyrian antiquities at the British Museum and a professor of Assyriology at the School of Oriental and African Studies, University of London. In 1956, Wiseman announced the discovery of four tablets of the Babylonian Chronicle which describe (for the first time known outside the bible) the capture of Jerusalem by Nebuchadnezzar in 598 to 597 BCE. He participated in archaeological digs in Iraq and even proposed a new location for the hanging gardens of Babylon. He taught courses on Old Testament History and Archaeology around the world and published works relating to the this.

Wiseman made several trips to Israel in the 1990s. Donald Wiseman was not Jewish, in fact he was fervently Christian and associated with the Tyndale House Foundation, a faith-driven public charity that distributes grants to Christian ministries around the globe.

Sure enough, I got called up and I was told I was going to be commissioned into the Education Branch of the RAF – if I passed the test. I was sent to RAF Uxbridge for a week and took all the assault courses. I am delighted to say that I passed as one of the first twelve, while most other applicants were rejected.

Having been accepted, I was waiting for the call, when I found myself talking to one of my good friends from the orthodox community, the one who had enjoyed quizzing my grandfather Reb Yankel on his superb biblical knowledge. He wondered whether I should consider doing something based on my rigorous religious training. I began to conjure the notion of combining military service with my friend's suggestion about 'taking up the cloth.'

I decided to share my thoughts with Chief Rabbi Israel Brodie who was a family friend. I visited his office to do so and met with his secretary, who was also an old family friend. I told him: 'I have seen the light and I think I want to become a rabbi.' Taken aback at first, he told me that Rabbi Isaac Newman had just recently resigned his commission as Chaplain to the Royal Air Force. So, would I be interested? This sounded very fitting for my role in the RAF. I realised that as a commission, it would mean spending at least three years in the RAF instead of the usual two allotted for national service. Even so, the thought intrigued me.

I duly went to see the Jewish Chaplaincy Board and the Chaplain-in-Chief of the Royal Air Force. Then, instead of going to the Education Branch, as previously planned, I went into the Air Force as a Chaplain. I did not intend to do it for more than the three years required, but in fact, the job has lasted a lifetime.

There was still the question of qualifications for the job as the Jewish Military Chaplain to the RAF! I consulted with Chief Rabbi Brodie. He undertook to verify my knowledge and he took me through the works of Malbim and Rashi, two prominent commentators on the Bible and the Talmud. Brodie was aware of my thorough Jewish educational background and knew my teachers and my family. Even though I did not go through the usual channels, he was happy to furnish me with a 'Letter of Authorisation.'

With this certificate from the Chief Rabbi, I had the authority to practise as a member of the clergy, not just in the RAF but anywhere. I had the right to bury, to marry and to lead services. Thus, I became a minister – something I had never imagined before I was drafted. It was the last thing on my mind! Yet it has shaped my life.

Chaplain to the RAF

When I joined the 'team', there were two full-time Jewish army chaplains: Reverend Moshe Davis, who was based in Germany; and Reverend Alec Ginsberg, who was based in London. And I – now Reverend Malcolm Weisman – was the new Jewish Chaplain for the Royal Air Force, replacing, Reverend Isaac Newman.

Alec Ginsberg and I shared the Woburn House office one floor below the offices of the Board of Deputies of British Jews. At first, I spent much of my time at home because I was based in London. I was attached to the RAF unit at Uxbridge, but I was not posted away immediately. This was convenient, especially as I spent my spare moments studying for my Bar exams. In fact, I eventually passed those while still serving in the RAF.

After that brief 'honeymoon' period, matters became more active. I realised, with pleasure, that travel, particularly motor travel under my own steam, would form a large part of my duties. This was not just in England. For instance, I used to drive from the UK to Germany via France and Belgium. When I had to be in Cyprus, they used to give me a Land Rover to drive, and the RAF provided me with a car and driver when I visited our military bases in Germany and in Singapore.

In the course of my travels, I always made a point of visiting the Jewish communities wherever I was stationed. That gave the job added attraction. I got to know the tiny Jewish community in Khartoum, for instance, which no longer exists. There was also a small community in Karachi, Pakistan with whom I spent a couple of days while stopping en route to Singapore.

Similarly, whenever I was visiting an RAF base anywhere in England, I would seek out the local community. Soon I discovered that most of these small communities around the country, were completely abandoned by the mainstream of Jewish life. When I asked Rabbi Brodie who looked after these places, he told me that nobody did. That is when I offered to support these small groups of Jews across the country. I felt that I could easily incorporate this activity with my visits to RAF bases. And that is how my small communities work arose – out of my military mission!

To call the chaplaincy job intense, would be an understatement. During the years of National Service in the 1950s through to the early 1960s, every

5. Here I am in my full RAF uniform at one of our RAF bases, 1957

fortnight some 6,000 youths were conscripted, with a total of 2,301,000 called up over the period of national conscription.

I used to meet hundreds of young Jewish men and some women going into the Royal Air Force. Every second Thursday afternoon, at five o'clock, I would greet every Jewish recruit at RAF Cardington, a small base in Bedfordshire, which at that time had gigantic hangars – for R101 airships, not yet jumbo jets. The new recruits were 'processed' there for two weeks before being farmed out to different basic training camps.

The RAF had six basic training camps in the country. However, all the Jewish conscripts were sent to one particular camp which was RAF Bridgenorth, near Birmingham where a synagogue had thoughtfully been established. Every fortnight twenty or thirty new Jewish airmen would arrive. There could be as many as 150 Jewish recruits at Bridgenorth at any one time. Once a week I visited the base, ran a service, and generally kept an eye on them. Many found themselves away from their families for the first time and were quite homesick, often never imagining that they would find themselves in the Royal Air Force. Basic training for them lasted eight long weeks. That was a demanding stretch for the young trainees. Sometimes I even had to act as agony uncle.

Rev Reuben Brookes of the Singers Hill Synagogue was the liaison between the Birmingham Jewish Community and the camp. He was the local chaplain on a day-to-day basis. He was the one who arranged for kosher meat to be provided for *Shabbat*.

If the young men put themselves down as Jewish, they were obliged to see the chaplain, whether they liked it or not. Some of them were not very pleased to be forced into this situation, and I must say, I was not so happy either. But I told them, 'Look, here we are, I'm the Jewish Chaplain for the RAF. You don't have to take advantage of my services, but I'm here if you need help.'

One or two people told me that they appreciated the fact that I was there, and they looked forward to seeing me when they went on to their further service stations. Quite a few told me, 'My grandfather was a rabbi' and I was meant to look impressed. I would ask 'What was his name'? I most often had never heard of him. I would nevertheless look very impressed, and say, 'That's wonderful', and they would say, 'We know all about Judaism because my grandfather is or was a rabbi, but we do not need to practise it.'

I worked out that every one of their grandfathers must have had a beard, and, to a person, with a somewhat assimilated Jewish background, anybody with a beard must be not merely religious, but a rabbi. Sometimes they used to tell me 'We eat chopped liver on a Friday night – and chicken soup too – so we know about the traditions. I used to get a lot of this, week in and week out. Two people impressed me with their candour, however. They said, 'Look, it is very kind of you to talk to us, but we don't believe in anything, so don't bother to make contact with us. We do not deny we are Jewish, but we are simply not interested.' (I write more about them in the 'Long-Haul' Chapter, in which I go on military journeys round the world, and we met again in Singapore.)

The late Rev Moshe Davis, a fellow and more senior (by about 16 years) Jewish military chaplain, was stationed with the British forces in Germany. He was a most remarkable person and a role model for me. He achieved so much and motivated so many by his thoughtful and friendly approach. Rev Davis never actually told anybody what to do, but instead led by example. He was wonderfully warm and full of enthusiasm for what he did. He gave lectures and sermons which were very easy to follow. He was not patronising in any way at all. People just loved coming to his talks. He managed to develop a very close friendship with each individual, which is what I try to do too. The result was that people came along to his talks and services because they wanted to be with him.

Rev Moshe Davis had spent about eighteen months working with the survivors at Bergen-Belsen at the end of the war. He did this sensitive and heart-rending work together Rev Leslie Hardman. Even though Davis served sixty or more years ago, I nevertheless used to meet many respected leaders of their communities, both religious and administrative, who had been inspired by him.

I learnt a lot from Moshe Davis. I could see that if you can get this kind of relationship, you're a long way towards creating an eager community. I tried to emulate him. When I am leading prayers in small communities round the country, I know that some of my most enthusiastic supporters are people who have had no previous background in Jewish life. They normally would not set foot in a synagogue, yet they seem to like to come to services when I am around.

The End of National Service

National Service ended in 1960, and the last drafted men were discharged in 1963 after deferred services were completed. That led to a precipitous fall in the number of Jews in the military. Comparatively few chose to volunteer for the army or air force after the mid-1960s. Understandably, the need for a fleet of Jewish chaplains disappeared. Shortly after National

Service ended, Dr Isaac Levy, Rev Moshe Davis and Rev Alec Ginsberg all retired, leaving me as the only one in office. At that time, I was thinking of leaving the military too, to concentrate on law. However, I suddenly found myself promoted to the position of Senior Chaplain, part-time, for the Jewish personnel in all three services: the army, air force and the navy. This is how my very rewarding career as a minister to the forces and small communities continued.

In my new capacity, I had to visit all the Jewish servicemen and women wherever they were, in the UK and abroad, to make sure they were keeping well and spiritually satisfied. Britain had troops all over the world in those days. Apart from the armies in Germany and Cyprus, we had bases which I visited in Malaya, Singapore, Hong Kong, Aden, Libya and Ceylon. I write about my longer-range military adventures across the world in 'The Long-Haul' chapter.

Moral Leadership Courses

It was fortunate that I had acquired a good basic knowledge of Jewish principles, history and ethics, because Moshe Davis, before he retired, had brought me to participate with him in what were called Moral Leadership Courses that he ran in Germany which I now had to preside over on my own.

These moral leadership courses had originated in the RAF in 1941 during the war and were held under the auspices of the various religious denominations. The first course, for Jews in the RAF and the Air Forces of other Allied Nations, was run by Dr Isaac Levy in August 1944, at Kfar Hanoar Hadati in Palestine and lasted for a week. Over time they were extended to all serving Jewish personnel and held in Britain and in numerous locations around the world, some arranged to last over the periods of the Passover and High Holydays festivals.

When I was a chaplain during the time of National Service in the late 1950s, we held the weeklong courses over the Passover and High Holydays periods in Germany and Cyprus. We brought all Jewish serving personnel of whatever rank together for these Jewish holidays. The army operated 'Church Houses' at its bases in both Kyrenia in Cyprus and at Lubekke near Dusseldorf in Germany. They could accommodate at least a hundred people and could be used by all faiths for religious purposes. We commandeered these for a week at a time in April for the days of Passover and in September for the Rosh Hashanah to Yom Kippur periods.

This was a busy time as not only did I run the festival services, but we also had to keep the troops educated and entertained each day for the whole period. This could include up to five hours of lecturing and other activity each day. We might visit a site of Jewish interest or have a sports afternoon and also had to prepare evening entertainment.

My wife Rosalie and our two boys Brian and Daniel would often accompany me to these courses, especially the ones in Germany as we would drive ourselves though France, Belgium and Holland to Germany – as a 750-mile round trip. I enjoyed driving and remember once having to go from our base in Germany to Amsterdam to collect our kosher provisions for *Pesach* and turning round and driving straight back. I was also to run shorter weekend courses like this at our other smaller bases in Aden, Gibraltar, Hong Kong and Singapore as well as in London.

These residential gatherings – our Jewish Moral Leadership Courses, continued long after conscription ended. Jewish service personnel were given special leave to attend these events and their spouses and children were encouraged to join them. The purpose was to reintroduce or reinforce Jewish values and identity to military personnel who were far away from their families and from Jewish surroundings for months, sometimes years, on end. This also gave them the opportunity to meet fellow Jews in the forces.

In the UK we first ran our courses for Jewish service personnel at Woburn House, helped by our chaplains' secretary. Later we used the beautiful Army Chaplaincy Centre in Somerset for our annual UK weekend meetings. This was the former stately home of Amport House near our base in Andover. There were 30 or 40 bedrooms to house our group and lovely spaces for our daily services and talks. (This building has now been sold off to make a hotel.)

Some senior officers have remarked that my annual *Shabbat* family get-togethers at the Armed Forces Chaplaincy Centre in the countryside, were for many Jews in the military – including some NATO guests from Holland, the USA and Germany – 'the only full *Shabbat* experience they are likely to enjoy for some months due to postings and locations.' (For some it may have been the only one they would experience at all.)

Hilary Fox of the Bedford Community reminded me of the story of Barry Harvey, a young refugee from Austria who joined the RAF. Once they let me know he was Jewish (the only one on his station) I immediately contacted him and went to meet him. As he was stationed near Luton, I put him in touch with the Bedford community who befriended him and ferried him to services. I also invited him to my next Moral Leadership Course.

Barry wrote an article about his meeting with me, for the Bedford Community Newsletter. In it he said:

Prior to attending the course, Malcolm, who was aware that I had not been able to have a Bar Mitzvah because of the dire situation for Jews in Austria before the war, arranged to prepare me for this rite of passage to take place during the course. He introduced me to a Jewish community where a kind lady taught me my parts of the Torah to enable me to take my 'Bar Mitzvah'. When the day arrived, the most special day in every Jewish male's life, it was a very big deal for me. We were all welcomed by Malcolm, and although I was extremely nervous, I felt supported. Malcolm conducted the service, and I was called up. I was in tears, not in sorrow but happiness. Malcolm had made me the proudest person that day, and if it was not for him, I would not be writing this. Throughout my RAF service, I always made sure that I attended all Malcolm's courses. When I went with David Young of the Bedford community to see Malcolm at his own special day in Oxford where they celebrated Malcolm's fifty years supporting small communities, I did not say a word, but this dear man remembered me straight away. It is an honour and privilege to know Malcolm, and to see him after all these years was great as I have always wanted to have the opportunity to do so.

Naval events

In 1993, I was especially pleased to be guest of honour and speaker at an event attended by 200 naval officers at HMS Dryad in Portsmouth. This is not a ship but a shore establishment. It was home to the Royal Navy's Maritime Warfare School. My speech highlighted that the armed forces were truly the first British institution to pursue the concept of tolerance of people of different faith groups.

Six years later in 1999, I found myself at another Portsmouth event with naval significance, although this time the occasion was more sombre. The local reverend of the Portsmouth Synagogue, Herschel Caplan, co-led with me a Service of Remembrance for the sixty-nine sailors aboard the Israeli submarine, Dakar, all of whom had died during an accident in January 1968.

The Dakar was one of three submarines that Israel had bought from Britain. This particular vessel sank inexplicably near Cyprus during its maiden voyage from Portsmouth to Haifa. We learnt at the ceremony that the seamen had befriended local Portsmouth congregants during the submarine's two-year refit before tragedy had struck. Adding to the poignancy of the occasion, London-based film director, Arnon Manor, recalled how his father had changed his plans and chose to travel early on the doomed Dakar. His intention was to return to Israel as soon as possible to see his newborn son, that is, Arnon himself. I was proud to represent Her Majesty's Armed Forces (HMAF) alongside representatives of the Queen and the Israeli Embassy on that moving day.

Throughout my military career, I have been supported not only by my family and colleagues, but also by an institution called Her Majesty's Forces Jewish Community. It was created in 1947, long before my arrival, to support and celebrate Jewish serving personnel in the UK Armed Services across the Regular, Reserve and Cadet Forces. Its thirtieth anniversary was celebrated with an informal dinner at the Ministry of Defence in March 1977. At that event, I was pleased to sit alongside the deputy Secretaries of States for all three services, as well as Jack Harman, adjutant-general to the Forces, and the principal chaplains of the Army, Navy and Air Force.

Moving to NATO

Two factors led to a profound change in focus for the armed forces, changing the nature of my work in the services. The first was the shift from conscription to a professional standing army. After National Service was phased out during the period 1960-63, comparatively few Jews chose to join the forces.

The other key factor was Britain's post-war withdrawal from its former colonies. Newly independent states formed their own standing armies and thus had less need for UK military protection. Therefore, in the late 1960s the British government closed key overseas military bases, especially in the Middle East. These included two RAF bases that I used to visit, in Aden and Libya. Both of these places had small yet notable Jewish populations.

However, these twin factors – end of conscription and closure of British colonial bases – did not lead to a reduction of our foreign deployments. However, such deployments in Europe now came under the umbrella of the North Atlantic Treaty Organisation (NATO). As a result, my military chaplaincy work expanded considerably in the 1970s in the European arena.

For instance, in 1977 I presided at a session of NATO Naval Senior Chaplains held near St Albans. The conference was also attended by the NATO commander-in-chief, General Haig and Dr Lancelot Fleming, former Bishop of Norwich.

I used to revel in the title Secretary-General of the Allied Air Forces Chiefs of the Chaplains Consultative Committee, having been elected to that post in 1993. I have also remained the lifelong Senior Chaplain to the NATO Armed Forces Committee. In this capacity I am invited to attend

NATO weekend conferences. I am always moved by how well I am treated these days. The organisers used to arrange for extended stays and go to great lengths to ensure that Rosalie and I could properly observe the Sabbath and that the food served was kosher.

I had the chance to rebuild ties with Continental European communities. This was not only a privilege, but also helped me in my own small way to restore long severed ties between British and European Jews. Since the fall of the Eastern Bloc and then the Soviet Union itself, NATO has gradually expanded eastwards. This development has had a profound and largely beneficial impact on the communities of the former Warsaw Pact. From 1997, Jewish leaders in Hungary, Poland and the Czech Republic have generally welcomed this trend. In their eyes, it meant coming under a Western envelope, and reuniting with their brethren in Western Europe, from whom they had been cut off for so many decades while living behind the Iron Curtain.

6. Two Yarmulkas greeting! At a NATO Chief of Chaplains' Conferences in Rome in mid-1990s, we had a special audience with Pope John Paul II outside the Vatican. Upon shaking hands with me, the Pope asked why I had not yet emigrated to Israel.

My NATO obligations meant that I often visited the British Army of the Rhine (BAOR) to meet Jewish personnel. BAOR grew out of the British invasion and then occupation armies during and after the Second World War from 1944 to 1948. After that, BAOR became a fulcrum of the West's defence against the Eastern Bloc. As BAOR came under the NATO ambit, I enjoyed meeting and comparing notes with fellow Jewish chaplains from the USA, Canada, France, the Netherlands, Belgium and other places.

BAOR ended in 1994, following the Ministry of Defence's 'Options for Change' defence cuts, and the appraisal then of military threats from the east. Since then, a reduced British Forces Germany (BFG) has taken its place. One sidenote is that the worrying Russian invasion of Ukraine in 2022 has arguably increased the importance of the BFG as a bulwark against Moscow and Putin's intentions – but that is another story.

Whenever possible on my European tours, I tried to connect with and visit local Jewish communities. They were often the last small outposts of what had once been large and vibrant populations. I had the pleasure of combining the military and civilian aspects of my European journeys, when I was invited to conduct a Jewish wedding between the daughter of the head of a local German Jewish community, Deborah Ahnsfeld, and a Corporal of the British Army, Malcolm Iveson. This took place in a town near the river Rhine in late 1989, after I had conducted one of our Moral Leadership Courses nearby. It was the first Jewish military wedding since 1945.

A widening religious perspective in the Armed Forces

In the chaplaincy of the 1950s, I had been one of a small handful of Jews amongst literally hundreds of Christian clerics. I was the sole source of information on Judaism and Jewish life and customs.

Fifty years later, recognising the changed demographic of the population of the United Kingdom, the Armed Forces appointed their first Buddhist, Hindu, Muslim and Sikh chaplains. I appreciated the day in November 2005 when I joined the Defence Secretary John Reid in welcoming them. Reid stressed at the time the importance of 'spiritual, moral and pastoral support' being available for service men and women of all faiths. I fully agree with that credo, and I also concur with his observation about the importance of morale. He said, 'It is not just a matter of a service man or woman being happy, it is not just a matter of trust and comradeship, it is also a matter of spiritual fulfilment.' Until then, Jews had been the only non-Christian religion who were permitted to have their own chaplains.

In 2015 I was posed with a most unusual task. This might sound like something out of Monty Python, yet it was true. I was asked if I could compose a three-minute Jewish burial service for use while under fire! Even more remarkably, I was asked whether I could – or rather, I was told that I should – give a similar final farewell to a Protestant, Catholic, Muslim, Hindu or any other faith soldier who had the misfortune to die in combat or training.

What did that mean in practice? Well, if I was in the field and discovered a dead Buddhist, according to his identity document, I, or whichever chaplain was on that rota, would take out my Buddhist burial card, or my Protestant card if he were Protestant, and so on. Then I would have to read it with all the respect due to someone who had literally just sacrificed his or her life for their country.

Just think of the presence of mind you need to recite three minutes' worth of the catechism, say, while bullets fly all around. An even larger challenge would be how to handle texts in different languages. Imagine having to deliver the traditional Muslim prayer, Surat Fatihah, presumably with the Arabic transliterated into Latin characters for a non-Muslim. By the same token I suppose a Baptist minister who encountered a fallen Jewish soldier might be able to recite the Kaddish if it were written out in Latin characters. That would be a quite a task on a 'normal day', even without the pressure of battlefield conditions!

Now consider the other suggestion from on high: Could I create a 'service' of just three minutes, summarising the essentials of a fuller ceremony. Well, that was another challenge. Somehow, I managed to meet the brief. And I daresay my many years up to that time, of devising short and halachically compatible services for small communities up and down the country and the world, made it seem less like 'mission impossible'!

Today (2022) I am a trustee of the Armed Forces Chaplaincy Centre, though my on-the-spot duties are rarer. I do still attend the inductions of new chaplains of all faiths and ethnicities into the services as an honorary officiating chaplain. And I still enjoy attending our annual leadership weekends for the UK military and NATO.

The Royal Navy Chaplain who became Jewish!

I would like to add a special story – about the Royal Navy Chaplain who became Jewish! Reverend William Walter claims that I was 'the influence' that prompted his full Beth Din conversion to Judaism. I first met Bill in the 1960s, when he was the Senior Christian Chaplain at Portsmouth Naval

Base. He invited me down from time to time, to talk about Jewish matters. One day he said, 'Oh, I would love to see some of your services', so I invited him to join me for a weekend in London, which he really enjoyed and thereafter came quite often.

One Friday night I noticed that he had something under his arm, and it looked like a *tallit* (prayer shawl) bag. 'But you're not Jewish', I exclaimed. 'Oh', he replied, 'I just want to wear it sometimes.' I had to explain to him that we did not normally wear it on a Friday night. I invited him to sport the garment the next day at the *Shabbat* morning service in the synagogue.

He became deeply interested in Judaism, together with his wife, who came from a devout Catholic family. In fact, her brother was a Catholic priest. Before long William and his wife decided to convert to Judaism; and in record time they were converted by the Beth Din. He was living in Farnham, Surrey, at the time, and he asked me if I knew if there were Jews in Farnham. 'Well', I said, 'I know there are one or two who are members of the Guilford congregation, but I really do not know who they are.'

Straight away he said, 'No problem – I'm going to find out.' He had already worked out a plan: he would go to the stationers WHSmith and ask the shopkeeper, 'Who among your customers buys the Jewish Chronicle?' Of course, I knew that many non-Jews buy the JC too, but I didn't want to dampen his spirit.

Not long afterwards he reported back: apparently the shop manager was very sympathetic, but said it was a confidential matter, and he could not divulge who his Jewish customers were, nor who amongst them bought the paper. When he saw how crestfallen Bill looked, though, he had suggested that Bill stand on the pavement outside the shop on a Friday. 'And what you do there is not my business.'

On our third debriefing, Bill proudly revealed that he knew that seven people in Farnham bought the Jewish Chronicle from WHSmith's. 'So, did you speak to them and did that reveal who was Jewish?' I asked. 'No', he replied, 'but four of them emerged, hiding the Jewish Chronicle, under their arms, so I assumed that they were Jewish. Three appeared, reading the paper very ostentatiously, and I assumed they were *not* Jewish.' I have always thought that was quite an astute observation about the low profile that many Jews like to keep in some of these smaller communities!

Clearly Bill could no longer be a Christian chaplain. After he converted, I got him a job as secretary to Rabbi Abraham Levy, spiritual leader of the Spanish and Portuguese (Sephardi) community at their Lauderdale Road, Maida Vale, headquarters. After that William went to teach *bar mitzvah* boys at Pinner United Synagogue. Rabbi Mickey Rosen and I officiated at the couple's strictly orthodox Jewish wedding, which was held at the Pinner synagogue. Later, he and his wife returned to Ireland. I believe they ran a strictly kosher home and that he used to *daven* (pray) every day. this was in their splendid isolation, as they lived a long way away from any established Jewish community. I understand that he only went to synagogue once a year, for the High Holy Days.

One never knows how far one's influence may stretch!

National Service changed my life.

National Service changed my life, as no doubt it did for many. Had there not been the post-war conscription in Britain, I most certainly would never have had any military connection at all, let alone a life-long one. Furthermore, it is clear that had it not been for my military service as a chaplain, I might never have become a minister either. My life would have taken an entirely different and less interesting trajectory.

I had the rare honour of being a commissioned officer in all three of HM Forces. I was a Squadron Leader in the Royal Air Force and also held a high rank in the Army and the Navy.

5

The Law – Barrister and Recorder SE Circuit

I had decided early on that I wanted to be a barrister. The journey to achieve this was not easy, but very rewarding. I had to battle to get to Oxford University to study law. I had quite a struggle to fund the first year there. After university, finding time to study for the law exams between my National Service commitments around the country as the Jewish Chaplain to the Royal Air Force and making the acquaintance of pockets of Jews near the RAF bases was quite difficult. Finally, in 1961, I was called to the Bar at Middle Temple.

The origins of my legal leanings probably began with a schoolboy jape I devised when I was School Captain at Parmiters School in Bethnal Green in the early 1950s. I decided that if the pupils wished to protest against either the detention or the 'lines' that we prefects had given them, we would set up a court to hear their pleas. The plan was that we would hold court in the small library every lunchtime. I appointed one of my prefects to be the prosecutor. Another served as defence counsel. If a student came to complain about what he thought was an unreasonable punishment, I would adjudicate. That seemed to me a fair way of doing things.

The trouble started as soon, as I discovered that the prefect that I had appointed to be prosecutor, was extremely vindictive. He was very hostile when he presented the prosecution case. I realised that there was going to be serious trouble if I let it go on. So, the court which had started on a Monday, and had a second hearing on the Tuesday, was abandoned by Wednesday. It lasted just two days, because I just could not risk the wrath of the real authorities if they heard what was going on up there. I have told subsequent headmasters the story, and they cannot believe it. Maybe that planted the seed in me – or more likely, it reflected my latent desire to advocate and adjudicate on behalf of the aggrieved.

I had set my heart on reading law at Oxford, but instead my school had deflected me saying it would be easier for me to study Law at the London School of Economics (LSE) which I duly did. However, I did not enjoy my time there. It was like being at school. The lecturer would call out your name to tick it off on the register. There were a hundred of us who started in the first year. We were told, in no uncertain terms, that at the end of the first year, thirty people would be thrown out. In the second year, another thirty would be removed, leaving just thirty or so for third year. Our lectures were intercollegiate, so on Monday we might be at LSE, on Tuesday at Kings College, on Wednesday at University College London, and so on.

I passed the first part of my Law Degree at LSE that year, despite having spent much of my time as editor of the LSE fortnightly newspaper called 'The Beaver'. This is a prestigious publication. Over the years the national press has picked up some of its stories.

I was still determined to continue at my first choice of University, Oxford. I was eventually accepted at St Catherine's Society. (In 1962, this became St Catherine's College, Oxford). Although they were reluctant to take me at first, I was eventually accepted when I mentioned I could play cricket. I thoroughly enjoyed my time at Oxford, being active in Student Societies and the Oxford Union. (More is written about this in the Oxford Days chapter).

After graduating in 1954, I was all set to pass my Bar exams and join the Inns of Court to launch my longed-for legal career. My plans, however, were interrupted by conscription for National Service. I opted for a role as a Jewish Chaplain to the Royal Air Force (RAF). (I write about my extensive and enduring military career in the 'Military' chapter.)

While serving the RAF with my chaplaincy duties, I developed a side interest, seeking out and helping small groups of Jews in small towns and villages in England and the Commonwealth wherever I could find them. While doing all this, I continued studying for my Bar examinations.

I was helped to pass these exams by rigorous instruction from a private tutor recommended by Jeremy Thorpe whom I had known at university. His father was a distinguished lawyer. Jeremy read Law at Oxford, though his first love was politics. He soon headed the Oxford University Liberal Society and was President of the Oxford Union, both of which I also joined. Jeremy was later elected a Liberal Party MP aged just thirty and later became leader of the party – before his sad downfall.

I was called to the Bar at Middle Temple in 1961. I soon learned that joining an Inn of Court was only one of the stages towards becoming a fully-fledged barrister. There was first the little matter of obtaining pupillage – a sort of apprenticeship for a barrister. In order to be registered, you needed to complete six months of civil law pupillage and another six months of criminal law.

7. Each of my three careers had its own costume. Here I am wearing my legal regalia, the gown, and wig.

Pupillage is similar to being articled to a solicitor. These days 'pupils' get paid for this, but not so when I was a young lawyer! Indeed, we had to pay our pupil master 100 guineas for each six months, for the privilege of being a pupil. Fortunately, I had received the Gladstone Pupillage Prize from adjudicators at the Middle Temple, who possibly saw some potential in me.

There is fierce competition for pupillage nowadays. My own chambers, 1 Gray's Inn Square, recently had 350 applications for just two or three pupillages. That is quite frightening. Sixty years ago, the situation was less formal. In my case, it was almost a family affair. I approached a very distinguished Queen's Counsel, Sam Stamler. I asked him if I could do six months of pupillage with him in civil law, and he took me on there and then. Maybe it helped that we knew each other from Jewish study groups; or at least, I knew his wife, Honor Brotman, whose father had been the Secretary of the Board of Deputies. My Civil Law apprenticeship turned out to be a bit haphazard as every now and then I had to disappear for a few days at a time, to do my visiting duties as RAF chaplain.

Next, through my friend Leonard Gerber, who later became a circuit judge, I met Cyril Salmon, another distinguished Queen's Counsel who took me on for my six months of pupillage in criminal law. Cyril was later to become distinguished Judge assigned to the Queen's Bench Division. He has knighted and later created a life peer, fittingly Baron Salmon of Sandwich! He was the son of Montague Salmon, one of the most remarkable entrepreneurs of the firm of Salmon & Gluckstein. They were first tobacconists and then major event caterers and food manufacturers and the creators of the famous Lyons Tea Rooms and Corner Houses that dominated Britain's high streets for nearly 100 years between 1894 and the 1980s. The firm, known as J Lyons and Co, also founded the Trocadero at Piccadilly Circus housing prestigious restaurants. They also built and owned London's landmark hotels, the Strand Palace, Regents Palace and the Cumberland Hotel at Marble Arch. J Lyons & Co was also a pioneer in introducing computers to business. Between 1951 and 1963, the company developed, manufactured and sold a range of LEO (Lyons Electronic Office) computers. Though having been ahead of the curve in this regard, and in many ways paved the way for computerisation in business, they left the field to the burgeoning specialised companies such as IBM and concentrated instead on their core businesses.

It did not take long before I realised criminal law was to be my true calling.

Joining chambers

Fortune smiled on me again after those twelve months of pupillage, when I began looking for Chambers. I met the esteemed divorce lawyer, Count Dmitri Tolstoy, great-nephew of the famous Russian author. The count had escaped from Russia in 1920 and settled in England. He was granted British nationality in 1946. By the time I made his acquaintance he was a respected Queen's Counsel. (His son is the historian, monarchist and occasional politician, Nikolai Tolstoy.)

Count Dmitri's Chambers were located at 12 Kings Bench Walk, and I joined him and stayed there for about four years. Later Tolstoy retired and I left that practice soon after the barrister Harry Lester took over. Around that time an MP called Willy Wells, QC, started a new set of Chambers in Middle Temple Lane. I was invited to join them, and I moved there.

8. Gray's Inn Square

Eventually I settled at 1 Gray's Inn Square. These Chambers were then run by Terry Boston. Interestingly, Terry and I shared a connection with the RAF. He was first a pilot officer, then a flying officer, and in 1960 he became a flight lieutenant (the same year he was called to the Bar in Inner Temple). When I joined the Chambers, Terry Boston was a senior Labour politician. He later became Lord Boston of Faversham. The set of Chambers was originally headed by Dame Rose Heilbron from Liverpool. Lord Boston succeeded her when she became the first Jewish female High Court Judge. Little did I suspect that within 20 years of qualifying, I would become the head of these Chambers!

Criminal Barrister and Judge

In defending criminals, you start at the bottom – at the Magistrates' Court. Here you deal with cases involving speeding or driving through a red light. Then, as your reputation gets known by various solicitors 'weightier' cases start to come your way. That is how you build up your practice. As you become more experienced, you would move from the Magistrates Court to the Crown Court or Quarter Sessions. Cases get more involved and tougher. You develop a relationship with particular solicitors for the defence. How far you go depends on what your instructing solicitors think of you.

As far as the prosecution is concerned, all major prosecutions were conducted by solicitors for Scotland Yard. It was considered to be quite a privilege to get on to what is called the 'Yard List'. This meant the right to conduct prosecutions on behalf of solicitors who served Scotland Yard. There was a waiting list to get onto it. I applied, and after two or three years, my Clerk told me, 'Oh, your turn has come, you've been given a Yard brief.' He told me that when I go to court, there would be a senior solicitor from Scotland Yard, sitting behind me, and if I failed this, I had had it. 'There is no second chance.'

Along came two briefs, for fairly minor cases in one of the local magistrates' courts. I went to court and, thank goodness, I passed the test!

A memorable case

Many cases spring to mind when I think back on my career as a criminal defence barrister. One of the most extraordinary concerned an eighteen-year-old boy who had escaped from Borstal. He then went on to commit – wait for it! – two hundred and fifty house burglaries over a short period of time, in and around Central London. It appeared that he had an amazing photographic memory too. He was able to give the police a detailed confession statement about each and every one of the houses that he had entered. All of these places had indeed been burgled, and there he was, admitting to doing them all.

My unenviable task was to defend him. When I got the brief I naturally assumed that this would be a case of mitigation. I thought I had to find something good to say about him. I must try and plead for as lenient a sentence as possible. Yet when I saw him, he protested: 'No, no, I'm not pleading guilty, I'm pleading not guilty'.

'Are you seriously going to say you didn't commit all of this?' I replied. 'No', he retorted, 'I am admitting that I did them all. But I have to tell you why I really am not guilty'. What followed was bizarre and illogical – though maybe it made sense on an emotional level.

'I have been in this Borstal for ages,' he explained 'and I hated the place. I couldn't stand the headmaster and so I escaped.' (All this I knew to be true). 'Well, I was on the run for a long time, and so I pleaded guilty to those crimes on the basis that, maybe, because of the severity of the case, I would not be sent back to Borstal, but I might go to a prison instead.'

Where did you get this information come from, I asked? 'Well,' he replied, 'one of my colleagues in Borstal was very proud of the fact that he had committed all these burglaries; he gave me all the details, and I remembered them all. I thought that if I admit to these crimes, at least I won't go back to Borstal.'

This was simply not the case, because he was not old enough. If found guilty he would have had to go back to Borstal anyway. Clearly my client's Borstal 'colleague' was not at all put out that someone else would pick up the tab for his crimes!

How would any jury on earth accept his innocence? And how could I, as his barrister, persuade them of the truth of his argument?

Suddenly I thought of a way out. The year was 1965, and newspapers were full of news about James Beauclerk, son of the Duke of St Albans, who had run away from Eton College. Young James insisted that he simply couldn't stand life at Britain's most elite public school and preferred to be a stableboy.

I decided to throw caution to the winds. I treated the jury to a forty-minute impassioned closing speech. This is what I said:

Here you have the story of this young man, the defendant, who has pleaded guilty to offences that he claims he didn't commit, because he was so determined not to go back to Borstal. He was horrified at what goes on at the that Institution. Now, think carefully about this, because here, on the other hand, you have read in the papers about a case in which the son of a duke ran away from Eton College because couldn't stand what was going on there. Think of it, here we have somebody running away from Eton because he couldn't stand it. Are you surprised, then, that my client wanted to run away from a Borstal? Obviously, life in a Borstal is much more terrifying than what goes on at Eton College.

The jury listened, left the room, deliberated, and returned a short while later. Their verdict was in: they acquitted my client. You should have seen the judge's face – it was something to behold!

I recall another two cases that were less successful, though for reasons wholly out of my hands. Both were set in the Commonwealth. The first concerned two Arab gentlemen who had been convicted of murder in Zanzibar. My potential clients were due to be hanged. I was to appeal against the death sentence. I was led by a Queen's Counsel (QC) who had close connections in Africa. The QC and I duly arrived at the place where we were to appear before the Privy Council in Downing Street with all our papers, specially bound and printed in special documents. Suddenly the Clerk to the Privy Council appeared and said, 'Oh, I'm terribly sorry gentlemen. Your clients were hanged this morning.' It was all quite tragic, and bizarre, not to mention disappointing.

The other Commonwealth case that landed on my desk was to be heard in Patna, a region of West Bengal famous the world over for its excellent rice. At short notice I was supposed to defend some alleged terrorists. They were members of the Ananda Marga group, or Path of Eternal Bliss, which was founded in 1955 as a Hindu 'socio-spiritual organisation'. By the late 1960s, when the trial was due to be held, this ostensibly peaceful group was accused of violent clashes with Communists and other violent actions. Then, just as we, the English lawyers were about to fly to India, British Government security ordered us to stay away. They had uncovered intelligence that we might be murdered!

Head of Chambers

In 1980, nearly 20 years after I qualified as a barrister, I suddenly found myself saddled with the job of Head of Chambers. I say 'saddled' because, while most will hear the term and imagine a hugely prestigious promotion, the job had several serious drawbacks, and I had not wanted to do it at all.

My predecessor as Head of Chambers at 1 Gray's Inn Square, Terry Boston, had already spent more than a decade as a Labour MP. He had since become the Shadow Lord Chancellor in the House of Lords, during the early years of Mrs Thatcher's Conservative rule. Terry found that he had too many strenuous political duties and decided he had to drop his Chambers post. He persuaded me, against my better judgement, to succeed him. (I could see that there probably was no one else in Chambers at the time who could have taken it on – or perhaps they were just passing the buck.)

Overnight, I was responsible for the finances of the group. There were no partnerships at the Bar, so one person, the Head of Chambers, had to take on the entire lease of the premises and be personally responsible for it. The rent for Chambers in the 1980s could be up to £50,000 a year, added to which the council tax was vast, because we were just on the edge of the City of London, so that was another £60,000 or so. I had to raise all these large sums including staff wages for our Clerks and the heating, water and gas expenses in order to keep the place going.

We had a big split in the Chambers at one stage, with some people walking out, which is not uncommon in the Law. I soon realised that if my Chambers went down the tube, and all the members decamped, I could personally be left with debts running into maybe several million pounds.

We used to assess the amount that members paid on the basis of their income. The minimum was about £600 to £800 a month. If you were earning, say, £100,000 a year, you had to pay up your share, which could be as much as £20,000 a year. That is how we raised our money. Collecting it all could be an arduous exercise, and of course you have to make sure that the work is coming in to pay for it.

Until the 1960s many Chambers were very small. There might have been six or eight good close friends, and they could pool resources and cover expenses. They would take a very small number of rooms in the Inns of Court, their expenses would be fairly limited, and you would cope. However, when you get to the stage where you have to employ a Chief Clerk, three or four Assistant Clerks, and you have up to sixty members, you are really a boss running a major business. One of these clerks would be working full time as your bookkeeper, so it's no small endeavour.

Other tasks falling to the Head of Chambers was having to hire and fire members. Sacking people who just were not meeting their obligations was the most unpleasant aspect of all. It could be a lonely job, and there were times when I did not like it at all.

Despite the stresses and strains, I am proud of what I achieved as Head of Chambers over the eight years that I held that position. I completely restructured the place. When I began, the finances were in a parlous state. At one point, we were down to as few as eleven members of Chambers – that is, only eleven full-time practising barristers. Over my time the numbers went up and up, and when I handed over to my successor, we had over sixty members.

Becoming A Judge

Reflecting on my earliest days as Recorder (a part-time Judge) there was absolutely no training such as there is today. Soon after I got my first judicial appointment as a Recorder in November 1981 the Clerk rang me and asked if I was 'interested'. 'In what?' I asked. He replied: 'Would you like to sit at such and such Crown Court next week?' When I asked him what I was expected to do, he just said, 'You'll find out.'

The case was held at the old Willesden Crown Court, which was conveniently just up the road from my home. At the end of the case, I had to deliver a sentence after a guilty verdict was given by the jury. Afterwards, I turned to the Clerk and said: 'I hope I was alright; that was my very first case.' He said nonchalantly, 'Yeah, you did alright.' Then he added, 'By the way, did you not have any instructions or guidance?' I said, 'No.' To which he responded, after suddenly remembering, 'Oh, I've got a little list here,' and he showed me a sheet of paper with advice to new judges. Nobody had ever considered giving me such an instructive document. When I saw it, I went pale, but, thank goodness, I had got it right.

The legal world can open up possibilities of work in fields of which you may never have dreamt. Some may be onerous, but others can be truly fascinating, even though they may seem like a bureaucratic chore at first. That was the case when I became a Parliamentary Boundaries Commission Adjudicator and also when I sat on the Immigration Tribunal.

Parliamentary Boundaries Commission Adjudicator

Constituency boundaries were reviewed every ten to fifteen years, in order to accommodate demographic changes. The job advertisement arrived at our Chambers and as it sounded interesting, I applied and got the post for the 1980s assessment.

The principle is equity. Strict guidelines have to be followed. The idea is that each parliamentary constituency should represent more or less the same number of voters. At the time 67,000 was the accepted benchmark. The results, however, sometimes led to certain constituencies being subsumed into new or existing constituencies. Some parliamentary seats simply disappeared off the map altogether! Our job was to make sense of an overwhelming load of data.

Once decisions had been made, we had to spend many long hours hearing petitions for and against boundary changes. We had to make sure they were not going across housing estates or dividing families. Naturally, this led to many conflicts, not least among MPs themselves. Furthermore, when seats vanished, former sitting MPs were left adrift. Such was the case with Stanley Clinton-Davis, a Jewish Labour Party MP for what was then Hackney Central, in East London. The constituency had been created in 1885, and Clinton-Davis was its parliamentary representative for four terms, from 1970 to 1983. During that time, he served successfully as Undersecretary for Trade.

Following our constituency review in the early 1980s the seat was abolished. I assumed Clinton-Davis would be bitterly disappointed at losing his seat – not at the hands of a disgruntled electorate, but merely over a boundary ruling. However, this dramatic and apparently disturbing change proved a blessing in disguise for him. At that precise moment, the Government was looking for a new Commissioner to serve Britain in Europe, and Clinton-Davis got the job! Following his many achievements as MP and in Brussels, he entered the House of Lords as a life peer in 1990. In due course, he rang me up and expressed his appreciation for my decision.

Another MP who had lost his seat along the South Coast due to my rulings also came to thank me. As a result, he was free to take up the post of Governor of Gibraltar!

My role involved hearing petitions and writing reports. It was a lonely job; but a rewarding one too, as it promoted fairer democracy in Britain, which I strongly support. Besides, how many jobs are there where you can alter 'facts on the ground' with the stroke of a pen?

Immigration tribunal

Another job I applied for and succeeded in getting, was being on the Immigration Tribunal panel. This meant sitting at the immigration desk at Heathrow Airport as an on-the-spot advisor to frontline immigration officials as claimants came through customs. You had to decide whether single people or entire families were genuinely eligible to be claiming asylum. I listened to what they had to say and what the government officials said. Sometimes there is no choice but to refuse the entrants, if they had no family already in the country, or if they had entered dubiously, or showed no obvious right to be here.

What connects Law and being a Minister?

You may well wonder, what connects the law with being a minister to small groups of Jews in the army, at university or scattered about the country. One obvious link is the ability to inspire them by delivering a convincing speech, often at short notice. In the debating society of the Oxford Union, I discovered I had an aptitude for speaking in public. That is, once I overcame my nerves before giving my first three-minute presentation.

Before long I found that public speaking was easy for me. This certainly helped my legal career. I have led both for the prosecution and for the defence in many major trials at the Old Bailey. I have noticed that my colleagues would often become stressed out by staying up all night, writing copious notes for their opening speech, or their closing speech. They would be looking at their notes closely and almost reading their jotted-down words verbatim to the jury.

By contrast, I had done no such thing. Sometimes I would have been out visiting a community the night before, returning home for a short sleep before waking up at four the next morning to gather my thoughts for the speech I would have to make that day. Of course, I would have studied the materials and discussed the case in a general sense, but I could do that very quickly. I have the ability to assemble my thoughts and address the Jury directly without the need for notes.

Wearing my rabbinical hat, if I am asked to give a sermon on a *Shabbat* morning at synagogue, I will probably start thinking about the portion of the week in the days beforehand. (The sermon usually had to reflect thoughts gathered from the portion of the Torah that would be read in the synagogue that week that are relevant to our life today.) I would not really concentrate on the actual words until the actual reading from the Torah scrolls had started during the service itself. Then I would concentrate on the story and meaning of Torah portion, sometimes I might even change my mind about the theme. However, by the end of the reading, and by the time the scrolls had been rolled up and 'dressed' in their covers and adornments and paraded around the synagogue before being replaced in the holy Ark, I would be ready to give my sermon.

Usually, I find that I do not need to write things down, which is very useful. Too many barristers, I have noticed, become almost prisoners to their pre-written notes. On the other hand, my lack of notes can be a bit awkward because there's no record of what I have said. This is why when people want to publish a talk of mine – and assuming it is not on *Shabbat*, when this would be banned – I recommend that they record it.

Discretion, and maybe even a flair for using euphemisms, are other qualities that both a good barrister and an able rabbi need to cultivate. Luckily, I find that I can absorb information very quickly. Sometimes as the rabbi officiating at a funeral or stone setting, I have been asked to talk about the deceased, whom I may have never heard of before. A note would be handed to me as I arrive. Fortunately, I can process this very quickly and get a mental picture of the personality. I can perhaps credit this talent to my legal training. Very often I would walk into Chambers at nine in the morning and be presented with the need to be prepared to go to Court in a matter of hours, having grasped all the implications of the case.

What, you may well ask, was a typical day? Well, the frank answer is, there never was a typical day! Each day was different and often entirely unpredictable. In a sense, being a barrister is like a 'resting' actor suddenly pressed into service; or a soldier on the frontline, patiently waiting days on end for 'action', and then at a moment's notice thrust into the heat of battle.

My days would be spent in court, while three or four nights a week I would be running around to attend to my other duties. Occasionally, I would take advantage of a 'blank' period if there were no immediate cases.

Or I might have a big trial starting on a Thursday or Friday, with the previous Monday, Tuesday and Wednesday off. I would do my preparatory work, and then I would jump into the car and visit a military base, and a university or a small community. It was a most peculiar existence, even abnormal. Not realistic at all, but I loved it. Images of that man in the Chinese circus forever spinning plates and rushing around from one pole to another, spring to mind.

I might call my Clerk at 4.30pm on a Monday and he might say 'There's a trial starting tomorrow morning at the Old Bailey, at 10.30am. We've got a brief here. It has come in, under your name as an expressed wish from a solicitor, so would you please prosecute (or defend) it.' I knew every telephone booth in the UK as that was what I needed to use to keep in touch with my chambers, my communities and my family. (How useful a mobile phone is today).

I might be on my way to a scheduled Jewish community meeting in say Bognor Regis. So as soon as the event finished, around 10.00pm, I would leap back into my car and drive to London, reaching my Chambers at 1.00am. I would pick up my brief and arrive home at 1.30am where I would look at the papers for the case before settling down for a good, though short, sleep.

I would get up at about 6.30 the next morning. I would probably leave home by 7.15am to get to court before the car park was full. Even when I first began my law practice in the 1960s, parking in Central London was a big problem. I would be carrying a heavy bag, with my wig, my gown and all my papers, and any other books I required, so I needed to park close by. Sometimes I would have to drop off our younger son at the City of London School, on my way to the Old Bailey, or the Inner London Crown Court, or to wherever I was going.

Court would finish around 4.00pm, and then immediately I would check my diary to see where I was meant to go next, wearing my ministerial or military chaplaincy hat – down to Devon or up to Oxford or Cambridge, or whichever locality needed my help.

At the other end of the law

I also had the opportunity to experience the law from the opposite end of the spectrum when I began to visit Jews who had been through the courts, had been convicted and were serving time at Her Majesty's pleasure.

This part of my 'legal' or rather 'ministerial' career began in the late 1950s. Chief Rabbi Brodie knew that I had begun visiting some army bases in the West Country. He casually asked me one day that if I were passing by Dartmoor in Devon, could I spare the time to pop in to check on the needs of some Jewish prisoners? Of course, I agreed to do so, which led to four decades as the visiting Jewish minister to nine of Her Majesty's Prisons. As I was driving some thousands of miles every week anyway, if I were in Eltham, Surrey, for instance, I could visit Ford prison and in Devon or Cornwall I could visit Dartmoor.

In 'serving my time', as Prison Chaplain, I came across Jewish prisoners from respectable families both non-observant and observant. I met Jewish robbers, drug dealers, even murderers, child molesters and rapists. You may meet the odd Jewish solicitor behind bars who has been struck off for fraud. Yet the stereotype of the canny white-collar criminal, is as typical of a non-Jewish as it is of a Jewish offender.

I noticed though, that Jewish offenders tend to be late developers. It is still rare to find Jewish juvenile miscreants. For some reason, things start to go wrong after about 21 years of age. Presumably, what little family pressure there had been, becomes relaxed, and freedom becomes synonymous with breaking the law.

Working with convicted criminals was not about telling them how bad they had been, nor was it about forgiving them. It was not my job to point out the error of their ways. They certainly knew that already. Instead, I tried to recognise the good in every person. A crime, no matter how heinous, should never define the entirety of a person. Jewish teaching emphasises *teshuvah* – return and repentance. If you can change even one life for the better, it is worth it. Therefore, I was keen to meet the prisoners and to see what I could do for them.

My approach was to have a chat over tea with five or six Jewish inmates – maybe robbers – or 'lifers' who had probably murdered a dozen people between them. Maybe, I thought, the meetings and activities that I would arrange such as a study session or a prayer meeting might assist in their rehabilitation. Sometimes a simple action such as lighting Chanukah candles together or joining in with a communal Passover seder can rekindle a gentler side that they had suppressed for so long. One or two of the prisoners that I befriended, have turned up trumps and done extremely well. I even officiated later on at the marriage of one young man.

Prison regulations state that an inmate is whoever he or she says he is. If they say they are Jewish, they are entitled to a visit from a rabbi. Many times, I have met with prisoners who are clearly not Jewish. Some eventually confessed that they opted for a Jewish identity because they thought that kosher food might taste better than normal prison rations. One case stands out in particular. There was a charming man who was clearly not Jewish. However, he spoke fluent Yiddish and excelled at the questions I posed at the prison *shiurim* (religious lessons) that I ran. It turned out that he had worked in a kosher hotel in Bournemouth and proved a quick learner. As he had only three months left to his sentence and was an example to the others, I was happy to continue to treat him as an 'honorary Jew'.

Besides kosher meals, there are a few extra privileges Jews in prison may enjoy. For example, Jews may opt for days off for *Shabbat* or a festival, but in so doing this could mean losing out on the most sought-after jobs. Pentonville and Wormwood Scrubs, in London, even have a 'synagogue' room where Jewish prisoners may go to pray. Some Jewish prisoners serving their sentences in open prisons have been invited by local small communities to make up a minyan for *Shabbat* or festivals.

In the 1990s there were said to be about 200 to 500 Jewish prisoners in Britain's prisons at any one time. Often a prisoner would protest piteously about racist bigotry from everyone including police, judges, juries, warders and fellow prisoners. His family might assure you that he would not be inside if he were not Jewish. You start to feel their pain, until it transpires that their 'innocent relative' has a list of convictions for grievous bodily harm as long as your arm! On the other hand, it is certainly true that overt displays of Jewishness – like *peyot* (sidelocks) or *kippot* (skullcaps) – can arouse a degree of prejudice. Prison is a pressurised microcosm of life in general and such bigotry sadly exists. Any perceived vulnerability or difference is seized upon, and the Jewish prisoner may be tormented by his fellow inmates.

Many prisoners are remarkably candid about how they got themselves into trouble. They blame no one but themselves. Quite a few have made new lives and found new partners after leaving jail. For some, however, no matter how hard they try, they sadly seem trapped in a life of crime. They end up going from one prison to another.

Although I found prison visiting a rewarding activity, it was becoming hard to manage as part of my busy schedule. I was therefore very pleased that in the early 2000s my eldest son, Brian, was able to take over this role entirely.

Brian takes up the story here. He says:

My work for my father, for which I am eternally grateful, started in the late 1990s. Dad had to visit several people along the south coast in various homes and hospitals and a few people in Suffolk. I had recently wound up my music business and was spending my spare time learning to fly at Denham! I was used to long distance driving and staying overnight, so dad offered me the opportunity to assist him, by visiting some of the members of small communities on his behalf and on behalf of the Jewish Memorial Council (JMC). I worked for the JMC for several years, driving to various villages and towns around England, visiting people in remote parts to offer company and support. Dad continued with all his normal visiting and driving to small communities, but this was in addition to visit more lonely, sick and isolated Jewish people. It was a wonderful time for me.

'*This led to dad asking me in 1999, to visit a prisoner at Her Majesty's Prison, The Verne, on Portland Bill. Following a successful visit, dad felt it would be beneficial for me – and for the prisoners – if I were to act as his deputy. He realised that I would be able to visit all his prisons on a more regular basis than he could.*

'*After a year or so and formally joining the United Synagogue Prison Chaplaincy Committee, as a Prison Chaplain, I then took on more prisons in my own right. At my peak, I was covering sixteen prisons, from York to Devon and the Isle of Wight. Nowadays, I am only covering a few prisons, having retired from many and a number of prisons closing over the years. I have found it rather challenging at times. As my father had done, I had to deal with (and am still dealing with) many bogus requests for a kosher diet to be issued by the prison.*

'*I also joined JAMI the Jewish Association for Mental Health in the late 1990s, continuing my interest in visiting people in hospitals and psychiatric units for the organisation. I am still working for JAMI, hospital visiting and co-ordinating hospital volunteer visitors.*

Brian said that he has much to be grateful to his father for – to which I reply, that it is I who have much to be grateful to my son Brian for. This has been an enormous help to me and is a true extension of my ideals and desires – that I could not possibly fulfil all by myself. So many people have been very pleased to have Brian visit, console and comfort them in hospitals, care homes and prisons.

6

Interfaith

To describe Christianity's historical relationship with Judaism as tempestuous would be something of an understatement. All the more reason, I firmly believe, that Jews and Christians should never miss an opportunity to get to know each other better.

I have always sought to educate and demystify prejudices and to help build a more harmonious future for the Britain we all love and share. I have engaged in such interfaith work from my earliest days as a Military Chaplain. When speaking to young conscripts from 1956, I was a struck by the ignorance of many about Jews and the Jewish religion (sometimes among Jews themselves). While visiting our RAF bases, I had many opportunities to talk not only with the young airmen – but with the many Christian chaplains as well. This led to many invitations to visit them in their churches around the country, to talk about Jewish life. I never refused.

Jews in Britain

Jewish people were first invited to settle in England by William the Conqueror in about 1070. The Jewish community was protected by and served the King. England's Jews were skilled doctors, goldsmiths, artisans and poets. However lending money was their primary function and source of income. Jews were permitted to give loans at interest, whereas Christians were not. In this way, Jews became fundamental to the working of the English economy. They provided loans for many of the most important figures at the royal court. This could be for the purchase of property, building castles and cathedrals, fighting wars and other projects. But when things got tough for the king or his courtiers, they could turn on the Jews to repeal their loans – or else!

The reign of Henry II (1152-89) is generally seen as a time when Jewish privileges were best protected. (There was an advantage to an English king for this protection. The Jews, unlike the rest of his subjects, could be taxed at whatever rate and whenever he wanted. When a Jew died, all his property went to the crown.)

The year 1180 seems to have marked the zenith of their prosperity and success. After that, things turned sour. The king and his nobles resented the prosperity of the Jewish communities and particularly wanted to cancel the pledges to the Jews for money owed which they could not and did not want to repay. Religious fervour fuelled by the Crusades swept through England, causing many Christians to feel and show enmity towards the Jews.

From 1189 when Henry II died, the situation for Jews deteriorated further. When his son, the new King Richard the Lionheart acceded to the throne that year, Jewish dignitaries bearing gifts were not allowed to attend the ceremony and instead were stripped, whipped and banished from the court. This gave a signal for violence against Jews to break out in almost all the towns in which they resided.

These riots actually caused a heavy loss to the English exchequer, both by the impoverishment of the Jews who survived and the plunder of the assets of those who were killed – making the position of the now more penurious Jews even more precarious.

King Richard I was the leading commander of the Third Crusade. Following the path his father Henry II had trodden in the Second Crusade, he set off for the Holy Land in April 1191. He was victorious in several battles against Saladin's Muslim armies, including the capture of Acre. Although the Crusaders had aimed to retake Jerusalem from the Saracens – they did not manage to achieve that ambition.

Richard was unfortunately captured, on his way back from the Holy Land when his ship ran aground at Venice. He was captured by his 'colleague' King Leopold of Austria – who was persuaded to hand him over to the Holy Roman Emperor Henry VI. Richard's support of King Tancred of Sicily had angered the Holy Roman Emperor, who rather fancied the Mediterranean island for himself. For such political reasons they saw the opportunity of extracting a large sum of money from England to have their King back.

To pay this enormous sum of 150,000 silver Marks, Richard's dutiful mother, Eleanor of Aquitaine, began to scrape together the money. Both clergy and laymen were taxed for a quarter of the value of their property, the gold and silver treasures of the churches were confiscated along with money, and additional taxes were imposed on knights. England also turned to the Jews, who they felt were prosperous at their expense – though they were by now quite impoverished. They were summoned from several cities to Northampton and made to pay a disproportionate amount of the ransom – three times as much as was demanded from the Burghers of London, by far the richest city in the kingdom. (Sir Walter Scott's novel Ivanhoe throws some interesting light on the role of the Jews in ransoming Richard.) When Richard returned in 1194, he tried to settle things down and allow the Jews to lend money at interest and to regulate loans from the Jews.

In the next century, although there were moments of respite, the situation for Jews deteriorated further. Pope Innocent III issued edicts calling upon all towns to compel the remission of all usury demanded by Jews from Christians. This would of course render the Jewish community's very existence impossible. They were also compelled to wear a distinguishing badge on their clothing. Many towns expelled their Jewish Community from 1269 onwards. Added to this was the spreading of fabricated and malicious rumours of Jews kidnapping Christian children and using their blood for Passover rituals, known as the 'Blood Libel'. This untrue insinuation resulted in many Jews being shunned, hounded, imprisoned, and executed. This influenced the views of ordinary people. The official stance of the Church was also slowly shifting from tolerance of Jews to increasing hostility.

Eventually on July 18, 1290, King Edward I, having returned from his own Crusade, with his own coffers depleted, decided that he had no further use for the impoverished and persecuted Jews. He duly issued writs to the sheriffs of all the English counties ordering them to enforce a decree to the effect that all Jews should leave England before All Saints Day (1 November) of that year 1290. Apparently, in return for this Edict of Expulsion, Parliament granted Edward a tax of £116,000 – the largest single tax of the Middle Ages.

The Jews were allowed to carry only their portable property. Their houses reverted to the king, except in the case of a few favoured persons who were allowed to sell theirs before they left. Somewhere between 3,000 and 16,000 Jews (depending on the sources) were expelled. They fled back to France and Spain and further afield. Some were tricked by ships' captains, offloaded on to sandbanks and left to drown when the tide rose.

Jews of Medieval York and the Clifford's Tower Commemorations

A particularly horrific event in these early times, was the massacre of the Jews of York in March 1190. The Jewish population who had supported the king and his courtiers, was hounded upon and fled to Clifford's Tower – where they thought they would have the king's protection. There they met their deaths, either being murdered, or they committed suicide lest they would be.

6. Interfaith

Eight hundred years later, as a Senior Executive of the Council of Christians and Jews, I was asked by Geraldine Auerbach, Director of the Bnai Brith Jewish Music Festival, to be the Religious Advisor for a long weekend of Jewish and Christian collaboration in commemoration of the Clifford's Tower events.

My friends and colleagues, including the Canons of York Minster, and leaders of the York Council of Churches readily engaged with the project. So did the History Department of the University of York and members of the York Anglo-Israel Society – the only association of the few Jews living in York at the time. (There had been an embargo in place for centuries against Jews living in York.) The significant Jewish Community of the nearby industrial city of Leeds also became partners. Geraldine was the mastermind who organised monthly meetings for all of us in order to create a truly memorable long weekend encouraging interfaith understanding in March 1990.

9. Our guests climbing stairs to our historic events in Clifford's Tower

It started on a Thursday afternoon with a ceremony inside Clifford's Tower itself opened specially for the occasion. Here, in the presence of the Archbishop and the Lord Mayor of York and other civic and religious leaders, my colleague Rabbi Norman Solomon, (who was also heavily involved in Christian/Jewish education) was able to recite the traditional Jewish prayer (the Kaddish) for those that had perished – probably for the first time in the setting where they had met their end. In this moving ceremony Cantor Ian Camissar of Leeds intoned the traditional melody for such occasions: *El Mole Rachamim* (God, Full of Compassion).

After this auspicious start to the interfaith weekend, there followed a reception at the Guildhall addressed by the Sheriff of York and the President of the Board of Deputies of British Jews, who at the time was Dr Lionel Kopelowitz, each stressing the need for tolerance and understanding between faith communities.

Many Jews from across the country flocked to York, joining with the Christian denominations of York's residents. The weekend included talks on medieval poetry and about the notoriously antisemitic passion plays. There were walks following Jewish trails and concerts including works related to, or specially written about the massacre in York. One of the highlights was a performance of Ernest Bloch's *Sacred Service,* sung in Hebrew in one of Britain's most important cathedrals, York Minster. Louis Berkman, Cantor of the Belsize Square Synagogue took the role of the cantor with a specially created choir for the occasion, comprising the Zemel Choir plus the Alyth Choral Society from London and the Bach Choir of York. All were trained and rehearsed by Malcolm Singer, who was at that time the Director of the Zemel Choir who made regular trips to York to rehearse.

The synagogue services for the Sabbath that weekend were truly remarkable. Both the Friday night and Saturday morning services were attended by more people than had ever got together for Jewish prayer in York in its entire history! Not only were there Jews of all denominations from all over the country praying together, but also nuns and priests, academics and the general public of York.

The Friday evening service was held at the Quaker School and conducted by Reform Rabbi Walter Rothschild. It must have been one of the most glorious services in the country that night, with the 40-strong Zemel Choir, a Jewish mixed choir from London under Malcolm Singer, providing the beautiful Sabbath music for the congregation of more than 500.

Everybody came out elated. Dr Edward Royle, the Professor of History at York University who had compiled a booklet on the history of the Jews of York for the occasion, came out enthusiastically showing the prayer book and saying, 'Even the words are the same!' This to me demonstrated how useful this weekend was in facilitating Christian-Jewish understanding.

A huge joint Friday night dinner for 200 participants was held at the ancient Merchant Adventurers' Hall with a hot kosher meal imported from Manchester. On the Saturday morning, I led an orthodox Sabbath service at a 'popup' synagogue at the Viking Hotel, again attended by a large congregation from many different faiths. For some explanation, we had arranged for an 'Ask the Rabbi' session at the end of the service. We felt this might be needed to clarify to the non-Jews what it was all about. I had three companions with me on the panel: my reform colleagues Rabbis Walter Rothschild, Jonathan Romain and also his wife Rabbi Sybil Sheridan. The service had run quite late, (on that particular sabbath there were two readings from the scrolls of the law) so many of the participants had gone home for lunch. Nevertheless, some of the remaining, mainly Jewish, attendees kept us on our toes asking questions for over an hour. (This was a rare example of collaboration between the different Jewish denominations.)

In the afternoon we had organised three separate bible study sessions for all, discussing the portion of the week. Each class was headed both by a Christian minister and a rabbi. This proved very popular for the attendees from all faiths. A Canon of York Minster excitedly told us that they had been 'drinking from the fountain' as the rabbis set about dissecting the story word by word, even letter by letter, as they usually do.

On Sunday morning I found myself and some Christian and Jewish colleagues racing around York, visiting several church services to see if they were, as promised, delivering their sermons on the theme of interfaith ideals. We must have visited about twenty churches in a couple of hours.

This incredible weekend ended on Sunday afternoon when the Archbishop of York, John Habgood, and I presided over an event we called 'Expressions of Heritage and Hope' in York Minster. We chose significant Jewish and Christian prayers and readings. The Zemel Choir, conducted by Malcolm Singer sang Hebrew psalms and Herman Berlinski, a Jewish composer, one of whose works had been performed on the Thursday night, and who had come over from America specially for the event, played the organ in the Minster. All members of the 2,000-strong 'congregation' were invited to light a candle that had been placed on their pews and come forward to 'plant' it in the soil mound they had constructed, representing Clifford's Tower.

We hope those glowing lights, and the experiences of the weekend, left a lasting impression of how Jews and Christians could live together in harmony with greater understanding of each other.

Commemoration of the 805th anniversary of the Clifford's Tower atrocity

A few years later I was again contacted by somebody who had read an account of the 800th anniversary commemoration in 1990 and seen a TV programme about the Jews of Medieval York. His name was Gyora Novak. He had the idea to present an oratorio in Clifford's Tower. He called it *Sh'maa! (Hear) – The Dirge of York*. He also had the inspirational idea to cover the mound on which Clifford's Tower stands with thousands of yellow Stars of David – in the form of small six-pointed daffodils, that would naturally bloom in March every year to honour the event. What a beautiful memorial – but how was this to be implemented?

This time, I used my military hat, and persuaded the Army to send three lorry-loads of soldiers, with spades at the ready, to plant two hundred and fifty thousand daffodils on the mound of Clifford's Tower. They were assisted by the Girl Guides and Boy Scouts of the city. We had a small window of opportunity for planting to make sure they would open to perfection at the right time. Talk about a logistical challenge – happily, it succeeded!

The mound was ablaze (in a good way) on 17 March 1995 for this 805th commemoration. We had created what a local editor wrote: 'The yellow hill of York each March, converting that hill of shame to a living, blooming, act of anti-bigotry, like nowhere else on earth.'

Nowadays, it seems that due to climate change and the exigencies of the weather, they bloom earlier and earlier each year, and you can now see them opening up in February – with a rather sorry brown mess by March! Nevertheless, all these years later most are still there to remind us of the ups and downs of Jewish life in York.

Jews Return to England

Between the expulsion of the Jews in 1290 and their formal return 366 years later in 1656 at the time of Oliver Cromwell, who had overthrown the monarchy and instituted a short-lived republic, there is no mention of Jewish Communities as such on English soil. Jews were officially able to return and could again set up businesses and places of worship. The number of Jews that came at first was quite small and were descended from the Sephardi communities of the Netherlands and Italy. In 1723 Jews were first given the right to be called British Subjects and were allowed a specially worded oath in court. But oaths for other purposes remained unchanged. It took centuries, however, for Jews to be accepted as full citizens and to take their places at universities and in Parliament. Up to 1833 no Jew could be a barrister and not until 1845 could a Jew be elected to local councils. It was not until 1858 that Jews could take their seat in Parliament – even though elected to the office. The last hurdle was overcome in 1871 when Jews were allowed to enter Oxford and Cambridge Universities as undergraduates.

On the positive side, at the turn of the 20th century, Britain had accepted over 140,000 poor and very religious, Yiddish speaking Jews, migrating from villages under the Russian yoke in Poland and Lithuania. This area, known as the 'Pale of Settlement', was where Jews were forced to live with restricted occupations and under threat of persecution. When Alexander II was assassinated in St Petersburg in March 1881, there was considerable unrest and particularly for Jews. The new Czar gave them permission to leave – and leave they did. This included all four of my own grandparents.

They were part of a miraculous relocation of nearly three million Jews out of the poverty and persecution of Eastern Europe to the freedom of America, Britain and its Empire. My grandparents were able to settle down in North London in safety and security. Their children benefitted from living in a free and largely tolerant society. With hard work and attention to their children's education, these immigrants were ultimately able to prosper and to contribute incalculably to society in many fields wherever they had settled. Many, including members of my family, excelled in the disciplines of medicine and science, business, academia and the arts often making significant innovations and discoveries and contributions to their chosen fields.

However, tensions remained. In 1930s Britain, the Nazi aligned British Union of Fascists known as 'Black Shirts' provocatively marched through the Jewish streets of London's Whitechapel and Ridley Road, Dalston. Many politicians and even royalty, including King Edward VIII himself, shared some of Hitler's anti-Jewish sentiments. So, it was fortunate for liberty, and for the Jews, that Churchill decided to go all out to defeat the tyranny of Hitler and Fascism.

English doors were not wide open to accept Jewish refugees from Europe. Thankfully however, after Hitler came to power in 1933, there were schemes to help as many as 45,000 educated and cultured European

Jews, who had been dismissed from their positions in academia, the arts and business, to find refuge in the UK. They too contributed greatly to British society, especially in university circles, art, science, architecture and music.

In an amazing undertaking, in 1938 the British Parliament accepted the arrival of 10,000 unaccompanied Jewish children fleeing from Nazi anti-Jewish threats in Germany, Austria and Czechoslovakia. The position was so dire that parents were prepared to pack a little suitcase, tie a label round their necks and let their children go. They might have been hoping to join them or to have them back when the troubles were over. Most of these children sadly never saw their parents again, as they had been murdered in the concentration camps. Today there is a statue to remember them at Liverpool Street Station.

British people from all walks of life, all religious backgrounds and from all over the country, stepped forward to care for these children who arrived on trains at Liverpool Street Station on what came to be known as the 'Kindertransport'. The Refugee Children's Movement took care to ensure that whenever a Jewish child was placed in a Christian home the child would not be subject to conversion attempts and that contact was established with the nearest Rabbi.

The Council of Christians and Jews (CCJ)

As a Military Chaplain, I had made a point of explaining Judaism to Christians, talking to new recruits and to Christian chaplains. I was often invited by them to address church groups around the UK about Jews and Jewish life. It therefore seemed natural that I should become aligned with the Council of Christians and Jews (CCJ) which had been officially founded in 1942 – at the very time of the worst atrocities ever meted out to Jews.

I became an active member of CCJ and was invited to address local grass-roots groups that had been founded all over the country. Whenever I visited a CCJ group in centres small and large including Edinburgh, Newcastle, Manchester, and Belfast, I always tried to make sure that the local Jewish community turned out in force. My brief was to talk about interfaith relations that were relevant at that moment – like particular festivals, or to give a thirty-minute presentation about what Judaism is, to those who know nothing and had never met a Jew. Later I was pleased to become a trustee and even later Vice President of the Council of Christians and Jews, a position I still retain.

It is worth considering the people and events that led to the founding of CCJ. Quoting from *The History of the Council of Christians and Jews – Children of one God*, written by my friend, Rev Marcus Braybrooke who was the senior executive of CCJ, I can tell you that even before CCJ was established, initiatives had been developing to bring Jews and Christians to a closer understanding.

The London Society for the Study of Religions, founded in 1904, included Jews in its membership. In 1924 the Presbyterian Church of England General Assembly had formed a subcommittee to discuss the lack of understanding between Jews and Christians. The committee wished to abandon proselytising and instead promote cooperative engagement.

Also in 1924, the Social Service Committee of the Liberal Jewish Synagogue, St John's Wood, had held a meeting for Jews and Christians 'to confer together on the basis of their common ideals and with mutual respect for differences of belief'. From this developed the Society of Jews and Christians in 1927, that provided a platform for a number of notable speakers.

The inter-war period was marked by a reappraisal by Christian scholars of the Jewish religion. In 1930 Rev Dr James Parkes published *The Jew and His Neighbour,* setting out the causes of anti-Semitism and its Christian roots. Parkes was a tireless fighter against antisemitism and helped rescue Jewish refugees during the 1930s and campaigned for European Jews during the Holocaust. He worked throughout his career to promote religious tolerance and mutual respect. (Parkes would later be placed on Hitler's list of those to be killed if the Nazis invaded Britain.)

The Parkes Institute at Southampton University, named after him, is one of the world's leading centres for the study of Jewish/non-Jewish relations. Its scholarly expertise ranges from antiquity through to the present day, and their archive is one of the largest Jewish documentation centres in Europe.

By the mid-1930s various groups made up of Jews and Christians were involved in giving aid to Jewish refugees from Germany, whose number rose sharply after the so-called Kristallnacht, 9 November 1938, when Germans rounded on Jews in their midst, wrecking and looting Jewish property, stoning, and killing Jews and burning down synagogues.

After this catastrophe, and following the passing of the Nuremberg Laws, Anglican, Free Church, and Roman Catholic Churches came together in 1938 to form a Christian Council for Refugees. The Council's secretary was W.W Simpson, a Methodist minister, who would dedicate his life to the improvement of Christian-Jewish relations. His 1939 pamphlet *The*

Christian and the Jewish Problem recognised the role of Christianity in Jewish suffering, involving factors such as deicide, the Crusades, the ghettos, the Inquisition and their influence on present day persecution.

Out of these diverse groups that marked Jewish-Christian dialogue and aid during the 1930s, a proposal was circulated with a view to forming a national organization. William Temple, who was then the Archbishop of York, invited leaders of various communities to discuss these suggestions in 1941. He outlined the mission of what was to become the Council of Christians and Jews. The Council would work against all forms of discrimination and promote the 'fundamental ethical teachings which are common to Judaism and Christianity'.

The Chief Rabbi Dr Joseph Hertz agreed with this approach and highlighted the central point as being 'the danger to civilisation involved in antisemitism, as well as the steps that might be taken by Christians, working in consultation with Jews, to prevent its spread in this country'. He also noted how Pope Pius XI had recently affirmed that 'Antisemitism is a movement in which we Christians can have no part whatsoever. Spiritually we are Semites.' Hertz made it clear that Jews and Christians would be responsible for their own religious teaching without mutual interference.

The formation of the Council of Christians and Jews was agreed on 20 March 1942, at a meeting chaired by William Temple, now nominated as the next Archbishop of Canterbury. The initial membership was composed of leaders of Christian and Jewish organisations. The Roman Catholic prelate, Cardinal Hinsley, agreed to be a Joint President subject to the condition that any statements be approved by him prior to publication. The formation of the CCJ was announced on radio and in the press on 1 October 1942. It was an auspicious moment, given that it coincided with the height of World War II and the start of the worst phase of Nazi persecution of the Jews.

Ten years later the late Queen Elizabeth became an official patron of the CCJ; and I have had the pleasure of meeting her personally at several CCJ events over my many years of work with the Council.

Sir Sigmund Sternberg

We cannot begin to talk about interfaith activity without thinking of and praising my friend Sir Sigmund Sternberg – or Sigi as he was known to all his friends and associates. Everything he did was in some way dedicated to improving relations between Christians and Jews. He was a driving force in the Council. However, his thoughts and actions went much further,

10. My Council of Christians and Jews colleagues at a reception hosted by Chief Rabbi (later Lord) Jonathan Sacks (left) in 2008. Between Rosalie and myself is Sir Sigmund Sternberg and on Rosalie's right former Archbishop of Canterbury, Dr George Carey and the Greek Orthodox Archbishop, Gregorios Theocharous.

operating on an international scale at the very highest levels and eventually encompassing more faiths as they expanded in the UK. I was a great supporter of and collaborator with Sigi in his interfaith work.

On the world stage, Sigi helped to arrange the first-ever papal visit to a synagogue, which was in Rome in 1986. He worked with others to establish diplomatic relations between the Vatican and Israel in 1993. He interceded with Poland's Chief Cardinal to facilitate the removal, by mutual consent, of a Carmelite convent in the grounds of Auschwitz. Many, particularly Jews, had considered this an intrusion in a setting where nearly two million Jews were killed during the Holocaust.

In 1985, Sigi had the rare honour of being named a Papal Knight of St. Gregory the Great at the request of Pope John Paul II. And when Pope John Paul II died, Sigi organised an exceptional service dedicated to his memory at the prestigious West London Synagogue of British Jews, in Upper Berkeley Street, which I was pleased to attend.

Sigi was born in Hungary in 1921 and had managed to arrive in the UK just before the War in 1939. Barred from undertaking further study, he started by dealing in scrap metal and eventually prospered in the metal industry. He became a member of the London Metal Exchange in 1945, and a naturalized British citizen in 1947. He created a charitable foundation that fostered excellence in both Judaism and also in interfaith relations. In 1976 he was knighted by Queen Elizabeth II. In 2008 he accepted the Responsible Capitalism Lifetime Achievement Award, presented by British Foreign Secretary, David Miliband.

For his work on inter-faith relations, Sigi was constantly being presented with medals, from countries ranging from Argentina to Ukraine. It was said that at almost every public appearance, the decorations he wore seemed to multiply. Sigi accepted all these honours from religious and civic leaders not for his own pride, but because they focused the givers' attention on the need for interfaith understanding. These acts of recognition endorsed and strengthened his international work in fostering interfaith understanding and helped this to be more effective.

The Interfaith Gold Medallion

Not only was Sigi gathering awards himself, but he was also presenting awards. In 1986 he instituted the prestigious Interfaith Gold Medallion. The purpose was to recognise those who have made an exceptional contribution to the improvement of understanding between the faiths in the United Kingdom, and across the world. The Medallion has been awarded to Heads of State and Governments, Royalty, and religious, civic, business, and philanthropic leaders. Recipients have included Pope John Paul II, Queen Elizabeth II, King Hassan II of Morocco, the President of Ireland, The Imam of Eton College, the Archduke of Austria and the President of Germany as well as the distinguished violinist and humanitarian (Lord) Yehudi Menuhin.

Each award is given at a prestigious ceremony hosted at palaces and embassies and attended by senior diplomats and politicians. The awardees make moving and heartfelt speeches on these occasions – thus, making sure the message of interfaith dialogue and tolerance is heard and documented far and wide at the highest levels. Even though Sigi passed away in 2016 at the age of 95, his son Michael Sternberg QC is the chair of the awards scheme which still continues.

Faith and Belief Forum

As the demography of Britain changed, so Sigi realised the importance of engaging not only with Christians, but also with Muslims. To this end he recruited the collaboration of his close associates, the Rev Dr Marcus Braybrooke, of CCJ, and Sheikh Zaki Badawi, Imam of the Regents Park Mosque. In 1997, ably assisted by the Jewish lawyer and community leader Sidney Shipton they founded the 'Three Faiths Forum'. Its mission was to foster friendship, goodwill and understanding between people of different faiths and beliefs, (especially between Muslims, Christians and Jews). This forum worked with religious leaders, communities, schools, students, business and other non-governmental organisations (NGOs).

As more faith groups settled in the UK, it became clear that the Three Faiths Forum should be further expanded. The organisation changed its name to the 'Faith and Belief Forum' in 2018 which continues to work towards a connected and supportive society where people of different faiths, beliefs and cultures have strong, productive and lasting relationships.

I have worked with Sigi covering the whole spectrum of his interfaith projects. I would represent him at many gatherings up and down the country, often speaking as part of a cross-faith panel consisting of Christians, Jews, Muslims, Hindus or other faiths, addressing questions from the audience about attitudes to certain problems like marriage, divorce, conversion, burial and discussing general moral, religious and political issues. I was particularly supportive of the Forum's programme to reach out to the citizens of the future – schoolchildren and university students.

I have accompanied Sigi on interfaith matters, meeting most of the High Commissioners and Ambassadors to the Court of St James. I felt particularly honoured when the Faith Forum (which also gave out awards) gave me their third annual award for 'outstanding achievements in the interfaith field'. The honour was made even more gratifying to me by the celebratory reception hosted at his home by the then Chief Rabbi Jonathan Sacks. Many important figures attended, including leaders of many different faiths.

In 1998 Sir Sigmund Sternberg won the prestigious Templeton Prize, for having 'advanced public understanding of God and spirituality.' Sternberg was the second Jew – and the first Reform Jew – to receive the prize, which was established by the philanthropist Sir John Templeton in 1972 to recognize achievements related to humanity's spiritual dimension. This is a financial reward of even greater value than that of the Nobel Prize. The first Jew to receive it was the Chief Rabbi Sir Immanuel Jakobovits in 1991. Chief Rabbi Lord Jonathan Sacks was also to win the Templeton Prize in 2016. In 2008 Sigi Sternberg received the St. Mellitus Medal from the

Bishop of London, in recognition of his continued promotion of interfaith relations.

A Jewish service in a nunnery?

One of my most intriguing interfaith invitations was being asked to conduct a Jewish service in a Dutch nunnery. I duly took a boat to Amsterdam where I was picked up by a nun and taken to her convent just outside the city. For two nights I slept in a cell like they did. They explained that they wanted me to run a strictly traditional Jewish service on both Friday night and Saturday morning. The only Jew in the room was me. However, we had lots of discussions and they seemed very satisfied. We were able to recognise the common ground between their prayers and ours.

Making history in Gloucester, Norwich and Winchester

With my connections via Cheltenham and via the Council of Christians and Jews, the clergy of Gloucester Cathedral invited me to help them create a special interfaith choral event there. This time I called on Geraldine for her assistance. We also brought a coachload of interested Jewish people to attend this beautiful concert in this glorious cathedral. On the way we stopped off in Cheltenham and were given a tour of the beautiful regency style synagogue by its president at the time, the late Michael Webber. Rosalie and I, and our sons were very fond of the Cheltenham community. We had taken a cottage in the area for several summers and I had conducted countless services in that beautiful little synagogue.

I also assisted Geraldine as religious advisor in presenting a choral concert in Norwich Cathedral in 2002, celebrating the 60th anniversary of CCJ. A new work had been commissioned specially for the event called 'Trust in the Lord' by Ronald Cass composer friend of Harry Secombe who had composed songs for Cliff Richards such as 'Summer Holiday'. It was conducted by Cathy Heller Jones and performed by her choir of the Liberal Synagogue, St John's Wood, together with choristers from the Zemel Choir and Alyth Choral Society. I have written more about the role that music in cathedrals can play in fostering good relations between Christians and Jews.

I was also delighted to be invited as the first Jewish speaker at Winchester Cathedral. In 2005 the cathedral of that Hampshire city, once called England's capital, at last welcomed me, as what is believed to have been its first Jewish guest speaker. It was quite some wait, seeing as the sacred building began life in 1079. I was introduced by the Bishop of

Winchester. I felt the weight of history as I approached the pulpit. I had chosen a subject I could address with some confidence. I spoke about 'interfaith developments within the NATO alliance'.

I emphasised the need to combat prejudice among faiths, I took as a model of good practice the very person after whom the annual memorial lecture was named, Donald Coggan. I knew Rev Coggan well before he became the Archbishop of Canterbury in 1974. We had worked together as chaplains in the armed forces where our paths had often crossed. I reminded the audience, that Donald Coggan had been a key figure in the early development of CCJ of which he later became vice-president from 1983 to 1987.

The struggle for tolerance and understanding continues. Not every Christian prelate in history has been as open and humane, gracious, humble and tolerant as Donald Coggan and the deans and canons of the cathedrals, minsters and abbeys, with whom we have had the pleasure of working.

I hope that as we go forward, we continue to evidence and build on the real advances in interfaith understanding in schools and on university campuses and in civic and faith communities around the country. I feel sure that the foundations laid by the wonderful work of people like Sir Sigmund Sternberg and his counterparts in other faiths, and the activities of the Council of Christians and Jews, will have lasting beneficial results for the whole of society.

7

Out on a Limb – Small Communities: origins and issues

To most Jews in Britain, I am known primarily for my work as a minister, supporting small Jewish communities in the UK. However, this aspect of my life though massive and rewarding, was just one third of my professional working career which included being a barrister and a military chaplain.

After graduating from Oxford in 1954, I was set on a career in law. In the late 1950s however, this smooth path was disrupted when I was called up for compulsory National Service. I had chosen to serve as a Jewish spiritual advisor. Having had a thorough Jewish education as well as some extra sessions of study on torah tractates with Chief Rabbi Brodie, he conferred upon me my ministerial authority. This enabled me to conduct services, marriages and funerals and all other rabbinic duties. I was then appointed as Her Majesty's Chaplain to all Jewish recruits in the Royal Air Force (RAF). You can read more about my army exploits in 'The Miliary' chapter.

This position involved travel to many dozens of Royal Air Force bases in the UK and abroad. Wherever I found myself, I had the urge to seek out any civilian Jews. I formed a bond with many, and they regularly invited me to come back the next time I visited the base.

What has brought Jews to country districts?

I wondered how Jews had come to settle in the smaller towns. One reason was the effect of evacuation during the Second World War from the big industrial cities. This was something which I had also experienced in my childhood. A previous reason was the huge migration of millions of Jews out of the Pale of Settlement in Eastern Europe at the turn of the Twentieth Century. Later there was a further influx of Jews fleeing Nazism from Central Europe in the 1930s which further enriched both the city and country Jewish communities.

In the major wave of immigration from Eastern Europe between 1880 and 1920, nearly 150,000 Jews had settled in Britain. Most gravitated to major cities like London, Manchester and Leeds. Many however, settled around their ports of entry such as Hull, Grimsby, Sunderland and Newcastle on the Northeast coast. All four of my grandparents arrived in Britain as part of this mass migration: the Weismans settling in London and the Segals and Rifkinds in Edinburgh.

Had they not left Eastern Europe, their fate, and mine, would have been disastrously different. The Jewish populations remaining in the places from which they came in Poland and Lithuania had to endure severe economic privation and to contend with wholesale evictions during the First World War as well as frequent attacks from the surrounding population. In 1940 and 1941 their villages and towns were overtaken by the Nazis. All the Jews were crowded into ghettos and every last Jew either dragged out and brutally murdered in the surrounding forests or sent to their deaths in the concentration camps.

The world, as we know it, would be a very different place if not for the amazing positive contributions made by the children and grandchildren of those courageous Jews who left the stagnation of life in the Russian controlled Pale of Settlement for the free world. Once they had access to a wide ranging and liberal education, they have made spectacular and groundbreaking advances in almost every field of human endeavour – in medicine, the sciences, economics, the arts and business. The number of Jewish sounding names of the experts who are called upon to talk on our radios or televisions about Covid treatment and vaccination, or about astronomy, physics, microbiology and other scientific discoveries is remarkable. What they have achieved for the betterment of the world is significant.

The immigrants engaged in and often revolutionised the local trades and industries at their ports of entry, such as fishing, cold storage, trading, farming and food processing which contributed greatly to the economic growth and prosperity of these towns. Their compatriots also filled the jobs needed to provide for the burgeoning Jewish community, kosher butchers and bakers, pickle sellers, rabbis, cantors, ritual circumcisers and animal slaughterers. Strangers at first, they became integral parts of the towns where they settled, establishing businesses in tailoring, jewellery and furniture making and distributing. They sat on local councils contributing to the civic advancements and good management. Their communities grew and prospered for nearly a hundred years.

One of the most significant ports of entry for Jewish immigrants was Grimsby in Lincolnshire, on the southern bank of the Humber estuary. Thanks to its deep-water Royal Docks that had opened in 1852, Grimsby became an important trading port sending coal to Northern Europe. In

Liverpool on the west coast, they were receiving grain from America. The boats from these destinations, returning empty to Britain and to America, offered cheap passages to Germans, Poles and Russians seeking a new life in the West. The Great Central Railway company offered cheap package deals right through from the continental ports of Riga, Libau, Hamburg and Rotterdam via Grimsby and Hull, thence by railway to Liverpool and onwards to America.

As early as 1854 a thousand transmigrants and immigrants were landing in Grimsby every month, a small number of Jews amongst them. A few settled in Grimsby. They set up businesses and by 1865 with barely 70 Jews in the town, they came together and formally established the Grimsby Hebrew Congregation. They gathered for prayers in each other's homes.

At the peak of the great Jewish migration of 1881 to 1920, Grimsby became the third largest port for Jewish immigration, after London and neighbouring Hull (its big brother community a few miles north as the crow flies, on the northern bank of the River Humber). Nearly 100,000 poor, fervently religious, Yiddish speaking Jews landed at Grimsby, generally bound for the United States of America. Most had travelled the cheapest way, by steerage, huddled together in the holds, existing on black bread and herrings that they had brought with them. The Great Central Railway company owned several of the ships that carried the transiting passengers. They also operated a very large shelter at the docks in Grimsby, accommodating up to three hundred people at a time, between the time their boat arrived, and their trains departed the next day. The weary travellers came off the boats weighed down with parcels, a *pereneh,* (eiderdown quilt) a big black loaf of bread and a tub of herrings. They were walked across the railway lines by the warden to this large, nicely decorated room under the railway arches. There were long tables and benches for them to sit at in the daytime. At night, mattresses were distributed, and they slept on the floor as best they could. In the morning they were directed onto a train bound for the west coast if voyaging further, or to Manchester or London if they were staying in the country.

Those that stayed in Britain or those that stopped in Grimsby might have done so because they were too ill, or too impecunious to travel further. Some may have been victims of deception, not realising that their tickets ended there. There was the ever-present risk of disease and infection, hence the community's first need was for a Jewish burial ground and indeed the cemetery has graves of those who had perished on the voyage. It was often by default that they remained in England and even more so, that they stayed in Grimsby.

7. Out on a Limb – Small Communities

Whenever the weekly boats arrived, residents would go 'down docks' to see *'unsere yidden'* (our Jews). They would look for *landsleit* – people from the same villages in Latvia or Lithuania or Poland that they had come from. They would lend a helping hand to the tired travellers, if they could, by taking a family home for a kosher meal and giving them a bed on their floor for the night, and then perhaps trying to persuade them to stay in Grimsby. The attractions of Grimsby may have been few, but it was a welcome haven for those in need and also a place to worship freely.

By 1881, the members of the congregation, though not so many in number, determined to build a proper synagogue. They formed a building committee and started raising funds from Jews and also from Christians. They paid £20 for the deeds of a plot of land from the estate of Lord

11. The Moses Montefiore Memorial Synagogue in Grimsby (exterior) consecrated in 1888 by Chief Rabbi Nathan Adler.

Heneage on which they promised to build a fine synagogue by 1885. There were the inevitable delays, due to resignations, deaths and feuds, but mostly due to lack of funds. Despite several appeals to Anglo-Jewry via the Jewish Chronicle and to the Chief Rabbis Nathan Adler (1845 - 1891) and his son Herman Adler (who took over his duties when his father became ill in the 1870s) who did their best to help, they were still without most of the money they needed. Nevertheless, to show they were still on track, in 1885, they invited Mr F.D.Mocatta, a philanthropist of London to lay the foundation stone amidst much civic pomp. Mocatta's relative, Sir Moses Montefiore the renowned Jewish activist and philanthropist had just died in July 1885 aged 101. Montefiore's mother had been part of the Mocatta family, and for this reason perhaps, Mocatta and the community decided that the synagogue in Grimsby was to be known, in his honour, as the Sir Moses Montefiore Memorial Synagogue. The Victorian Romanesque-style building, designed to accommodate three hundred worshippers, was finally completed and consecrated by Chief Rabbi Nathan Adler in December 1888. It has served the community with its ups and downs ever since. Reaching a peak of 450 in 1909, the numbers have slowly decreased ever since. I have been visiting Grimsby on and off from the early 1960s when the community had about 120 members.

A new lease of life

During the Second World War, many Jewish children, like I was, were evacuated from the big cities. Sometimes their parents joined them. After living for several years in small towns and villages, they had established themselves there and decided not to return to the metropolis after the war. Such was the case in many places like Cheltenham and Harrogate.

The 1930s also brought an influx of about 50,000 refugees to Britain from Germany, Austria Czechoslovakia and elsewhere in Europe, who were fleeing Nazi persecution. Many of these were highly educated and skilled often emancipated Jews. Some had to take on domestic duties in stately (or less stately) homes around the country. Others created or transplanted businesses, especially in the fashion trades, pharmaceutical production and light engineering. Yet others were displaced professionals, intellectuals, academics and artists. They provided a welcome injection of intellectual rigour into the fields of music and art and to many universities around the country. They also changed the dynamics of the British Jewish community and strengthened both the Orthodox and the Reform movements in the major centres as well as around the country.

Today the majority of Britain's two to three-hundred thousand Jews (the second largest Jewish population in Europe after France, and the fifth largest Jewish community worldwide) live in England. There are about six thousand in Scotland, two thousand in Wales, and a few hundred in Northern Ireland. Outside of London there are significant communities in Manchester, Birmingham, Southend-on-Sea, Liverpool, Bournemouth, and Gateshead, with dozens of smaller groups spread across the country. I have had the great pleasure of visiting most of these smaller places and befriending the Jews who have landed up in all these parts of the UK.

By the time I took on the role of seeking out and supporting small groups of Jews in isolated spots in the early 1960s, many of these communities were already dwindling and in dire need of succour. Others had already ceased to exist. Children and grandchildren of the founders had not returned after completing their schooling or going to University or to take jobs in bigger centres. Those remaining were the older generation of the original largely orthodox settlers. Newcomers, if any came to these places, might be from families born in the UK and might have very different Jewish perspectives. As a consequence, some accommodation needed to be made in order to avoid splits in the communities, making them even smaller! Some groups were to have a refreshing new lease of life when new universities were established around the country, and others actually started from scratch under my care.

How did my work for small communities begin?

While visiting RAF bases, across the country, I had discovered groups of Jews, living in isolated areas who were completely cut off from any mainstream support. They were utterly on their own. Jews who live in London or in major provincial towns and who wish to live a Jewish life, have no difficulty in doing so. There are many Jewish institutions, synagogues, businesses and shops to supply their needs. However, there is no such support in outlying districts where there were small groups of Jews who wanted to retain their Jewish identity. To my mind, this was a situation that needed serious attention. I felt strongly that the rabbinate and leaders of the mainstream community should not abandon isolated people, saying, in effect, 'You are a waste of our time'.

It proved very difficult to persuade the powers that be, to help these small groups. I wrote to the then President of the United Synagogue asking him to support Jews in Potters Bar and Maidenhead and similar places. He basically said words to the effect of, 'Let them move to Golders Green.' (A more populous Jewish area in North London).

Brushed off, I therefore approached Chief Rabbi Brodie directly. I asked him, 'Who looks after these places? They seem to be completely out on their own, with no visits from any rabbinical personnel'. 'Nobody!' he said. At that, I suggested, 'I might as well undertake to look after them if you would like me to. I could easily fit this in with my Air Force base visits'. Chief Rabbi Brodie welcomed my offer. Thus, in the early 1960s, the whole of my life changed. Although at the time, I was hard at work on my legal studies, preparing for the Bar exams, as well as working as a Chaplain to the Royal Air Force, I was nevertheless very pleased to be given this opportunity of nurturing Jewish life in far-flung places.

Support for my venture

How I would manage this work still remained an issue. I realised that there would be substantial expenses incurred in travel and accommodation, and considerable time and help needed to communicate with people in remote places. I wondered whether I was expected to work as a volunteer, without any financial or administrative assistance.

By 1960, conscription for National Service was being phased out, with the last conscripted soldiers leaving the service in 1963. Consequently, there were far fewer Jewish recruits entering the Air Force who might need attention from me. My full-time chaplaincy post serving the RAF was therefore reduced to part-time – but now I was asked to serve all branches of the Armed Forces, the Army, the Navy and the Air Force Whilst I might have more time available to attend to the communities, I would have less personal finance to do so.

Chief Rabbi Brodie immediately offered me £150 pounds a year. Well, that didn't go very far. His perception was that I would just be visiting one or two locations nearby on a voluntary basis, places like Bognor Regis or Hastings. In those days petrol was only about a shilling or two a gallon, and £150 would be the equivalent of a couple of thousand pounds today. However, it was still not nearly enough, it barely covered my petrol expenses for a month.

Fortuitously around this time, in 1962/63, another opportunity arose. There was an expansion of higher education, and many new universities sprang up in places like East Anglia, Sussex, Kent, Lancaster, York, Warwick and Essex. Michael Beloff, in his book on the subject, labelled these new institutions, 'Plate-glass Universities'. The Hillel Foundation, which supports Jewish students on campus by providing hostels and other Jewish facilities, was looking for a spiritual leader for these new seats of learning. (A Jewish University Chaplaincy service, such as now exists covering the whole country, had not yet been established.)

Immediately I made myself available and Hillel gave me the job of chaplain to these new universities. I was grateful for the post, but compared to the need, the funds offered, were still not sufficient. They did however, offer more help though, in the form of the use of an office and the support of a secretary at Hillel House in Endsleigh Street, Euston. This helped me to keep in contact with the University Jewish Societies, and also with people in the countryside.

The Jewish Chronicle (JC) Britain's oldest and renowned weekly Jewish newspaper played a big part in making my work widely known. They had a dedicated Campus Correspondent, Lionel Simmonds who liked nothing more than to accompany me on my visits to the various universities. He wrote regular columns 'On Campus' about my activities – which often also included visits to the small groups of Jews living in the surrounding areas.

Once the word got out, on the grapevine, and especially through the JC, that I was available and ready to visit and attend to the Jewish needs of people across the country, more and more requests came rolling in. Before long fifty small communities across the length and breadth of the country were asking for my support.

The northernmost community I visited was in Aberdeen, Scotland, the most southerly, in Jersey in the Channel Islands. To the east I looked after Norwich and to the west there were several small groups in Wales, and most westerly, the Cornish village of Zelah, known only to a few English people. It had five families who could not even muster a *minyan*.

Soon I was looking after a far-flung flock of three or four thousand individuals, who had no other assistance for leading a Jewish life. As the extent and value of my work became apparent, at long last, in the later 1960s, the Chief Rabbi decided to formalise the outreach to the smaller and long neglected pockets of Jews, by creating the 'Office for Jewish Small Communities' (OSC) supported by the Jewish Memorial Council. In my new capacity with the official title of 'Chief Rabbi's Minister for Small Communities'. I was then given the use of an office and a secretary at the Jewish Memorial Council on the second floor of Woburn House. This building in Euston, at the time, housed the headquarters of many Jewish communal organisations. This arrangement was very convenient as my three command centres, each with secretarial assistance, were very close to each other. My Military Jewish Chaplain's office was on the third floor of Woburn House and my university activities office was around the corner at Hillel House. As well as financial support from the Jewish Memorial Council, I was fortunate also to receive generous funding from a number of individual well-wishers in the mainstream Jewish community, as well as from some individuals in the small communities. Thus, I was well bolstered and equipped and no charges were ever made to any communities for my visits. By 1963 I was also established in Chambers, working as a full-time barrister and I was, in addition, continuing with my military chaplaincy at home and abroad. Nevertheless, I could never refuse a request for help from an isolated individual or a group of Jews around the country.

I always tried to visit as many of my communities as often as I could. Some I would manage to visit eight or ten times a year, driving some 1000 miles every week. In a few cases, it was due to my efforts and intervention that isolated families in rural areas were brought together and enabled to organise prayers and Jewish education for their children. My policy was to attend communities only in places where there was no resident minister. I also responded to requests to visit from individual Jewish families living in what I called 'splendid isolation'. As a result, I enjoyed several good coffee-stops on my way to communities, punctuating my long journeys and assuaging their concerns about Jewish matters.

Sometimes I have been invited to help small groups of Jews around the country, such as at Bognor Regis, at the very conception of creating a community. Other times I might be needed as the midwife to see that the community is safely born such as occurred at East Grinstead, Hastings and Chelmsford. In yet other instances, it was to give fresh impetus and to steer them in a practical and hopefully sustainable direction. And just sometimes, like in Sunderland, I am called in when things are really bad, though by that time it is usually too late to avoid the demise.

My working ethos

Jews have always had their cultural diversity and religious divisions. The tensions generated between different groups with fervently held beliefs, may in some way, have vitalised and helped the very survival of Jews and Judaism over the centuries. However, in the small groups I have nurtured, I would always try to bring together all the people who wanted a Jewish dimension to their lives. I would try to help them to become a self-sustaining, overarching 'Jewish Community', one that was not defined along the spectrum from Liberal and Reform to Orthodox. In the big cities these elements keep strictly separate from each other.

My role as the Minister for Small Communities was primarily to lead them in Jewish prayer and support them 'Jewishly' through the life cycle events of marriage, childbirth, bar and bat mitzvah, death and bereavement with its funerals and stone settings. Although I was the Chief Rabbi's emissary, and therefore coming from an orthodox framework, I strove to give everyone who came within my ambit a meaningful Jewish experience on both a social and a spiritual level, getting to the heart of what Judaism is about, and not concentrating on any particular ritual. My 'toolkit', which I carried in the boot of my car, was a set of prayer books of the standard orthodox service, a small *sefer torah* and a few *tallit* and *kippot*. If I was coming for *Shabbat*, I would try to bring some Jewish delicacies like chopped herring and some plaited or round *challot* depending on the time of year. Around Rosh Hashanah time (New Year) we choose a round *challa* signifying a round or complete year.

When I would meet a new group of Jews thrown together by circumstances and locality, just as I had done in the army and at the universities, I would first find out how much Jewish knowledge they had and their level of Jewish connection. While there were often a few who knew the orthodox ritual and could lead a service, and frequently several who were nominally orthodox, I also found some who might have come from a reform or liberal background. There may be a few who had no knowledge or connection and who would probably never have become attached to a synagogue, or any Jewish life, had they lived in a city. I usually found I needed to start from scratch, nurturing a Jewish identity and commitment amongst people from all these differing backgrounds.

At a conventional Orthodox service, you would find high-speed praying all in Hebrew. However, I needed to be sure that all my congregants would understand and could follow what was happening. Therefore, as in my military and university experience, religious services of necessity had to be shortened and three quarters of the service needed to be in English rather than mostly in Hebrew. We dispensed with the traditional patterns, and I paused at intervals, to explain the meaning of different parts of the service.

This approach proved very popular with all members of my small communities who became absorbed in these services. The result was that they became more engaged in and committed to the group. I was pleased to notice that, as time went on and as the local attendees became more familiar with the words, they would say to me: 'We like this, do not jump that paragraph, let us do it.' That way of dealing with services, helped members of the communities to feel confident to lead the services themselves when I was not available. The communities and I developed a firm friendship and trust between us. Although from differing environments, they became eager to come together and to learn and practise what I imparted to them. It was very satisfying to see how my stimulus enabled them to work together in a real community and to see how even with my infrequent visits, but constant contact, they remained attached to Jewish life and traditions and could pass these on to their children.

Time and again, those with little previous Jewish background or commitment have become my biggest supporters. They regularly turn up at services or functions in advance of the nominally observant Jews. I visit them in their homes where they may have had a traditional 'full English' for breakfast, but I can still have coffee with them; and engage with them on Jewish matters. I am not prepared to ignore them. Frequently I have seen such people returning strongly to their Jewish faith.

The ultimate expression of community compatibility occurred when the Jews of Oxford came to build a new synagogue complex in 1973. They explicitly decided to incorporate all strands of Jewish life within it. They operate as a single community but enable separate strands to use the spaces in the building to worship in the way they feel most comfortable. There might be an Orthodox service taking place in the main sanctuary and a Reform or Masorti one going on in another space. The one stipulation is that all services must end at the same time so that they can enjoy a *kiddush* (refreshments) together afterwards. I was honoured that they asked me, their Honorary Minister and University Chaplain, to inaugurate this unique facility. You can read more about this in the chapter of my 'Oxford Days'. Exeter is another place which welcomes all, no matter their Jewish background. The Exeter Community often alternate services in Orthodox and Reform styles.

Small community issues

As well as arranging meetings and talks and helping them to run events and especially services, there are other concerns of people in outlying places, for which they sought my help. Education for their children was one of the most pressing (and expensive) needs for these fledgling communities. I needed to find the people to provide it. For those within range of a big city, I helped to recruit students or teachers prepared to travel to the community's classroom or private home once or twice a week.

Kosher food was another issue. Thanks to the development of the frozen foods industry, provision of kosher food is no longer the problem it once was. I helped communities to arrange a suitable supply. The Aberdeen community, for example, nearly 500 miles away, had its meat sent on the night train from London. The Channel Islands community had their meat flown in from Bournemouth, a south coast resort with a large Jewish community. Meat for Exeter was sent from Brighton.

These small-scale communities also needed trained cantors and ministers to lead the High Holydays services. My own commitment in earlier times was to conduct these services at my military bases in Cyprus and Germany. With the help of my various secretaries, I recruited most of the cantors and ministers who officiated on major Jewish festivals in many of the universities and small communities. In later years I was pleased to offer my services to conduct the High Holydays services for the Jersey Jewish community.

How do many of these smaller communities ever survive financially? The great problem I have found, is that most small communities cannot generate enough income from subscriptions from their members alone. The members in country areas often do not have the financial wherewithal or the dedication to pay a substantial membership fee. In fact, some communities do not even request subscriptions. In the days of postage, one community just used to charge £5 a year to be on the mailing list. Thankfully, as I received funds to support my visits, I did not need to charge the communities at all. Had I needed to charge for each visit, it would have destroyed their financial viability completely.

One way that synagogues in earlier times, and still today, used to increase their income, in addition to subscriptions, is for congregants to make a voluntary contribution to the synagogue when they were given a *'mitzvah'* (an honour such as when they were 'called up' to read from the *Torah*). This could be on a special occasion of the congregant – such as their wedding or *barmitzvah* anniversary or a *yahrzeit* (the anniversary of a family death) or simply if the wardens invited them to be so honoured. The amount of their contribution could be of their choosing and had no upper limit. Communities relied on richer members making greater contributions and the less well-off more modest ones. It balanced out.

To ensure they received a contribution, the foundational constitutions of some synagogues, drafted in the 19th century, stated that if you did not accept or turn up for your honour, you would be fined. Many a community managed their finances in this manner. For instance, Cheltenham's constitution had a rule that 'If a person persisted in talking during the service, he would be fined after receiving a written warning'. If after repeatedly receiving a written notice to desist from talking, you continued, you would be fined half a guinea. That was a lot of money in those days. Another of Cheltenham's rulings stated that the community could nominate you for election to the synagogue council, even if you refused to take up the office, you also got fined!

This situation occurred at Bevis Marks Synagogue in London when Isaac Disraeli refused to pay the fine imposed on him for not wishing to take a seat on the board as offered to him. He subsequently withdrew from the congregation and had his family baptised, opening the way for his son Benjamin to embrace and be accepted in political life and to become Prime Minister – twice.

It was, and still is a fact, that most Jewish ministers, have to find some additional sources of employment in order to make a living and support their families. As well as teaching the children of his community their *alef bet*, (Hebrew alphabet and language) they might also teach languages to adult members and also to non-Jewish students as well. Some ministers today have a weekday job.

Be prepared for all eventualities.

In my sixty years of attending to small Jewish groups across the country I have witnessed the shifting of Jewish life in the UK. I have observed the movement of people from small towns to the cities. I have seen the drift away from an erstwhile almost universal orthodoxy to more diverse ways of expressing Judaism. In younger generations I have noticed the rise and importance to many (especially in small communities) of the more understandable and welcoming services of the progressive movements. And at the same time, I have watched the rise of strict orthodoxy in younger graduates of Bnei Akiva and other religious Jewish youth moments.

In some places, the Jews I visit may be very cultured and worldly, and in others, quite the opposite. In some tightly regulated ultra-orthodox communities they do not watch television, or read the newspapers, so they do not know what is taking place in the world. But in both cases, they know they are Jewish and long for a space where they can express their sense of identity. If they do not favour a religious service, they might want to gather for a social chat, for coffee and a bagel, or even to share some Jewish jokes.

Each community, though faced with similar problems, might, according to their makeup and history, deal with them in completely different ways. I soon realised I would have to tailor my role to fit the local cloth. For instance, when I arrived to greet a group in Weymouth, they told me that they wanted an evening of Jewish 'reflection', but on no account was there to be any mention of God. I was just to talk about 'something Jewish'. Naturally that called for some compromise and innovation on my part, which was not difficult. Once they were happy to come together and enjoy each other's company as Jews, we could suggest some more ambitious activity.

Another problem I faced was, of course, that several of the people in some small communities were quite elderly. Although I was the one who may have had a 'trying' day in court and had got straight into my car to hurry down to see them, and they presumably had had a quiet day at home, it was I that had to be on my toes and try to keep them awake! To do this, if it was a service, I would select a few appropriate familiar prayers, in Hebrew or English, and then get them to sing along. If I gave them a talk, it had to be very engaging – otherwise after about five or six minutes they would all be asleep.

From a tiny spark

To make a community work, you need one or two dynamic leaders who want to make it happen. Often, they are women who know how to get the job done. In my experience it is often the energy and drive of a woman who may not even have been born Jewish, who leads the group and keeps the community active – and also keeps her Jewish husband involved in Jewish life. Sadly, when a dominant and powerful personality dies or moves away, that can lead to the collapse of the whole group.

Sometimes from a tiny spark on the verge of being extinguished, a mighty blaze can ignite. The following story is a perfect example. As happens so often in my long and geographically dispersed career, it involves meeting someone in one community who pops up again in another, sometimes a decade or more later. It was in Jersey that I first met a young lady who was not technically Jewish, because she had a Jewish father but a non-Jewish mother. She herself had married a non-Jew, which at first sight might seem to further dilute her Jewish identity. Nonetheless, she felt compelled to join the local Jewish community. Crucially, her non-Jewish husband stood by her side. Though he might have been reluctant at first, he supported his wife. I became very friendly with the couple. Later when they moved to Bournemouth, they both became genuinely enthusiastic about Judaism. Both went through full orthodox conversions. He now wears a black hat and has grown a beard. His son is now very active in an ultra-orthodox community in London. You never know what can happen.

On the whole, I think that I have succeeded in bringing and keeping groups of diverse Jews together, and in helping them to have a meaningful Jewish life. I like to think this is because I learned never to judge Jews who are less religiously observant. Time and again I hear of Jews who sincerely wished to re-engage with their lineage and heritage, but who were put off by rabbis who unthinkingly demanded absolute conformity to their own notion of 'orthodoxy'.

I am very gratified when I am approached by people who say – you don't remember me – but you changed my life. And they describe our encounters at crucial stages in their Jewish journeys.

I have to admit though that I have not always been able to sustain a community. You will read in the chapters on the communities that I visited,

12. Interior of Grimsby Montefiore Synagogue refurbished 100 years after its consecration and rededicated in 1989

of places and people who just could not come to terms with change. Some small communities have split into even smaller ones. Others have simply disappeared altogether. A few small communities have steadily increased in number as more Jews took up employment in outlying districts and new universities around the country, increased the communities with Jewish staff and students. Some communities have reached a critical mass and have become and remained sustainable – at least for a while.

I wonder whether working from home during the Covid Pandemic and the increasing pollution and gridlock in the cities will lead more Jewish families to prefer to live in the countryside once more.

We talked about the Jewish Community in Grimsby at the start of this chapter. To end it, I can report that in March 1989 I was delighted to be invited to Grimsby to give the address of rededication for the Moses Montefiore Memorial Synagogue. This was a very special double celebration as it both marked the centenary of the synagogue's life and activity in Grimsby and also its refurbishment after an arson attack the previous year had left the interior burnt and blackened. The event drew nearly 300 people, filling the synagogue to capacity.

Jonathan Arkush, the barrister and communal leader who regularly led the High Holydays services in Grimsby, conducted the service with a male choir from his Elstree and Borehamwood Synagogue. Guests of community president, Leo Solomon, included the Mayors of Grimsby and Cleethorpes and Dr Lionel Kopelowitz, who was the President of the Board of Deputies of British Jews. I told the community in my address that 'It is quality, not quantity that counts' and that, though small in number, they could be very proud of their achievements.

8

Old Communities in Modern Times

Exeter, Norwich Cheltenham and Guildford

Not all the small communities I have tended to are recent establishments. For instance, Exeter's synagogue dates from 1764. The Norwich community was created in 1813; Cheltenham was established in 1823; Guildford early in the twentieth century. But these towns also had significant Jewish communities, centuries earlier in the Middle Ages.

William the Conqueror, believing that their commercial skills and incoming capital would make England more prosperous, invited a group of Jewish merchants from Rouen in Normandy to England in the 1070s.

They would basically be beholden to and under the protection of the king. They were not permitted to own any land. Their roles would have been to collect taxes for the king, supervise the economy of mining and other industries, and to facilitate trade with Europe. However, their main function and occupation was to be bankers. They were brought here for the purpose of lending money, for which they were allowed to charge interest. They were needed to fund various royal and noble enterprises such as fighting crusades and building castles, monasteries and cathedrals. Catholic doctrine held that money-lending for interest was the sin of usury, thus Christians were not allowed to do this. They did not mind Jews sinning, so Jews dominated this activity which was crucial to the English economy. Paradoxically, the Christian laws were based on Jewish laws prohibiting lending with interest – at least to fellow Jewish believers.

Jews were administered by a special court and did not have the same legal status as ordinary English people. On one hand, this provided a measure of protection for Jewish communities, but only so long as kings were willing to make good on this protection.

William's successor, King Henry I (his fourth son) issued a protective charter to Joseph, the Chief Rabbi of London, and all his followers, ensuring their freedom of movement throughout the country. He also granted them relief from ordinary tolls, (although they were subject to special Jewish taxes). He gave them free recourse to royal justice, and permission to retain land taken in pledge as security.

Feeling secure in these privileges, which were further endorsed by Henry's successors, King Stephen (William the Conqueror's nephew) (1135 to 1154), and after that Henry II (1154 - 1189) prosperous Jewish communities developed in several towns across England including London, Lincoln, Canterbury, Northampton, York and Gloucester, and the places where I visited small communities such as Exeter, Norwich Cheltenham and Guildford.

Exeter, Devon – (175 miles Southwest of London)
Welcoming all Jews

Of all the small communities that I care for, Exeter, on the river Exe in Devon, Southwest England, is rightly regarded as one of the oldest. As we have seen, William the Conqueror brought Jews to England and it seems that part of their role might have been to manage the tin mining industry in Devon and Cornwall. However, Rabbi Bernard Susser in his fascinating thesis on 'The early settlement of Jews in Devon and Cornwall', quotes scholars who say there is evidence of ancient Jewish trading posts there a thousand years before, in fact, going right back to biblical times!

Some say that Jews first visited England in company with the Phoenicians about the time of King Solomon in search of tin and lead. Scholars suggest some connection between the inhabitants of Devon and Cornwall and the dwellers on the Palestinian coast in their food habits, which they still hold in common. Both areas use saffron in cooking and in these two regions, as well as in Brittany, which was also under Celtic influence, clotted cream is manufactured! Another indication of association between the ancient Israelites and Celts is the similarity in sound and meaning of many words and phrases in the Hebrew and Celtic languages.

Researchers also note that there were smelting ovens in Cornwall and Devon known as 'Jews Houses'. The tin from a Jews House was known as 'Jews House tin'. Interestingly a farm on which such a Jews House oven was discovered in 1826 was locally known as 'Landjew'.

Susser notes that Jews may have had at least one well established trading centre in Cornwall even in the pre-Roman period, as the town Marazion was known in ancient times as 'Market-Jew', and the main street of Penzance which leads to it is even today called Market-Jew Street. This name Marazion itself is suggestive of Hebraic origin, meaning either 'sight of Zion' or 'bitterness of Zion'.

Nor is this the only town in Cornwall whose name is said to be Hebraic in its origin. There is also the village of Menheniot, which name, according to a correspondent to the Jewish Chronicle, is derived from the two Hebrew words, *min* and *oniyot,* which mean 'from ships' [JC, 1 June 1860] Also, the pronunciation of the name of the Cornish town of Mousehole is 'Muzzle'. This might also be influenced by Hebrew, as 'Muzzle' is the homonym of the Hebrew word *mazel* meaning 'luck'. Come to think of it, I used to visit a tiny village in Cornwall called Zelah, which certainly has Hebrew connotations. Zelah is the name of one of the fourteen cities of the tribe of Benjamin (Joshua 18:28) and Zelah is also mentioned in 2 Samuel 21:14, as the place where Saul and Jonathan are buried. This could of course be mere coincidence, and difficult to prove. Another consideration to add is that in the nineteenth century, the cryptic Hebrew expression *Makom Lamed* (meaning the 'L' Place) coined by local Jews when referring to London, has passed into general Cornish usage.

There is also some archaeological evidence of Jews in Roman Britain. They have found coins and pottery from the Near East at the time of the Roman presence in Dorset and Devon which show an early connection between those areas. This indicates that Exeter was one of the first ports of call for sea-traffic coming from the Mediterranean sailing up the English Channel. The coins originate from towns with a high percentage of Jews in their populations in those ancient times. [Applebaum, Roman Britain, p. 190.]

Medieval times

Devon was an ideal spot for Jews to settle in the middle of the twelfth century. Tin mining was still in operation in Devon, as it had been since biblical times. It is possible that rich Jews from already established centres in England provided some of the capital for one of Britain's first capitalist industries. They would also have sent their agents to safeguard their interests. If so, these agents probably formed the nucleus of the subsequent medieval Jewish community in Exeter. It has been shown that after the expulsion of all Jews from England in 1290, there was a steep decline in the Devon output of tin from 87 'thousandweight' (precursor of the ton) in 1291 to less than half of that in 1296, a decline which has been attributed to the expulsion of the Jews. [*Victoria History of Cornwall* (1906), p. 525.] Furthermore, the name of at least one mine owner, Abraham the Tinner, who owned a number of stream-powered works in 1342 and employed several hundred men, suggests that he was of Jewish origin.

The first mention of a resident Jew in Exeter was in 1181 when Piers Deulesalt paid ten marks that the king might take care of his bonds. Interestingly, the name Dieu-le-saut, meaning 'May God save him' is the French translation of the Hebrew name Isaiah. By 1188 there were enough Jews to form a distinct community. The earliest recorded act of the new community was to pay the authorities one gold mark in order to be allowed to set up a *Beth Din* (Jewish court). [Adler, 'Medieval Jews', p. 222.]

Their main means of livelihood was the interest they received from money which they advanced on the security of lands, rents and chattels. Hundreds of documents survive relating to the loaning of money. In the thirteenth century strict records were kept of all Jewish possessions and credits. In each of the designated towns two Jews and two Christian clerks, called chirographers, were appointed to safeguard the royal interest under the supervision of a representative from the newly established central authority.

Orders were given that all deeds and contracts (chirographs) were to be drawn up in duplicate and the counterparts deposited in a chest (archa) secured by three locks. At Exeter in 1276 there seem to have been only two Jews actively engaged in money-lending: Auntéra widow of Samuel son of Moses, and Isaac son of Moses, apparently her brother-in-law. By 1290, there was hardly a shadow of the formerly prosperous community of Exeter, the sole representative being a Jewess named Comitissa. Besides her house in the High Street, no other house was either owned or leased by Jews in Exeter, nor was there a synagogue.

Two centuries after 1290, it is suggested that secret communities of Spanish Jews who had been living and thriving in Spain for hundreds of years settled in Devon as well as in other parts of England after they have been cast out of Spain in 1492. When Sir Francis Drake circumnavigated the world in 1577 his navigator was Moses the Jew, from the Barbican in Plymouth.

Once Jews were officially 'allowed' back to England in 1656, by Oliver Cromwell, and could practise their religion openly in this country, it seems that Jews from Italy and Holland began to settle in Exeter, where they established a snuff business. They were joined by immigrants from Germany and by 1757 the community was sufficiently organised to take the lease of land at Bull Meadow in order to create a Burial Ground that is still maintained by the congregation today. Six years later they acquired some land in the parish of St Mary Arches where they built a synagogue

13. Exeter Synagogue, exterior

that was consecrated in 1764. This building still serves as the religious and social centre for the Jews of Exeter today.

Though never large, the community continued to operate for over 100 years. In 1855 Rev Meyer Mendelssohn, born in Germany in 1833, became the minister of Exeter Hebrew Congregation at the age of 22. He was distantly related to the famous composer Felix Mendelssohn and his equally famous grandfather the German Jewish philosopher Moses Mendelssohn. He had arrived in Britain from Germany in 1850 at the age of 17 and completed his studies at Jews College in London. But 23 years after he took up office in Exeter, the community had declined and by 1878 when there were less than ten contributing families, Rev Mendelssohn was sent by the then Chief Rabbi, Nathan Adler to serve in Kimberley South Africa, where diamonds had recently been discovered. By 1889, regular services in Exeter had ceased. Meyer Mendelssohn made a terrific impact on the Kimberley community where many Jews, mainly from Germany and Britain had arrived on the scene.

Exeter's flame was however relit six years later in 1895 by Charles Samuels, founder of a picture framing firm. He remained the community's leader until his death in 1944.

Modern Times

When I first visited Exeter in 1963, the community comprised barely 20 families and there was very little Jewish activity. Despite having this beautiful old synagogue, they could only open it on the High Holydays of *Rosh Hashanah* (New Year) and *Yom Kippur* (the Day of Atonement) and occasionally for *Chanukah*, the festival of lights.

I visited Exeter regularly and as our activities became widely known, more people came forward. Over the next fifteen years or so, several Jewish people moved into Exeter's ambit. The developing Exeter University was one of the reasons for the growth of the community. Jewish staff and students and other newcomers had arrived. They came from diverse backgrounds – some from a strictly Orthodox movement, while others were brought up in Reform or Liberal surroundings.

I encouraged the community leaders to see themselves as serving the needs of all persons of the Jewish faith. I would like to think that my guidance has encouraged them to have a strong and broad-minded Jewish identity.

By 1980 regular services had been re-established. The leaders had vowed to keep the community together as a whole. They developed an innovative programme of running a Reform style service one week and an Orthodox one the next. Similarly, for the first day of Rosh Hashanah the service may be an Orthodox one, and the next day Liberal, or the other way round. Some members attend all the services. On that basis it has attracted even more people and the community has really grown. It became quite active and has remained so.

The ancient synagogue, first consecrated in 1764, in Synagogue Place, Mary Arches Street, is now a Grade II listed building. The community undertook extensive renovations over 200 years later in 1998. In July 1999 I was honoured to be invited to rededicate the refurbished synagogue. The community leaders acknowledged that I had given them the impetus and encouragement to make Exeter Jewish Community both inclusive and outward looking.

Despite having such a beautiful old synagogue, in the centre of town, one Devon couple in the 1970s chose to hold their Jewish wedding on a farm on Dartmoor – quite unusual for the times! The ceremony took place in a cowshed. Relatives from the cities, who had arrived in their finery and high heeled shoes were somewhat perturbed at having to traipse through a muddy field – and in the pouring rain – to get to the *chuppah* (the canopy under which the wedding is solemnised). Afterwards we used the same shed for a high tea and a jolly barn dance. It was a romantic idea, loved by the younger generation but some of us were not thrilled to have got a soaking in the process! Quite recently, in October 2021 I received a phone call from the Jewish Chaplain in Bristol, asking about the legitimacy of those very nuptials. I was able to confirm that I had performed the ceremony myself 'according to the laws of Moses and of Israel' and that the whole event was strictly in order according to Jewish law.

Exeter Synagogue has celebrated other major civic events including its 250th anniversary in 2013 at which Rosalie and I were honoured guests. There was yet another rededication in 2019 after it suffered an arson attack in July 2018. Staff members at a nearby bingo hall, Mecca, heard an explosion at the synagogue and used a fire extinguisher to battle the flames before the police and fire brigade arrived. Prompt response by the community limited the damage that had been caused by a man who tried to ignite a fire by pouring an inflammable substance into the building. The civic and faith communities of Exeter where quick to condemn the assault and showed tremendous support for the Jewish community. Thankfully nobody was injured and the damage to the building was not extensive.

At these events, the Honorary Officers remarked how the community retains a strong sense of identity despite a membership of only 120 spread thinly across the south-west of England. They still pride themselves on welcoming all shades of Judaism, holding both progressive and traditional services with both community leaders and visiting rabbis. Since 2014 and up until the onset of Covid-19, the Exeter community held both a Friday evening and a Saturday morning service each week, which were run according to the preference of the person leading the service. For the High Holidays these days, the community runs an inclusive service that serves everybody well.

Is Exeter's future assured? It could be. Having a university on the doorstep helps boost the numbers especially during term time. There are young Jewish families in the area, and the community caters for children.

I was also invited by a daughter of a North London rabbi to the nearby town of Totnes, 30 miles from Exeter, on the banks of the River Dart, as it makes its way to the South Devon coast. She asked me to help her to set up a Jewish community there. I was delighted to meet twenty-two Jewish people which is pretty good for such a small place – two men and twenty women! I was able to help them organise deliveries of kosher food and establish their community, which existed for a while.

NORWICH – (120 miles Northeast of London)
Medieval Jewish Heritage in Norwich

The Jews of Norwich have a long and interesting history. The first synagogue was founded in the 11th century in the city centre close to the Castle. The Jews lived together in the White Lion Street area of Norwich, to be close to the king's representative. They acted as the king's revenue collectors and important money lenders.

When buildings on the present Primark site were demolished In the 1960s to make way for a new Littlewoods store, remains were found of glazed tiles and parts of pillars which dated back to the period of the twelfth or thirteenth century. They could have been part of the synagogue which was destroyed either by fire in 1286 or by demolition in 1290, when the Jews were expelled from England.

Jews also engaged in cultural pursuits. The first recorded Hebrew poetry written in England was by Meir of Norwich. A building in King Street, (now Wensum Lodge) was the home of Jurnet, one of the richest Jews in England at the time, The house was later owned by his son, Isaac, in 1197. The family was very rich and lent money to successive kings to build castles, cathedrals and churches, including Norwich Cathedral. Many records are still available in the Westminster Abbey Muniment Room, documenting the Jurnet family's lending.

So much for the good things – now for the bad. The first known 'Blood Libel' in world history originated in Norwich. This fabricated and ludicrous story alleged that Jews abducted and murdered Christian children for their Passover rituals. The death of a young man, William, on the Eve of Pesach 1144, was blamed on the Jews, who were said, preposterously, to have used the child's blood to make matzah. The Jews were protected by the Sheriff, and they were allowed to take refuge in Norwich Castle. He refused to allow proceedings to be taken against them. However, the damage was done in the eyes of the public.

Following the expulsion of the Jews from England in 1290, Jews could only officially return to England in 1656 at the behest of Oliver Cromwell. Jews did not appear in Norwich until nearly a century later in 1750 and they have had a continuous though small presence there ever since.

In the latter part of the eighteenth century, a small community met in rooms in the city. There was also at that time a cemetery mentioned in the local paper on Mariners Lane. However, the first purpose built small synagogue was established in 1828 in Tombland Alley, close to the Anglican

Cathedral. There were only about thirty members at the time, yet 21 years later in 1849 they decided to build a much more substantial synagogue building in St Faiths Lane, on the corner of a small street which was later renamed Synagogue Street.

This significant building served the community for nearly 100 years. At the beginning of the twentieth century, the congregation numbered thirty-three member families amounting to 147 people.

In 1938/39, the Norwich Refugee Committee, which included Jews and Quakers, succeeded in bringing 90 Jewish refugee children out of Austria. Several members of the community had welcomed these children to live in their own homes. Ironically the synagogue was destroyed by the Nazis in a German bombing raid in 1942. After about a year of temporary accommodation they worshipped at the Spiritualist Church, Chapelfield North, where many American Jewish servicemen also attended services and social events up to 1945, when they left Norfolk.

In 1948 the Norwich City Council leased the present site at 3 Earlham Road to the community. (It is interesting to note how the Spiritualists – and often the Quakers, have helped out Jews in need, whether here in Norwich, or as in Guildford, Welwyn Garden City and many other places.) A prefabricated building was initially put up, with an undertaking to build a permanent synagogue within ten years.

I have been visiting the Norwich community since 1967, whenever they have been without a resident minister. By 1951, the community had managed to build a Communal Hall with a flat above it to house a minister. But nearly twenty years after the land had been granted, the permanent synagogue had not yet been built. The community had encountered several obstacles of finance, sudden deaths in the ministry and lay leadership and potential land subsidence. A bus had actually fallen into a chalk pit that had opened up in front of the building while the community was preparing a Purim party!

However, with renewed resolve, a beautiful synagogue was created. The Eastern Daily Press said that the consecration of this building in 1969, was a memorable occasion. The paper reported: *'The new synagogue is an impressive building of which a larger group would be proud. The service was taken by the Chief Rabbi Dr Immanuel Jakobovits with the Chief Rabbi's Minister for Small Communities, Rev Malcolm* Weisman *and the local reader/teacher Mr H Silman'*.

Today there is a small but active congregation, of over sixty members, swelled by Jewish families associated with the University of East Anglia. The community is independent and not affiliated to the United Synagogue,

14. Chief Rabbi Immanuel Jakobovits and I at the consecration of the new Norwich Synagogue in 1969.

except in the case of a synagogue marriage. However, it maintains an orthodox form of service, using the Orthodox prayer book, and its male and female congregants usually sit separately. In more recent times, families and couples may sit together in a designated area. The kitchen in the communal hall is kept kosher.

As members live over a very wide area of Norfolk, and very few live within easy walking distance of the synagogue it is accepted that they would have to drive to reach the synagogue. This would not normally be condoned on the sabbath in most orthodox communities – but in small and very widespread communities like Norwich, all those willing to make the journey to attend the service are warmly welcomed. Their cars may even be parked right inside the synagogue grounds, rather than out of sight round the corner!

In October 1994 I was invited to address the community on the 25th anniversary of the consecration of the synagogue. It was a great celebration with a dinner and dance attended by many past members, at which they acknowledged my involvement with the synagogue over the previous two and a half decades. I was also delighted to attend both the fortieth and fiftieth anniversary celebrations. Since then, there have been some young and energetic ministers and lay leaders and the community is holding its own and even growing.

In early January 1997, Jack Stern, the President of the community attended a very interesting event in Norwich Cathedral. As part of the service of dedication of the newly refurbished Chapel of the Holy Innocents in the Cathedral, the church apologised to the Jews for believing in and spreading the word of 1144 Blood Libel (mentioned earlier). This was a significant point in inter-faith relations.

Norwich now has a devoted part-time minister, Reverend Daniel Rosenthal, who is also a qualified cantor. He lives in the flat above the communal hall and looks after the community's spiritual needs. They hold regular religious services, educational activities and cultural events. I still visit from time to time when I am invited.

Cheltenham Gloucestershire – (100 miles Northwest of London)

Staunchly Orthodox

Gloucester, the county town of Gloucestershire, is another of the towns that had a thriving Jewish presence in the Middle Ages. Gloucester was among the lands of the Queen Dowager Eleanor from which the Jews were expelled in 1275, fifteen years before the general expulsion in 1290.

The current Jewish community is based in Cheltenham, about 8 miles northeast of Gloucester on the edge of the Cotswold hills. It reaches back to the early 1800s when Cheltenham became a fashionable spa town. Jews arrived as entrepreneurs setting up emporia right next to the pump rooms, selling the latest gadgets, fashions and toys to the aristocratic clientele who came to take the waters. One of those was the Duke of Wellington, 'who made large purchases!'. One Jew did very well when opening the Montpellier Bazaar, three doors away from the Davies Library. He advertised 'articles of the best manufacture (such as ladies and gent's dressing, writing, work and netting boxes) at the lowest remunerating profit, to merit a continuance of that patronage which he has hitherto received'. Jewish doctors and dentists, and lawyers then arrived to look after the health and wealth of those seeking cures in the waters. It was an affluent community. Some members of Sephardi heritage had estates in Jamaica.

In 1823 the hundred or so Jewish families formally established the Cheltenham Hebrew Congregation (CHC). In 1824, they purchased land in Elm Street for a cemetery that is still in use. By 1826 it was said that the 'Descendants of Abraham' worshipped God in an apartment in a fine part of town that they rented for the purpose. As the town was attracting ever more visitors and the accompanying Jewish tradespeople, businessmen and professionals the room proved too small for the expanding congregation. In 1833 they bought a plot of land off St James Square where they hoped to build a synagogue.

On 5 August 1837, the Cheltenham Free Press wrote that *This day in the morning was laid with due and masonic ceremonial, the first stone of the new synagogue for members of the Hebrew persuasion from the design of WH Knight.*

15. The imposing exterior of Cheltenham Synagogue.

Cheltenham is noted for its Regency architecture. The architect William Hill Knight was the most notable in the town at the time. He had designed the Cheltenham Public Library, and Montpellier Walk. Knight was duly invited to design a synagogue in Regency style. This fine building's facade features Doric pilasters and a pediment. The interior includes a typical Regency dome. At the centre of the dome a lantern made by Nicholas Adam provides natural light.

The Georgian Torah Ark and the Bimah dating back to 1761, were donated by a Synagogue in Leadenhall Street, London. (That congregation was in the process of building a new synagogue that was dedicated in 1838.) Thus, Cheltenham has the oldest Ashkenazi synagogue furniture in Great Britain. The cost of wagon freight from London to Cheltenham was £86.

The Cheltenham Free Press reported on the consecration which took place on May 1839 as follows:

The reader, followed by the honorary officers, carrying the Rolls of the Pentateuch walked in procession seven times around the synagogue chanting a psalm during each circuit, after which they deposited the Rolls in the Ark. The body of the Ark is of imitation jasper and the pediment is supported by elegant Corinthian columns, the capitals and bases of which are chastely gilded and the doors are hid by a rich Indian curtain. The reading desk is painted in imitation bird's eye maple. The synagogue is furnished with two brass chandeliers and eight large white candlesticks. Besides this there are two frames upon the wall, one containing a prayer for Her Majesty Queen Victoria and the other a prayer in Hebrew repeated on the days (sic) of Atonement. The Dome is one of the principal ornaments of the building and is finished in superior manner with cornice and fretwork.'

A number of unusual elements of the original furnishings still survive. Among these are the original rattan upholstery of the pews and bimah seats, and the plaques on the walls. Victoria's name is superimposed over the names of previous British monarchs, the earliest of which is George II.

Architectural historian Sir Nikolaus Pevsner (son of a Russian-Jewish fur merchant) judged that the Cheltenham Synagogue is one of the architecturally 'best' non-Anglican ecclesiastical buildings in Britain. Its Grade II* listing calls it: *An outstanding example of a small provincial English synagogue'.*

The town was founded in the 1820s when it was a popular spa, However, as the nineteenth century progressed the town's character changed, and it became a less affluent place. The later Jewish population was made up of traders rather than the professionals and businessmen of the previous community. The community dwindled to just two members and in 1903, a decision was taken, to close the synagogue.

With the Second World War came a new lease of life. There was an influx of orthodox evacuees from London. Refugees from Nazi Europe also settled in Cheltenham and there were Jewish soldiers stationed at nearby bases including many Americans. A skeleton committee that still existed, decided to reopen the synagogue building for regular services. The war years saw a thriving community. In 1941, there was even talk of having to hire a hall for an overflow service. At the end of the war, many of the evacuees and soldiers left Cheltenham. However, happily, several families liked the place so much that they decided to remain. They formed the backbone of the vigorous orthodox community in the post war years.

My first visit to Cheltenham was in the middle of one of the worst winters known in England that century – the winter of 1962/63. Snow ploughs had pushed huge mountains of icy snow ten feet high on either side of the road. For three months the snow and ice lay on the ground. I found that the community was 'frozen' too, with very little Jewish activity. Apart from the celebration of a few bar mitzvahs and weddings, hardly any services were taking place in their beautiful and historic synagogue building.

I am pleased to say that that with my encouragement the community was inspired to seek more potential members and to re-establish positive Jewish life and regular synagogue services in their beautiful building. I found it a special experience leading services with such congenial people in such a charming little Regency synagogue. So attached did my wife Rosalie and I become to the community in Cheltenham, that for some years we rented a cottage nearby for three months during the summer months and I ran the services there every week. Our adult sons Brian and Daniel would visit when they could. Sometimes we would have as many as twenty-five to thirty men in synagogue for a Friday evening service. We would even have fifteen to twenty men on *Shabbat* morning which was good for such a small community. I became an honorary Cheltonian. I was the Jewish spokesman in a local church, and I gave interviews to the local newspapers, television and radio stations.

In 1984 the congregation of less than 100 members managed to raise the funds needed to repair the roof and refurbish the synagogue building. I was delighted to have been invited to rededicate it in 1985. The Jewish Chronicle reported that:

Cheltenham Hebrew Congregation members and its many friends in the local community came together to celebrate the Rededication of the Synagogue following extensive repair to its Grade II-star listed building. The service was led by Rev. Malcolm Weisman.

The Lord Lieutenant of Gloucestershire Dame Janet Trotter had sent loyal greetings to the Queen Mother in advance of her 90th birthday on behalf of Cheltenham Hebrew Congregation and had in turn received a reply expressing Her Majesty's warm good wishes to all for the Rededication.

Dr Elizabeth Jacobs spoke of growing up as a Jewish girl in Cheltenham and commented on how an influx of Jewish servicemen and evacuees from London brought new life to the Jewish Community in the 1940s.

Rabbi Mark Daniels made a toast to the community and the part it plays in the life of Cheltenham. This was particularly apt as also present were the Mayor of Cheltenham Councillor Duncan Smith and representatives of the University of Gloucestershire, Cheltenham Borough Conservation Office, local churches and Gloucestershire Constabulary.

Cheltenham Synagogue always ran a very meticulous United Synagogue style Orthodox service. In later years with several new members not being of the orthodox persuasion, several people said, 'We do not understand a word of what's going on. I said to the officers 'Why don't you shorten it and do it with an explanation – maybe put a bit of English in for some of the people.' They said, 'We cannot do it; we are a traditional Orthodox shul.'

Finding the right compromise between tradition and flexibility can be a real challenge for long established places like Cheltenham. Their constitution opens with a clause stating, 'We follow the *minhag* (tradition and custom) of the Chief Rabbi in London'. This means that if they want to change their religious affiliation from strictly orthodox, it is not easily done – and as far as I know nobody was inclined even to try.

In places where the numbers are small, I always do my utmost to keep the people who come from orthodox and liberal families together in everybody's interests. I try to create a 'halachically compatible' Jewish community that serves them all well. But sometimes, even my considerable skills that are often remarked upon, are not enough to prevail against hard held beliefs and strong personalities. In 2008, some dozen members finally broke away and formed the Three Counties Liberal Community. This left 68 members of the Cheltenham Hebrew Congregation (CHC). Soon they were running entirely parallel activities.

I am glad to know, however, that both groups are still active and energetic and that the relationship between the two is really cordial. CHC has provided a Torah Scroll for the Liberals on a long-term loan. Halachically Jewish men, belonging to the Liberal community, have responded to CHC requests to make up a *minyan* to mark *yahrzeits*. They work in harmony together each year for Cheltenham's Act of Remembrance for Holocaust Memorial Day. Several Jews in Cheltenham are actually members of both communities!

In 2011, I was pleased to take Chief Rabbi Lord Jonathan Sacks to visit the Cheltenham Hebrew Congregation in their beautiful synagogue and to meet their energetic Chairman Michael Webber.

Over the years Rosalie and I have enjoyed many wonderful and warm events with the members of Cheltenham Hebrew Congregation. We have been with them for solemn commemorations like *Tisha B'av*, when we mourn the destruction of the temples in Jerusalem or prestigious civic services, or just celebrating a warm Cheltenham *Shabbat* or a 'Tea and Talk' with the enthusiastic members. I especially remember the 'Pudding Evening' in 2015 where the whole meal consisted of a dozen delicious desserts! In 2014 I was honoured at a very special event. It marked the 175th anniversary of the consecration of Cheltenham Synagogue in 1839.

Jenny Silverston, current Chairman of the Cheltenham Hebrew Congregation wrote in 2022:

Malcolm has been supporting CHC since around 1963, taking services, giving lectures and joining in with our events, the joyful and the sad. We presented Malcolm with a certificate and a basket of flowers and wine in appreciation of his support for our community. We knew Malcolm too well to make it a retirement event!

I was touched that Jennifer continued:

What makes Malcom's relationship with Cheltenham so special is that we feel he loves Cheltenham as we do. We also feel that Malcolm understands that our community is not just a scaled down version of a large Jewish community. We value the wisdom that he brings to issues put before him and the close friendship and support he gives members. When he is here with us Malcolm gives fully of himself to us.

Jennifer really has expressed the essence of what I try to do for each community that I attend to (though I know communities like to feel that I am there only for them). I try to give them confidence and I take pride in what they are doing. Very often they really punch well above their weight and play a big part in the wider communities where they are situated, enabling so many more people to understand and appreciate Jews and Jewish life.

Today in the 2020s, CHC has around 60 members which has stayed constant for the last ten years. Rabbi Mark Daniels remains a friend to the community. Although there have been the inevitable deaths of elderly members, new and younger people have joined, and they have members from all over Gloucestershire.

Jennifer reiterates that the CHC constitution decrees that members must be Jewish in accordance with the Office of the Chief Rabbi. She adds though that the Cheltenham Hebrew Congregation is pleased that Liberal Jews have their own community which means that more Jews can find a community that suits them.

It is not possible to tell what the future holds for any small community, but I am so pleased to see that the Cheltenham community is energetic and active beyond what its size may suggest. I hope they go from strength to strength. They are gearing up to celebrate their 200th anniversary in 2023. They are very excited about this. I hope I will be able to share this exceptional milestone with them.

Guildford, Surrey –
(32 miles Southwest of London)
A 'Do-it-yourself' Congregation – Core A3

If there were to be a place where Jews who want to leave the metropolis may want to settle these days. It would be a place like Guildford in Surrey. It is a very nice place to live. The town – a conurbation of 147,000 by 2018 – is well within the commuter belt of London. The borough has some truly beautiful surroundings. Guildford to Waterloo is just thirty minutes on a fast train. Maybe there are signs of new Jewish life there.

Medieval Jewish Guildford

The first Jews in Guildford probably arrived during the 12th Century. The town was one of the major centres of the wool trade. Jews would have been an important minority, connecting England with markets in Europe. For instance, a Jew named Isaac of Southwark, lived in, and had a woollen business in Guildford. He made and or traded a product called 'Guildford Blue', throughout Western Europe. Right up until the 17th century, this cloth

16. This is believed to be the ancient synagogue in Guildford.

made from the wool of local sheep and dyed blue with woad that was locally grown was the main industry of Guildford. The steeply banked land near Guildford Castle still called Racks Close, was once filled with drying racks for Guildford Blue.

It is widely believed that Guildford's Jews built a synagogue in the High Street during the heyday of Jewish presence in Medieval England in about 1180. It is thought that Isaac might well have created and funded a synagogue in the town.

During excavations in 1995 archaeologists discovered an ornately decorated chamber with steps down from street level on the site that is now occupied by the bookseller Waterstones. What leads us to believe this was a synagogue, is that there is seating all round and on the east wall is an alcove. There is a pillar where scorch marks demonstrate that a light was often burning in this place. The assumption is that the alcove is the *Aron Kodesh* (Holy Ark) and the mark is from a *Ner Tamid* (Everlasting Candle) which is always left burning before the Ark. If this is true, then Guildford has the oldest synagogue remains in the British Isles and one of the oldest in Western Europe, although sadly, there is no way we can really substantiate this.

Guildford Museum presented a stone from this building to the current Jewish congregation in York Road. Waterstones bookstore displays some items illustrating this medieval chamber. It's a pity it is now concreted over, rather than having a glass covering, so we could all see it.

There are other references to Jews in Medieval Guildford in the ancient legal papers, the 'Calendar Rolls'. By the late 12th century, anti-Jewish sentiment had begun to grow. Jews had to dress in distinctive clothing and were often attacked. Guildford is even infamous for giving the name to a major tax on the Jews of England during the Middle Ages, known as the 'Guildford Tallage'. The last recorded mention of a Jew of medieval Guildford was a man called Josce who was murdered in 1283 – possibly for his money. Soon after, in 1290, all the Jews of England were expelled by decree of Edward I.

Modern times in Guildford

There is no reference to Jews in Guildford from 1290 right up to the 20th century, when during the Second World War, evacuees from London formed a thriving orthodox congregation called the Guildford United Synagogue Membership Group. They met at Ayer's Hall, Bury Street, Guildford. However, by 1947, it had ceased to exist after most of the evacuees had gone home.

Guildford was one of the very first places I was invited to visit as a spiritual advisor in the early 1960s. When I arrived, I discovered a gathering of some thirty ladies and a few men, who were very enthusiastic about Jewish life, though their facilities were rudimentary.

They used to meet on the first Tuesday of every month for a social get-together in a small, corrugated iron hut, with a coal stove in one corner. This was an outbuilding of the Spiritualist Church on York Road kindly lent to the Jewish group.

Before long I was joining them each month for their Tuesday meetings, giving them a chat or hosting a guest speaker. Over the months I nurtured the idea of holding synagogue services, which they had not yet considered. They agreed to try out an Eve of Sabbath service one Friday evening. They felt they knew how to run a service, as most of their members had come from a traditional orthodox Jewish background. The son of one of the community presidents, Theo Rubin, in fact went on to become acting head of the prestigious Orthodox training institute, Jews College or as it is now called, the London School of Jewish Studies.

Nevertheless, I felt they needed to know the practicalities of running services, so I began holding instructional sessions at their regular Tuesday meetings. On the appointed Friday evening, as I could not attend myself, I

8. Old Communities in Modern Times

17. Guildford New Synagogue that I helped in a small way to build

invited Rabbi Edward Jackson who was at that time in nearby Kingston, who agreed to come to Guildford and lead the service. Surprisingly, some sixty or more people turned up in this hut. The service was a roaring success and after that we continued to hold services in this cabin in Guildford about once a month. Sometimes I went down to conduct the service, or members of the now growing community, led the service themselves. They determined to run their group along strictly orthodox lines. They insisted on separate seating for men and women. They also determined that only *halachically* Jewish people could be members. (Other communities welcome everybody who wants to attend a service and do not ask questions.)

It soon dawned on me, that if they had any aspiration of continuity, let alone expansion, the makeshift shed just would not do. The community set about trying to find appropriate alternative premises, when their hosts, the Spiritualist church, forced their hand by giving them notice to leave. Next, the Spiritualist community themselves folded and sold up. This resulted in the little Jewish community being able to purchase this same shack for a nominal sum – now additionally blighted by having a leaking roof. The President Theo Rubin was faced with a quandary. He and his congregation at last owned a building, but it was in a parlous state, and they had no money to do much about it.

They consulted me and I am glad to say that I managed to persuade the officers of the Jewish Memorial Council to grant Guildford an interest free loan of £5,000. That was quite a lot of money in the 1970s, though still not enough to pay for a professional construction team. Necessity being the mother of invention, Theo trained the members to be builders! Every Sunday morning, they rolled up their sleeves and began to knock down the tin structure bit by bit. After some months they had built four brick walls. Then they put up a roof, all by themselves.

When I visited, I was roped in as well. They say it is good for a Minister to have a hands-on approach. In the case of Guildford, the saying acquired a literal meaning that I could never have imagined. It even meant wielding a hammer and nails. Now, fifty years later, the building still stands and serves the community. I may even still have the odd splinter to show for my labours.

Happily, some of the younger congregants proved to be handy carpenters and it was soon fitted out. The synagogue building was ready for me to consecrate in 1979. The community then commenced regular weekly services and also held services on the High Holydays and arranged social events there. But as the community shrunk from the late 1980s onwards they did so less often.

I had begun visiting Guildford in the early 1960s with my thirty ladies, growing to sixty people at the first service. Once regular monthly Friday evening services were underway, this grew to over a hundred attendees. The establishment of the University of Surrey in Guildford in 1966 had brought some new blood in Jewish staff and students. I am glad to say that I, as the first university Jewish chaplain to the new Universities, was able to help to create the Kosher flat and Jewish prayer room on campus in the 1970s.

One of my special memories of Guildford is of leading a procession down Guildford High Street in June 2006 from the medieval synagogue ruins in the town centre, escorting a new *sefer torah* to the historic Guildhall. It was a joyous occasion, walking under a giant *tallit* (prayer shawl) that was held up by pole holders acting as a movable *chuppah* (bridal Canopy) above the 'bride' of the holy scrolls. All traffic came to a standstill as some non-Jews looked on in wonder whilst others even joined the procession. Goodness knows what they made of the parade, but to me it seemed that the happy spirit was infectious. The scroll had been saved from destruction by the rabbi of a small community in Czechoslovakia. His family in Britain decided to donate it to a small community in this country. I felt sure it would be treasured and well used in Guildford. Once inside the Guildhall some 70 guests heard a fascinating talk by Guildford Museum curator, on the city's recently unearthed twelfth century (potential) synagogue remains. Clearly the consensus is that it actually was the medieval synagogue. The audience included such luminaries as the Mayor and Bishop of Guildford.

Today the focus of Jewish life in Guildford has shifted from the synagogue to the Jewish Common Room on campus which has provision for holding services. With the arrival of Rabbi Alex Goldberg, who grew up in the town and received his rabbinic ordination in 2019, as the Jewish Chaplain to the University and the Dean of the special section for 'Religious Life and Belief', there has been renewed Jewish energy in Guildford.

During the pandemic the university was able to create safe spaces for faith services in the 'Religious Life and Belief Centre' and outdoors. It was gratifying to see that even during some of the lockdowns, Rabbi Goldberg was able to hold services. During lockdown, a new community started up, holding services online. They have around fifty-five younger families in their group. They call themselves 'Israel in the Astolat' that works through a WhatsApp group. ('Astolat' is the name of a legendary place in the Arthurian romances, possibly located in Surrey.) This group arranged regular Friday night and festival services on Zoom.

All in all, today there are about 275 people in and around Guildford who connect with Judaism in some way. They are evenly distributed, with some crossovers, between the Campus community and the WhatsApp group. Guildford Synagogue and its community, still exists. They have only fifteen to twenty members, and many are now elderly. Most services these days take place on campus, though if there is to be an occasional service in the synagogue, Alex will join the community there rather than compete.

Rabbi Goldberg is looking forward to leading full services for the High Holydays in 2022. They hold a large communal meal on *Rosh Hashana*. They also have a *Sukkah* on campus and create a cultural '*Sukkah* in the Square' event during the festival. All the High Holydays services will be on campus except for *Yom Kippur mincha* and *neilah* concluding services, which will be held in the synagogue.

By all accounts, it seems my confidence in the continuity of Jewish life in Guildford may yet prove justified.

9

Smaller Communities – an Internal Diaspora

If London is the root and stem of the British Jewish community, and the major centres of Manchester, Leeds and Glasgow are the leaves, then smaller Jewish conurbations can be regarded as the flowers in a larger plant. They form an internal Jewish diaspora. Received wisdom holds that such blooms as small communities are destined to wither away. Yet in my experience, scattered congregations, or even clusters of individuals, continually surprise us with signs of longevity, ingenuity, and sometimes unexpected new shoots.

The advantages of living in country districts can often outweigh the drawbacks. Common challenges shared by those living in the countryside have bred a spirit of co-operation and a sense of unity which people in larger communities can only aspire to. Often the countryside and a small town offer a better quality of life than a crowded city and the cost of living is usually lower. It is a special pleasure to me to be able to interact with them and try to enhance their Jewish experience.

Here are some of my encounters with the smaller communities (in alphabetical order): Bath, Cambridge, Chatham, Chelmsford, Colchester, Lancaster, Northampton, Peterborough, Reigate, Stoke-on-Trent, Sunderland, Yatesbury.

Bath, Somerset (120 miles due west of London)

A new University

Jews began to settle in Bath from the mid-eighteenth century, although the first synagogue was not established until the early nineteenth century, but by 1874, services had effectively ceased. Later, in the mid-twentieth century, a new congregation of evacuees was established, but this also closed and there is no longer a defined Jewish community in Bath. However, from 1966 there was a flicker of new life when a new University was established in Bath which attracted a handful of Jewish students who were on my radar and visiting list. Fiona Frank wrote to say that she was a student at Bath University in the 1970s and her mum had insisted that she get in touch with the Jewish Society. She said:

One of the best things about this was meeting Malcolm Weisman who was really kind. He told me how much respect he had for my uncle who lived in Jersey. He made me feel like there was a point in getting involved in some Jewish life because you were going to be part of a country-wide network. Roll on years later and I find him a regular visitor to my next home in Lancaster in the 1990s. He instantly remembered me from Bath, chatted to me about my uncle in Jersey - he must know absolutely everyone and never forgets anything!!

Bath University now has a friendly liberal leaning Jewish student community. The Jewish Society runs events throughout the year including Friday Night Dinners, trips to Bristol, socials and access to any events run by the Union of Jewish Students. I am glad I was able to help this development in Bath.

Cambridge, Cambridgeshire
(60 miles north northeast of London)

An umbrella organisation

Cambridge, like many other small British communities grew out of the orthodox stable. At the beginning of the twentieth century almost everybody was orthodox, even if they were not meticulous in following all the rules. There was really little choice. I was pleased to visit this beautiful city and I hope that I encouraged and helped the Cambridge Jewish Residents Association (CJRA) to run their services, children's classes and social events in cooperation with the University students. The synagogue building is actually owned by the Cambridge University Jewish Society (CUJS).

There was a move towards Reform Judaism in Cambridge in the late 1970s. Some residents began to organise services away from the orthodox synagogue. I was called in by the Cambridge Jewish Residents Association, the main orthodox body to try to avoid, or ameliorate, a split. As in the case in Oxford, where all denominations belong to the same Jewish community and worship separately under the same roof, (see my Oxford Days chapter) I was hoping that there could be an umbrella Jewish organisation in Cambridge under which all could comfortably operate.

I would say I was partially successful in this. The Cambridge Jewish Residents Association did remain as an overarching organisation for all Cambridge Jews including the students – but under that umbrella, two separate groups were created, namely Cambridge Traditional Jewish Congregation (Orthodox) and the Beth Shalom Reform Synagogue. They each worshipped in a separate location. I hope that in some way I was able to mitigate the upheaval and upset that a complete split might have caused.

I formed close friendships with many members, and I continued my interest in helping the Cambridge Jewish Community. In my judicial role, I sometimes served at court in Cambridge. On occasions when attending sessions there, I was delighted to stay overnight or for the Sabbath with my friends in Cambridge who seemed very pleased to accommodate me.

One of my good friends in Cambridge was Professor Norman Montague Bleehen of St John's College. We had first met when we were both students at Oxford University. While I fulfilled my National Service as an RAF Chaplain around the world, Norman did his as a medical specialist in the Royal Army Medical Corps serving in British military hospitals in post-war Germany. As the 50-year limits of the Official Secrets Act in his case has now passed, I can mention that in Berlin, Norman was the UK medical representative of the Four Powers Commission in medical charge at Spandau Prison which held the Nazi war criminals Rudolf Hess, Baldur von Schirach and Albert Speer. Consulting his commanding officer about the suitability of a Jew for the post, he was told 'This is the army, and this is your job'.

During Norman's last illness I hope I was of some comfort and consolation to his wife Tirza. The family asked me to officiate at his burial in 2008 and subsequently also at his Memorial service in the Cambridge Synagogue which is close to Norman's college. This was a very large and prestigious affair which was attended by many of the Fellows as well as many friends from near and far. The Master of St John's, Professor Christopher Dobson, spoke movingly on behalf of the college.

Chatham and Rochester, Kent (40 miles southeast of London)

Joining the Navy

Chatham in Kent has a very special synagogue. The land in Rochester High Street was bought and the synagogue designed and constructed by the dedication of one man – as a memorial to his son. The son was Lazarus Simon Magnus, born in the naval dockyard town of Chatham in 1826. His father Simon Magnus was a successful coal merchant – very important in the age of steam trains and ships.

There is some evidence of Jews in the Kent ports of Rochester and Chatham in medieval times. The community really developed however, during the eighteenth and early nineteenth centuries, when some Jews were listed as 'Naval, or Admiralty, Agents, deriving profit from the purchase of prize money shares from Royal Navy ships crews, when captured enemy vessels were sold off.' (As recorded in Geoffrey I. Green's book, *The Royal Navy and Anglo-Jewry, 1740 – 1820*). When such 'agencies' ceased, these people tended to become ships' chandlers, dealers in supplies and equipment, or military tailors. Some of their companies are still in existence today in naval dockyard ports.

Simon Magnus's son Lazarus had a first-class British education. It was at the time of Jewish emancipation when Jews could be recognised as equals. This led to many Jews taking an active part in British civil society. Lazarus became a successful businessman. His main aim, in every project he took on, was the promotion of the public interest. He was highly respected as a magistrate and for his role in civil defence. He was elected Mayor of his local borough of Queensborough three times. He was also appreciated for his generous donations to both fellow Jews and society in general. He became a significant player in the international fields of communication (undersea telegraph cables to America) transport (railways in Kent, San Francisco, and Buenos Aires) and in energy.

Lazarus Simon Magnus was a personal friend of Isambard Kingdom Brunel, one of the most daring and successful engineers of the nineteenth century. It was Lazarus who rescued a major Brunel company on the brink of financial collapse – his Great Eastern Shipping company, and by so doing, brought to fruition the giant steamship – the Great Eastern – that was not to be equalled in size or speed for another fifty years.

Lazarus was very well respected by a wide community and achieved so much in just 39 years. In a sad turn of events, in 1865, trying to relieve a terrible toothache, he accidentally inhaled too much chloroform – which killed him. Shops were said to have closed on the day of his funeral. A year later at his stone setting, Reverend David Woolf Marks, the minister of West London Synagogue, suggested in his speech that Lazarus Simon Magus be commemorated by building a synagogue in his name. This would serve two purposes, to be a permanent place of worship for Jews in the area and enhance the façade of the High Street.

His father, Simon Magnus, took this on board. The community was formally established in 1865 when the building of the present synagogue began. It was near the site of a previous synagogue and cemetery that had existed in the town for more than 150 years. The beautiful new synagogue in memory of Lazarus Simon Magnus was formally opened and consecrated in 1869.

This synagogue is still the home of regular services as well as social and cultural events. They do not have a resident minister and I have been pleased to support them whenever I can. I had the honour of officiating at special services celebrating both their 100th (in 1965) as well as their 150th (in 2015) anniversaries. In 2015, the synagogue chairman as well as Rabbi Cliff Cohen of Ramsgate Reform Synagogue, joined me in leading the civic service at which two hundred people attended, twice the number expected. There was standing room only. It was particularly moving as Alfred Magnus, a descendent of the synagogue's founders, Lazarus and Simon was one of the honoured guests.

18. I am third from left with community members at Civic Service in 2015 commemorating 150th anniversary of Chatham Memorial Synagogue.

Chelmsford, Essex (40 miles northeast of London)
Awakening a Sleeping Beauty?

Chelmsford in Essex needed only a little nudge to get going. As a military chaplain in the early 60s, I would regularly visit and run services at the neighbouring army barracks near Colchester which is 65 miles northeast of London. I made sure that any local Jews were invited to attend. We soon got a small community going in Colchester. (See below)

I noticed that two or three members from nearby Chelmsford were always present whenever we held a service or an event. They would drive the twenty-five miles to join us. A fifty-mile round trip is a real commitment. I wondered what made them make that special effort. Once we became further acquainted, they asked me whether I could help them establish a community in Chelmsford itself. We placed an advertisement in the local newspaper, announcing plans to start a Jewish community there, and inviting all who were interested to contact us. Disappointingly, there was no response at all, although the Chelmsford contingent continued to attend my visits to Colchester and were still as keen as ever.

A year later, we posted the advertisement again – and suddenly, we received twenty replies all at once! What, I wondered, had made these people suddenly react to this advertisement now. Most had been living in Chelmsford for years. It was not as though they were just newcomers, looking for a synagogue.

We held a preliminary meeting in 1974, and all twenty turned up. As a result, the community got going strongly from the very start. Before long, those twenty began to search for and collect other families, until we had about fifty families. That was a great achievement. This was one of several places that followed my suggestions and decided, from the start, that it would provide for local Jewish people of all shades of religious observance and background. It is a non-affiliated congregation that is open for membership to all co-religionists. Non-Jewish partners are welcome to all events and services. Even more gratifying was the way they managed to run their own affairs, helped by a little instruction from me.

Once, towards the end of Chief Rabbi Jakobovits' term of office, I drove him up to Colchester for a combined meeting with the community and with Jewish students at the University of Essex. We had arranged to go to Chelmsford on the way home, to hold an evening service, and for him to meet the community. In the event we found ourselves running late in Colchester, so I telephoned ahead to tell Chelmsford that the Chief Rabbi had not yet finished his talk. I asked if they would go ahead and start without us in the meantime. When we finally arrived in Chelmsford, at nearly ten o'clock, we were delighted to find them still assembled and that they had actually completed a full evening service all by themselves. We were very proud of them.

In 1987, thirteen years after the community was founded, we celebrated the community's *Barmitzvah* together at a joyous *Chanukah* party attended by over a hundred and twenty congregants, friends, and guests. The town's deputy mayor judged the children's fancy dress competition. By this time the community was thriving and running three levels of Hebrew classes for juniors.

Decades later, in 2014, I was invited to officiate at Chelmsford's 40th anniversary celebrations. They organised a full weekend programme at the local conference centre. The *Shabbat* service that I led, was held in the Hall of the Baptist Church across the road. One of the members chanted all the passages from the week's portion of the *Sefer Torah*. It had taken a long time to get the community to that stage of proficiency, but it can be done!

It was evident that the founders who were all fairly young at the beginning in 1974, by 2014 were now forty years older. Now, sadly, most of them have passed away, but I am glad to say, there has been some replenishment. The membership of the Chelmsford Jewish Community has remained fairly stable at between fifty and sixty members. They still hold regular services on Friday evenings and occasionally on Saturday mornings and for all major festivals. They also run a well-attended Holocaust Memorial Day event for the town. Not having a resident rabbi, their team of lay readers conduct the services. I visit whenever I can.

Colchester, Essex (65 miles northeast of London)
Punch and Judy – and a dental connection

There had been Jews in Colchester, one of the oldest towns in England, during the Middle Ages. The earliest notice of Jews in the town is in 1185, when Benedict of Norwich paid a heavy fine for selling goods without licence to, among others, Aaron, Isaac and Abraham of Colchester.

The current community dates from Second World War, when the Shomberg family began to entertain soldiers stationed nearby to Friday night meals. Several Jewish families were evacuated to the town, swelling the numbers. I started visiting and befriending Colchester Jews in the late 1950s when I visited the nearby RAF base. I began to hold religious services for the Jewish military personnel stationed there from the UK, the USA and the Commonwealth, to which we invited the local families.

The Colchester and District Jewish Community was formed in 1957 and first met in members' houses. I encouraged them from the start to be an independent community, not aligned to any particular branch is Judaism, enabling them to serve all the Jews in the vicinity, who might have come from a wide range of Jewish backgrounds. In the 1960s when the University of Essex was established, it attracted several Jewish staff members and students. As I was the first Jewish Chaplain to the University, my visits to Colchester became even more rewarding.

By the mid-sixties the congregation had grown to some eighty families covering an area of many square miles from Chelmsford to the Southwest, to Ipswich in Suffolk in the North East. We all felt that it was time that a permanent home for the Colchester community should be created in the town.

Some land was duly purchased from the Spiritualist Church, and I am pleased that I was able to help them obtain some of the funding needed to build their synagogue in Fennings Chase, Priory Street, in 1969. They were very pleased when I brought the then Chief Rabbi Jakobovits to set the foundation stone and were also delighted that I introduced them to Lieutenant-Colonel Oliver Sebag-Montefiore whose family seat was nearby at Brook Hall, Finchingfield, Essex, and who became their President for the first twenty-five years. Oliver held closely to his Jewish heritage. He married the daughter of Sir Robert Waley Cohen at the Central Synagogue, Hallam Street in London. His brother Hugh on the other hand, became the Rt Rev Hugh Montefiore, Bishop of Birmingham.

I was pleased to hear Ruth Stone, a longstanding member of the community, say of my support to Colchester:

I have so much admiration for Malcolm! He was a regular and much-loved visitor to Colchester over the years, both as a rabbi and friend. His dentist was based in Colchester, so after dental treatment he often used to go to visit my mother Norma Stone, who was the Honorary Secretary and sometime Chairman of our small shul. Always a gracious and eloquent man, he could command a room without ever raising his voice ... The night my mother died, he came up from Kent, just to spend an hour or so with her and give us comfort. I shall never forget his kindness.

John Gottesman former chairman of Colchester Jewish Community, with whom I am still in regular touch, was kind enough to say:

Since the 1960s, Malcolm has always been our friend and mentor, in times of joy as well as in times of sadness for our members. With his 'Quest' programmes he introduced us to other nearby communities from Kingston-upon-Thames to Rochester in Kent and Norwich in Norfolk so we could share experiences and solutions. For more than sixty years he has been a supporter of this, and every other small community from Scotland to Cornwall, Gibraltar, Malta, and the Channel Islands. What a man!

Maurice Sunkin, a senior and highly respected member of the small Colchester community, is a professor of law at the University of Essex. Maurice has kindly written:

In his various roles as minister for small communities, minister for university students and Jewish chaplain to the army the Rev Malcolm Weisman has had a long association with the Colchester and District Jewish Community, the University of Essex, and the local army garrison. I understand that his connections with Colchester had a dental dimension as well.

In all these capacities Malcolm has been unstinting in his generous and enthusiastic support, for which he is much loved, admired and respected. I think it's true to say that The Colchester and District Jewish Community would not have flourished as it has without the benefit of Malcolm's learning and wise counsel. He has always displayed a real understanding of small communities and has a much-needed ability to find ways to combine the spiritual with more pragmatic pressures that communities like ours inevitably face. His generosity is unparalleled. As is his willingness to simply join in.

At one of our Chanukah parties we had a Punch & Judy show. We were slightly nervous that Malcolm and his dear late wife Rosalie, who were visiting for the occasion, might consider the show to be not quite appropriate. What, after all, has Punch and Judy got to do with Chanukah? In the event we need not have worried at all. They both really enjoyed the fun and in fact Malcolm almost fell off the Bimah in fits of laughter.

Maurice went on to say,

On a more serious side Malcolm consecrated land for our Colchester burial site and has led many a funeral service there for much loved departed souls. Malcolm's energy has been simply remarkable. We know that while he has been enthusiastically supporting us in Colchester he has also been working with and for communities around the country. My wife and I were reminded of this when during a summer holiday in Cornwall who should we bump into but Malcolm and Rosalie! They, of course had been visiting a small community far from Colchester. Although we were all out of context Malcolm immediately greeted us with our names and a cheerful "Hello, how's Colchester?" We were amazed – but not surprised.

My family and I have had many happy associations with the members of the community in Colchester and District Jewish Community. Today they are a warm and welcoming group of eighty members of all ages, from diverse backgrounds and spread over quite a wide area. They enjoy coming together with their shared interest in Judaism Their small but beautiful synagogue in Colchester that they built in the 1960s is still the focus of their social, religious and educational activities. I look forward to spending a *Shabbat* with my friends in Colchester very soon.

Lancaster University (250 miles northeast of London)
The first multifaith chaplaincy centre

As Chaplain to the new Lancaster University in the 1960s, I was very pleased to meet the Jewish students and staff. Professor Stanley Henig, who was a founder member of the Department of Politics in 1964, was one of first Jewish academics that I met. I telephoned him at his lodgings within days of his arrival in Lancaster. We talked about future plans for Jewish life in Lancaster. We have had a wonderful collaborative partnership for nearly sixty years, including the time when Stanley was appointed as the Deputy Pro-Chancellor of Lancaster University from 2006 to 2011.

Stanley who was teaching politics, soon decided to practise it instead! From 1966 to 1970, Stanley was elected as the Labour Member of Parliament for Lancaster. He left the University but remained in the city and was a significant figure in the Lancaster and Lakes Jewish Community. This is linked to the University Multi-Faith Chaplaincy Centre and connected with the Jewish staff and students on campus. I relished visiting Lancaster – a five-hundred-mile round trip – which I did frequently.

Paying tribute to my work there, Stanley Henig has kindly said:

Over the years Malcolm has been a regular visitor and an inspiration to generations of students. Malcolm's role in the establishment of the Multi-Faith University Chaplaincy Centre at Lancaster was crucial. He played an important role in determining the structure and purpose of the various rooms within the centre and, critically, he was largely responsible for successful appeals to raise the Jewish financial contribution.

The Jewish rooms include a synagogue, a kosher kitchen, and a large general social room. These facilities are shared between the University Jewish Society (UJS) and the Lancaster and Lakes Jewish Community.

I had the special honour of consecrating this little synagogue complete with Holy Ark and *Bimah* in the presence of Her Majesty the Queen who had come to Lancaster in 1969 to open the Multi-Faith Chaplaincy Centre with which I was so intimately involved. The Queen and I spent about twenty minutes together. She showed a genuine interest in Jewish life and practice. She asked many pertinent questions about the Jewish appurtenances she had been shown. I have written more about this visit in my chapter on my meetings with Royalty.

Amusingly, in this photograph of the event, standing next to me and the Queen at the reading desk, was the president of the university's Jewish Students Society, Raymond Franks, who sported a beard. I don't think Her Majesty or anyone present was confused about our respective identities.

19. Here I am explaining to the ruling Monarch various appurtenances of a synagogue when she opened the Multifaith Chaplaincy Centre at Lancaster University.

However, I am told that some people who saw the photograph, assumed that the bearded student was the pious Jewish chaplain, and a still youthful-looking me, was the student representative.

I was very proud when the Lancaster Students Jewish Society was voted 'UJS Developing JSoc of the Year' in 2016 and also 'Emerging Society of the Year at the Israel 2019 awards!'

Stanley concluded:

I don't think that any of this would have happened without Malcolm. This was the very first of such Multi-Faith Chaplaincy Centres in the UK. Since then, I am pleased to say that the model has been repeated at several other of the newer universities such as Warwick, East Anglia, York and Aberdeen.

I was delighted to have been made an Honorary Fellow of Lancaster University in 2006 for my work on the Multi-Faith Centre. Fiona Frank, who was an active participant in the Lancaster and Lakes Jewish Community and the Lancaster University Jewish Society paid tribute to my work, saying:

He can run a service that's absolutely inclusive across all denominations and none, and doesn't make anyone feel excluded. I always remember him telling us at one Saturday morning service how it is not the Jews that kept the Sabbath, it is the Sabbath that has kept the Jews. And when I do Shabbat, wherever I am, I think of him.

Northampton, Northamptonshire
(70 miles northwest of London.)

Digging up bones

Records from 1159 show that Jews lived in Northampton at that time and had to pay heavy taxes. However, as we know, all Jews were expelled from England in 1290. In more modern times the Northampton Hebrew Congregation dates back to 1888. The community totalled about 150 people at the time. Two years later the congregation bought a corrugated iron building in Overstone Road which they used as a synagogue for nearly 80 years.

Not unexpectedly, according to the historian Dr Michael Jolles who wrote a history of the Jews of Northampton, a city famous for manufacturing shoes, several Jews were involved in the shoe trade in one way or another. Some supplied leather, some supplied and repaired manufacturing equipment for boots and shoes – and one even started a cardboard shoebox factory. Others were market traders and shopkeepers. In the 1930s several Jews fleeing Nazi Europe strengthened the community.

In 1939, literally thousands of Londoners were evacuated to Northampton and surrounding areas. This included a fair proportion of Jews from the East End. The community bent over backwards to make their co-religionists welcome, though they greatly outnumbered the ones already there. Several Jews stayed on after the war relocating their businesses to the area. In the 1960s, when the Northampton Jewish community numbered over 300, they decided to demolish the old synagogue and build a brand new one on the same site.

I have had the pleasure of visiting and advising the Northampton community for over 50 years. I would visit as regularly as I could, holding *Shabbat* weekends, giving talks to the members and attending their annual general meetings. They would help me organise my 'Quests', whereby we would bring several small communities from a region together for a day. They particularly loved the one we organised at the US airbase at RAF Alconbury 35 miles away in Cambridgeshire in 1982 which they found so interesting and helpful. (I write about these 'Quests' in a later chapter.)

I helped the community to set up a branch of the Council of Christians and Jews in Northampton. One of the highlights that the community members remember was a *Seder* meal for Passover with which I assisted.

In 2004, I assisted in opening an extension to their cemetery and conducted a service of dedication. I have conducted many a burial there, for members of the community. A most interesting internment though was from much earlier times. Following the discovery by accident, of the original medieval Jewish cemetery and the remains of some medieval Jews, I was able in 2010, to help them arrange for their reburial in the town's current cemetery. The following year we erected a tombstone to these medieval Jews, and I had the honour of conducting the service unveiling the stone. The inscription under a Star of David reads: 'The final resting place of three 12th century Northampton Jews, discovered during excavations in 1992, now at peace with their people 16th May 2010.

John Josephs, the honorary life president of the community wrote:

In 1988, we celebrated our centenary and Malcolm was in the forefront as usual, arranging for the then Chief Rabbi Jakobovits to attend. Malcolm also helped us to arrange our 125th anniversary celebration in 2013, and again he arranged for our current Chief Rabbi Ephraim Mirvis to attend. If I could sum up Malcolm's approach to his work with small communities in one phrase it would be with regard to his positive attitude to everything. Whenever we suggested something, however outrageous, he never said no, always "how about this?

PETERBOROUGH Cambridgeshire
(85 miles due North of London)
One of the first communities I ever visited

Peterborough was one of the very first small communities I got to know, because of my visits to the nearby Royal Air Force fighter base at Wittering. I would, as you know, always seek out any Jewish families in the area and give them a helping hand if I could. I found there were very few Jews in Peterborough, though there had been a synagogue in the town since the 1950s. The Congregation, linked to the United Synagogue, had been established just after the Second World War with about twenty-five members who were mainly war evacuees from Central and East London.

When I started visiting them in the early 60s, there were about 22 members. They really enjoyed coming together but I soon noticed that they preferred to meet on a social basis. They were not keen on services or even a formal talk. The moment we started to pray in the synagogue, the ladies in the upstairs gallery would launch into conversation. However, the fact that they wanted to come together regularly on Friday evenings helped to build a sense of community.

There are still a few orthodox Jewish families left in Peterborough, including the son of Professor Sir Ludwig Guttmann the pioneering neurologist who developed advanced rehabilitation through sports for paraplegics and those with spinal injuries. By the 1970s the synagogue had closed. In 1991 a small Liberal Jewish Community was established in Peterborough. They are still active with a membership that has grown to approximately fifty.

The Peterborough City Council arranges a multi-faith seminar every summer in the local town hall for which I am usually asked to represent the Jewish Community. Sometimes they also hold a multi-faith exhibition where religious objects are prominently displayed. Peterborough Multi-Faith Council meetings conclude with all the groups attending providing traditional food relevant to their religion and denomination. Afterwards, we all go and have a delicious nosh-up.

Reigate, Surrey (25 miles south of London)
Mitteleuropa in deepest Surrey?

The beauty of small communities is that each has its own unique character, depending on the history, location and makeup of the group. In Reigate, there was a distinctly German intellectual and cultural flavour. I discovered that unless I arrived with a high-powered cerebral talk once a month, they were not going to attend. They did not want services. An impressive in-depth lecture was much more to their taste!

It often takes a few dynamic individuals to keep a community together. In Reigate's case the leaders were two strong women. One of these, the community secretary, was crucial to its success. While it lasted, Reigate stood out as a tiny hub of well-informed and well-educated, if not particularly observant Jews. When these two women left, momentum began to falter, and the community effectively collapsed.

Stoke-on-Trent, Staffordshire
(170 miles northwest of London)
Out with the old and in with the new

The Stoke-on-Trent and North Staffordshire community, dating back to 1873, is one where I was called upon to both deconsecrate in 2003, their (once new, but now old) synagogue in Hanley and also consecrate the new one in Newcastle-under-Lyme in 2006.

In 2002, just when the remaining few members of the community were despairing as to how they could possibly manage the cost of replacing the boiler and repairing the 80-year-old building in Birch Terrace, along came a wonderful solution. They received an offer from a property developer who wanted to build a great shopping mall in Hanley. The community gladly accepted the deal and sold him the crumbling building that had been regularly used and enjoyed by generations of Staffordshire Jews, for services, study and social life.

Thereafter, they decided to build a new synagogue at the location of their cemetery in Newcastle-under-Lyme. In a process led by Stoke's dedicated president, Sydney Morris MBE, a well-known figure in interfaith relations in Staffordshire and who ran his family's bespoke tailoring business in the town for 50 years, they duly demolished the old cemetery prayer hall and designed and built a brand new fully functioning synagogue on that site.

Being in the Potteries, a special feature above the entrance of the old synagogue was a mosaic *Magen David* (Shield of David) made by the Henry Minton porcelain factory. It was carefully dismantled and transferred to the new building. Also refitted, were the antique stained-glass windows, the Ark and the *Bimah* and many of the interior fittings. The old front doors with stained glass fanlight above now grace the new porch. I had the double honour of helping the community with the transition with all due ceremony.

When Edwin Lucas, a member of the Stoke Community whom I had met in the late 70s, heard about the preparation for this book, he reminded me of his wedding there on a summer's weekend in 1995. He said he was so inspired by the community in Stoke, that although he no longer lived there, he and his wife-to-be had chosen to be married there – and had insisted that I be present to do the honours. It was the first wedding held in the old Birch Terrace synagogue for about 40 years.

When Edwin turned up in shorts I was not surprised as it was a hot day. However, he then revealed that he had left his wedding trousers at home! What is more, his best man had also brought the wrong trousers, as they had been hanging on the wrong hanger. Edwin said:

I wore my best man's trousers. The president of the shul Sydney Morris, who fortunately was a master tailor, found and hurriedly altered another pair, so that we both looked smart for the occasion.

There was yet another problem Edwin went on to describe:

Where was the Ketubah (the wedding contract) that we were required to sign? We thought Rev Malcolm had organised it – and he thought Sydney had organised it. Alas nobody had! Fortunately, Sydney Morris's son, Martin came to the rescue. He had made up a guidebook to show visitors what goes on in a synagogue. He had been meticulous at describing a Jewish wedding and thankfully there was an illustration of a Ketubah in the book – which we duly signed! We had a lovely wedding with Rev Ernest Levy from Glasgow together with Rev Malcolm delivering the ceremonials.

The giant shopping mall destined for Hanley has still not been constructed. Meantime, in 2016, I was able to celebrate the 10th anniversary of the new synagogue building in Newcastle-under-Lyme with the Stoke-on-Trent community, together with the Bishops of Lichfield and Stafford and other civic dignitaries.

Martin Morris, who took over the presidency from his late father Sydney, said,

When I organised our tenth anniversary service in 2016, Malcolm Weisman accompanied the Bishop of Lichfield who was the co-chair on the Council of Christians and Jews at the time, in conducting affairs. Malcolm's humility, his humour and his warmth are always appreciated whenever he has given our tiny community the benefit of his vast knowledge over the many years. 'I am proud to call him my friend, as is our whole community.

I too value my great friendship with Sydney and Martin Morris and all the valiant members of the Stoke community. I am sure that Sydney Morris would be most pleased to know that Jews in the Potteries are continuing to hold services on a regular basis and that they remain a positive force for good interfaith relations in Staffordshire.

Sunderland, Tyne and Wear –
(280 miles north of London)

'The Angel of Death'

I am often called in to communities when things are going wrong. More than once, I have intervened and managed to arrest a decline, only to see the inevitable downward trend resume. Sometimes it is simply too late. Other times people even mix up cause and effect and pretend that I am to blame for a community's demise! Such was the case in Sunderland.

Sunderland is a port city on the northeast coast of England at the mouth of the River Wear (thirteen miles southeast of Newcastle). It was thriving in the eighteenth and nineteenth centuries because of the Industrial Revolution, the growth of the railways and the development of the harbour and of course, the nearby Durham coalfields. It was a vital export centre for coal to Danzig and other northern European ports. The empty boats returning were ideal for Jewish emigres seeking a better life.

A vibrant Jewish community steadily developed in the town, numbering up to 2,000 between the wars, with several large congregations of orthodox Jews. Even in the early 1960s almost 1,400 Jews still lived there. However, the numbers dramatically diminished thereafter to a mere handful by the year 2000.

First to arrive in Sunderland in the 1770s were Polish Jews escaping from the Cossacks. Ten years later came the Litvak Jews in the 1780s escaping pogroms and severe economic hardship. They were mainly from Kretinga, a *shtetl* (village) in northwest Lithuania, near the port of Memel, where Jews were involved in international trade.

These two groups, the Poles and the Lithuanians, having arrived in Sunderland, within ten years of each other, formed two distinct communities – with much friction between them. The Polish Synagogue was opened in 1781 (and was active for 80 years) The Sunderland Hebrew Congregation was established by the Lithuanians ten years later in 1791. In 1821 this became a member of the overarching nationwide mainstream orthodox 'United Synagogue' organisation. By the 1850s the Polish congregation and other smaller congregations decided to join forces with the stronger Sunderland Hebrew Congregation, and they sought funds together to build a new synagogue in 1861.

By the time of the massive immigration from Eastern Europe between 1880 and 1920 the Jewish Community in Sunderland was thriving. There was a disastrous fire in the *shtetl* of Kretinga in 1889 that had left hundreds of Jews homeless and hopeless. Their brethren already prospering in Sunderland, set up a relief fund and helped them emigrate en-masse to join them in the North of England.

These new immigrants from Kretinga were among the poorer members of the community. However, they were generally men of deep religious learning and fiercely attached to their own Orthodox tradition and rituals. A dispute arose in 1889 over the reciting of certain Psalms in the Sunderland Hebrew Congregation, following the afternoon service on Rosh Hashanah. This dispute on the details of ritual, precipitated a break-away which resulted a year later, in 1890 in the creation of the Sunderland *Beth Hamedrash*, known as the 'Greener Shul'

In many other places in the UK (and also worldwide) the more pious and fervently religious newcomers did not feel comfortable in the lofty prayer halls of the already acclimatised congregations of the already established shuls of previous migrations, so they created their own prayer groups and built their own synagogues on the models that they had been used to in Eastern Europe. They often called their congregation the *Beth Hamedrash*, (hall of study) sometimes with an added name referring to a person or institution in Jewish life in Eastern Europe. This community was usually referred to by the established congregation as the 'greener' shul. The 'greeners' referred to the established congregation in the UK as the 'Englishe' (English) shul. The Sunderland *Beth Hamedrash* lasted nearly 100 years, right up to 1984 when it too joined the stronger shul in what was thenceforth called the 'Sunderland Hebrew Congregation incorporating the Beth Hamedrash'.

When the Sunderland Hebrew Congregation was in rapid downfall, I was invited in to try to resolve their dilemmas. The community already was an amalgamation of the three large orthodox communities that had existed separately in Sunderland for two centuries, but Jews were leaving the area in droves and those left behind were at a loss as to what to do.

In the early 2000s, when I walked into their magnificent synagogue, on Ryhope Road, someone joked: 'Go away, we don't want to see you here!' They pretended that I was the *Malach Ha-Mavet* (the Angel of Death) coming to close them down. But they knew that the writing was on the wall.

This exceptional, and now listed, synagogue was built in 1928 at the time when there were 2000 Jews living in Sunderland. The architect was Marcus Kenneth Glass, who had designed the Jesmond Synagogue in Newcastle (now flats) and the Clapton Synagogue in London (which was demolished just before it was going to be listed). Glass was a Jewish immigrant who had arrived in Newcastle from Lithuania as a toddler in the 1890s. It is built in what is described as a mixture of Art Deco and Byzantine style. The semi-circular stained-glass windows to east and west are superb.

By the time they called for my help, the community had dramatically dwindled. In the 1990s there were still a few hundred Jews left. The 2001 census showed that just forty-five Jewish people remained on Wearside. In September 2000, they had actually sold this Grade II listed building for £65,000 to an American Jewish charity, the Shlomo Memorial Trust. The community was permitted to continue to use it, paying a peppercorn rent.

When I entered, once the mirth had passed, we got to the root of the problem. They just could not manage the upkeep of such a large building anymore. They could not heat this huge edifice and so the Sunderland Jews had retreated to the basement; and even then, they often had to wait for a long time (in the cold) for a minyan to turn up on a *Shabbat*. They would eventually give up and go home.

How could I help, they asked me? Based on similar situations I had experienced in many smaller communities, I immediately suggested that they start on time and run a full service, omitting the things you cannot do without the required ten-man *minyan*. for example, some special prayers such as the *Kedushah*, *Baruch Hu* and the *Kaddish*. They could read the portion of the law for the week from the *Chumash* (the book of the Five Books of Moses – the beginning of the Hebrew Bible) but not directly from the Scrolls of the Law. In this way you can still enjoy a meaningful service. They took this up in Sunderland. Unfortunately, the challenge of covering expenses for maintenance remained.

20. Sunderland Synagogue in Ryhope Road

21. One of the huge semi-circular stained-glass windows of Sunderland Synagogue, Ryhope Road.

As seemed to be usual, in Sunderland, the views of the various synagogue officers differed very much on whether, when and how they should call an end to the community – and also on where the fittings and appurtenances might go. Finally, and decisively, one of the stalwarts ruled in 2006, that Sunderland Hebrew Congregation should close down forthwith. He arranged a celebratory farewell kiddush dinner on a Friday night in March that year followed by a final Saturday *Shabbat* morning service. The next day an outraged congregant rang me up. He said that he and other members would have preferred the finale to have been held on a Sunday afternoon as that would have enabled many more ex-Sunderlanders to have travelled to attend this closing ceremony. That would have made sense, but others felt that the closing services should be for faithful members that had remained to the bitter end – not for those who had already jumped ship. They could never please everyone.

Whichever way they decided to end it – the time had come when those left in the city could neither manage to maintain a community nor look after its synagogue. For a while thereafter, those Jews remaining in the area continued to conduct certain prayer services in members' homes. In 2008 though, Jewish communal life in Sunderland, finally came to end after 240 years. The new owner of the large and beautiful synagogue building was hoping to build flats inside it. They had successfully done this before, in other obsolete synagogues. So far nothing has happened. The magnificent building has stood empty and abandoned since 2006.

Yatesbury, Wiltshire (90 miles due west of London)
The Gruneberg Farming Chevra

The German Jewish spirit could be found in unexpected places. I became acquainted with the four German Gruneberg brothers who lived with their families in four houses on a farm, or farms, outside Yatesbury in the Cotswolds near Chippenham in Wiltshire. They had fled Europe at the start of the Nazi period and reached England before the war. They had been farmers in Europe and so settled together on a farm in four houses within walking distance of each other. They grew a range of crops and kept sheep and cattle as well. I have to confess that on the many occasions when I visited them, I never got my boots dirty by trudging out into the fields!

I was alerted to their existence in the early 1960s when I started my pastoral duties, visiting the Royal Air Force (RAF) base at Yatesbury as the

Jewish Chaplain. The main difference from the other German Jewish community that I called on at Reigate, Surrey, was that the four brothers Gruneberg were deeply attached to traditional Jewish observance.

While they wore regular farming attire in the fields, the brothers always covered their heads with a skull cap or hat. They treated the Sabbath as sacred and Jewish Holidays were strictly observed with prayers and no work. Living deep in the country there was no possibility of joining a far-away synagogue, so they became their own tight knit community. They were completely self-sufficient celebrating the Sabbath and all Jewish holidays in their isolation. When I offered to bring some *challot* (Jewish Friday night plaited bread loaves) from the Jewish hub of London for the Sabbath, or *Hamantaschen* for *Purim*, they declined politely, saying they had baked their own, thank you.

Their twelve children went to local schools and made friends with the local youngsters – but they were not allowed to join the young farmers' clubs, nor could they go out on a Friday night. The family was adamant: '*Shabbos is Shabbos*, and you are Jewish – we do our own thing.' The four families would get together over the Sabbath and have a really meaningful time. For their children's Jewish education, which was so crucially important to them, they used to recruit a student from Oxford, who would come every Sunday morning all the way from the university town to teach them. Because of their solid example, the children remained fully religiously Jewish and within the Jewish community. To my knowledge, not one of them has married out of the faith. The lesson is clear: if you have that kind of commitment, your religious beliefs can remain intact even in isolation. I always marvelled at the Grunebergs' independence and can-do spirit. At one stage I used to visit them every few weeks, making a special diversion and stopping off whenever I was driving to Cheltenham or Bristol. Occasionally I would even stay with them overnight, I can never forget their warm hospitality.

Reflections

I have lived to see many budding, flowering and also withering small communities over the last nearly 70 years. Sometimes the demise is inevitable when dealing with shifting and aging populations which are scattered about the country. The elders pass away and their children move elsewhere – and hopefully will have joined other communities. The once mighty Sunderland Hebrew Congregation is no more, just as there is no longer an orthodox community in nearby Middleborough on the East

Coast or Blackpool on the West – nor in Newport and other places in Wales. There had been flourishing orthodox communities in the mid-twentieth century with sometimes hundreds of members in these places, with their own rabbis and cantors and synagogue buildings. But these simply do not exist anymore. New Reform or Liberal communities have sprung up in some of these places.

I am pleased to say, however, that I have also seen several communities reach a stable and sustainable level and carry on doing excellent work in keeping Jews of all ages in far flung places together as a group. I have also seen with great pleasure that the new universities where I was once the sole chaplain in the 1960s have attracted active Jewish staff and students. These have had a revitalising and enduring impact on several Jewish Communities for instance in Guildford, Exeter, Bath, Norwich, Colchester and other university towns. The cycle of Jewish life continues.

10

Seaside Communities, Wales, Scotland and Geographical Quests

Hugging the Coast – Jewish seaside communities

Visiting the seaside grew in popularity with British People in the first half of the 20th Century. Providing for these holidaymakers with boarding houses and shops selling food, clothing and souvenirs seems to have been a promising proposition for newly arrived Jews from Eastern Europe. Around a hundred years ago, popular resorts like Whitley Bay, Darlington, Middlesbrough, North Shields, South Shields, Blackpool, Portsmouth, Southampton, Eastbourne, Margate and Ramsgate all had thriving Ashkenazi orthodox communities each with substantial synagogues and a full-time minister and cantor. But that is a thing of the past now. They have all ceased to be. Numbers of Jews living in these seaside towns have decreased so much that communities simply cannot justify having their own rabbi or synagogue building and are scarcely economically viable at all. Here are some anecdotes of my time in seaside communities.

Bognor Regis, West Sussex (85 miles Southwest of London)

The charm of turning a living room into an 'instant synagogue'

Bognor and District was one of the first of the small communities that fell into my remit and one which I helped to found in 1962 out of a group of disparate families and individuals. During the early 1940s there had been a number of short-lived Jewish congregations in the area, formed by wartime evacuees from London but they had ceased to exist.

When I came to visit in 1962, we began holding meetings in various homes where we collected about thirty or forty enthusiastic people from Bognor and along the coast as far as Chichester. For a few years in the 1970s, the congregation was buoyant. They used a room in a vacated Council Library in London Road, Bognor Regis as a dedicated synagogue.

They consider themselves a 'Traditional' community, but with no affiliation to any particular movement, leaving them freedom to innovate. Until the Covid pandemic struck, I used to go there about three times a year, to spend an evening with them, to give a talk on a Jewish topic or run a short service. Maybe just seven or eight people could attend, but in my view, it is still worth driving eighty-five miles each way. They could not make it to a bigger centre further away in Brighton or Portsmouth. They too, particularly enjoyed a wintertime visit from me during the eight-day Chanukah festival.

One particularly enjoyable *Chanukah* event there a few years ago took place in the small sitting room of Jack Jacobs' home. Halfway up the wall was an electric socket and two hooks. When he hosted a service, he used an old-fashioned TV cabinet and hooked it up as an Ark. A *ner tamid* (eternal light) was plugged into the socket above this Ark. He turned the armchairs around to face it and, hey presto! you had an 'instant synagogue'! This really showed me how dedicated and innovative people can be. We have celebrated barmitzvahs in this house and in other people's houses. On rare occasions if they had a special function, they would hire a hall or a hotel room. I remember one wedding that was held in a local hotel that was fully koshered for the occasion. Sadly, most of the people in this area are very elderly and the future of the Bognor Regis community is not assured.

Eastbourne, West Sussex (55 miles due south of London)

Is the tide running out?

Along the south coast many communities consist almost exclusively of people who have retired to the seaside, similar perhaps to Miami, but on a smaller scale. Eastbourne at the turn of the century was a thriving and elegant British seaside resort. The five-star Grand Hotel was, and still is, world famous. Concerts were broadcast regularly from there by the BBC and all the musical directors of the Grand Hotel Eastbourne Orchestra seem to have been Jewish violinists, some of whom became national heartthrobs.

First there was Simon Van Lier from 1903, then Albert (born Abraham) Sandler from 1925. He became a BBC radio celebrity. Leslie Jeffries (born David Jaffa) was the long-serving resident musical director there from 1934 until 1954. The Grand Hotel concerts continued for fifty years. They were broadcast live on the BBC from the Great Hall every Sunday night from

1924 to 1939. The programme was called 'Grand Hotel' and, it was at that time one of the most popular shows on the BBC.

There were several Jewish-owned hotels and boarding houses in Eastbourne. Jews also ran businesses and shops, amongst them three furriers. In 1918 they founded the orthodox Eastbourne Hebrew Congregation (EHC) and in 1922 purchased a three-story building at 22 Susan's Road, in the centre of town where they created a synagogue on the first floor and a community hall downstairs.

For seventy-five years Eastbourne had a resident minister. The longest serving was Rev Chaim Zack, who was the minister in a part-time capacity for over fifty years, from 1946 to 1997. He was the longest serving minster to one congregation in the whole of the UK. Rev Zack was married to the daughter of Cantor Jacob Koussevitzky whom I had had the pleasure of listening to at Dalston Synagogue in London in my youth. Rev Zack also ran a jewellery shop in the town.

Membership usually fluctuated at around fifty. The highest attended services were during the war years when British and American soldiers were billeted nearby. One Pesach, a communal Seder was attended by 150 people, a hundred of them being army personnel.

Ronnie Taylor the current (and life) president and his wife Linda, like many congregants came to Eastbourne for work related reasons. Originally from Manchester, they moved to Eastbourne in 1982 for Ronnie's job as an adviser to the then Dental Estimates Board. They immediately became involved in the Eastbourne Hebrew Congregation.

After Rev Zack retired, I would visit from time to time. The Eastbourne community in pre-Covid times held a service every Saturday at 10.00am in a traditional style. They prided themselves on being an open and friendly community welcoming all who wanted to attend. They accepted that to engage with all comers, including holidaymakers, they have to adapt by reading some parts in English instead of Hebrew and reading the portion of the law from the book in Hebrew or even in English whenever the quorum of ten adult Jewish men required to read directly from the scrolls, is not present. Often, they have a short discussion about the week's portion as well. The service was always followed by delicious refreshments and socialising.

Rosalie and I would regularly do a *Chanukah* trail', spending an afternoon or evening during the eight days of the festival with the various communities along the south coast. We would start in Canterbury, go down to Hastings then on to Bexhill and Eastbourne. From there we would visit the community in Worthing, ending with a final flourish of *Maoz Tzur* (a traditional *Chanukah* song) in Bognor Regis and Portsmouth, bringing Chanukah cheer to the whole region. All these communities would arrange a special party for the day we spent with them, and a great time was had by all. At Eastbourne, their Newsletter reported that:

The delicious refreshments were organised by Linda Taylor and her many helpers. Lazar and Nina Liebenberg provided entertainment on the keyboard and 'a hearty rendering of Maoz Tzur was led by Rev Weisman and there was even a valiant attempt at dancing a hora by a few brave participants!

Ronnie Taylor, long time president wrote:

Malcolm has been a very good friend to the Eastbourne congregation and also to the Jewish people of Hastings and Bexhill for a very long time. Being the Minister for Small Communities, he took us under his wing and made many visits over the years to take services on occasions.

He officiated at my granddaughter's Bat Chayil in 2002, a Bar Mitzvah in 2005 and a wedding in 2006. He very often came to our Chanukah parties, also to give talks, and even came to appear as the Jewish representative at an Eastbourne Interfaith Forum. I must say he outshone those of the other denominations. Malcolm always comes over as a highly intelligent and understanding Minister, and we have greatly appreciated the contributions he has made to our now very tiny community.

In the twenty-first Century, in view of the aging population, they moved the actual synagogue down to the ground floor and seating arrangements became more flexible! Recently Ronnie told me that the inevitable has happened, and that they have had to sell the building. The Eastbourne Hebrew Congregation still continues. They still hold their regular services, but at a different location.

A Liberal Jewish Community was established in Eastbourne in 2001. Members come from the town of Eastbourne itself and from the wider East Sussex area, including Hastings/St Leonards, Bexhill, Uckfield, Wadhurst, East Grinstead, Lewes, Seaford and surrounding areas. They meet once a month for services, sometimes on a Friday evening and sometimes on a *Shabbat* morning.

Eastbourne's big brother, further west on the South Coast in Dorset, is Bournemouth (100 miles southwest of London). This has the largest Jewish population of any seaside resort. Bournemouth used to have several kosher hotels and still maintains a thriving synagogue. I have been invited there from time to time to give a talk or for a special occasion, but as they have a resident minister it is not part of my remit.

Worthing, West Sussex (60 miles south of London)
A place by the sea

The Worthing Orthodox Jewish Community was another group established by evacuees during the Second World War. It continued for a number of years thereafter reaching a membership of nearly ninety families in the 1970s. At that time many Jewish people from up-country, including my wife's parents, had holiday homes in Worthing and Littlehampton, to the west of Brighton. I would go down once a month on a Friday to run *Shabbat* services there, held at the Quaker Meeting House.

In the 1980s many of the most active members either passed away or sold their properties and moved to London or elsewhere to be nearer their friends or children and grandchildren. The Worthing and District Hebrew Congregation that had been affiliated the United Synagogue officially closed down in 1980. However, all was not lost. They continued as an independent community, held together by a newsletter and events on special occasions and their wish to come together as Jews.

In 2002 when Ian and Barbara Gordon arrived from Stanmore, there were just three or four active couples on the committee, but the mailing list connected to more than sixty people. There was no formal membership or fee, but people were asked to pay £5 to cover the postage, to be on the mailing list. Ian ran services and held the community together. They specially enjoyed my visits at the festival of Chanukah and would bring in all those far flung 'members' plus non-Jewish friends and neighbours for a great party. They also ran a very jolly and well attended communal *Seder* at Passover.

I was pleased to have visited the Worthing community often. Rosalie and I would stay with the Gordons at their home. I have seen the community through some trying times. They said,

Malcolm thinks nothing of coming down to be with us for the day and driving back the same night! His advice and counsel is so wise and helpful. He is simply an amazing ambassador for the entire Jewish Community.

Since Gerry and Sharon Crest also arrived in the area in 2010, the community is even more active. These days, called Worthing and District

Jewish Community, (rather than Hebrew Congregation) they are a warm and welcoming group. Gerry runs a Friday night service in a local community centre in town once a month. They can attract more than thirty attendees. Their social events are also popular, attracting up to sixty people. It's good to see that the Jews of Worthing and district, from whatever background, still have the infrastructure and energy to enjoy coming together as Jews.

The End of the Pier?

I have tended to the needs of many seaside communities over the last sixty years and witnessed the members aging and the numbers decreasing year by year. In the summer, there may be an influx if the resort is popular with Jews. However, not all holidaying Jews plan to go to synagogue. Yet it is surprising how many do wish to visit a synagogue and find a home away from home. They like to meet old friends year on year, and to mix in that convivial atmosphere of sea and spray, take pleasure in walks along the pier and enjoy the ubiquitous fish and chips.

In the 1970s when cheap flights and package holidays in sunnier climes came onto the market, fewer Jewish visitors were attracted to British seaside vacations. Nowadays people recall such holiday resorts with nostalgia. Will there be new factors that change the situation? The experience of 'working from home', the desire to 'reduce one's carbon footprint', or to economise in post-Brexit Britain – as well as the fact the climate change has made Britain a bit drier and warmer – may encourage more Jewish people to live in the countryside or at the seaside and to take holidays locally.

Around the UK – Wales

Bangor, North Wales (270 miles northwest of London).

The smallest synagogue

Jewish life certainly has existed and continues to exist in Britain beyond Golders Green and Stamford Hill, also beyond Manchester and Leeds – even beyond the borders of England. A century ago, in the 1920s there were said to be 6,000 Jews in Wales. Many distinguished Jewish poets, novelists, politicians, comedians and musicians came from Wales. Today there are only a couple of hundred left, many of whom are very elderly.

By the time I was called to support the once thriving Jewish Community in Bangor, North Wales, I found the tiniest synagogue possible. It was situated in a church porch. When I attended, there were just six seats, three on each side with the readers desk in the middle. The *Sefer Torah* was kept in the home of the founder and leader of the community Mr Pollecoff and was brought out for the services each time. This little 'synagogue' has since been moved, seats, bimah and all, to the Manchester Jewish Museum.

The City of Bangor in North Wales and surrounding areas had enjoyed a rich Jewish history. Nathan Abrams, Professor of Film, at Bangor University, has written that Jews escaping persecution in Eastern Europe settled in the UK recognising the opportunity of a better life for their families. Eventually they transformed the high streets across Britain, as was also the case in Wales. In Bangor the High Street at some point hosted such national retailers as H.Samuel, Marks and Spencer, Dixons, Tesco and Burtons. All these firms were founded by and at one point owned and/or run by Jews who had provided the entrepreneurial energy, ambition, financial acumen, willingness to take risks and vision essential in building modern businesses in Britain.

Bangor also had its own homegrown Jewish businesses. Possibly the first was the Hyman Brothers' watchmaking business in 1820. In 1851, John Aronson opened a fine jewellery shop. There was also a purveyor of kosher meat which was so good it was even exported to London. Bangor's first delicatessen was opened by Jews, and three diamond cutting factories were set up in Bangor by Jews fleeing the Nazis or who were evacuated here during the Second World War.

The most well-known of Bangor's own Jewish entrepreneurs were the Wartskis and the Pollecoffs. Pollecoff sold clothing and other items. The Wartskis were silversmiths and goldsmiths and dealt in diamonds. They sold jewellery on the high street in Bangor and also had a drapery store.

Isidore Wartski bought the Castle Hotel opposite his shop and soon that section of the High Street became known as Wartski's Square. He had a transformative effect on the city and became its Mayor. He helped build new housing developments and dropped the tolls on the Menai Bridge.

As the case of Isidore Wartski shows, Jewish immigrants prospered, and integrated extremely well into the commercial, civic and cultural life of the wider community and swiftly acculturated into Bangor life. They even learned Welsh and participated in local Eisteddfodau. Their influence extended to politics and local charitable organizations, contributing greatly to the general life of the city. Today however, hardly anything remains of a Jewish Community in Bangor – as in many other small places in North and South Wales. Now even that tiniest synagogue is no more.

Montgomery, Mid-Wales (190 miles northwest of London)
A Nature Trip

The little town of Montgomery, just over the border into Wales from Shrewsbury in Shropshire, received a Royal Charter In 1227 to build a protective wall and ditch (Offa's Dyke) and to hold fairs and markets. The original medieval street plan has scarcely changed in almost eight centuries. Nearby is the famous Montgomery Castle, whose origins precede the charter by four years.

My own association with Montgomery began in the mid-1960s, when I joined a meeting of governors of my old school, Parmiters. We were gathering, not far from the little border town, to take a look at the Welsh Field Centre near Aberystwyth owned by the school, which hosted schoolchildren on week-long nature trips.

We checked in to the Dragon Inn Hotel in Montgomery and I fell into conversation with its owner, Mike Michaels. Before long it emerged that he was Jewish, so I asked if there were other Jews in the area. 'Oh, yes there are', he replied, 'and occasionally we have a little meeting here on *Shabbat* mornings.' He explained that his hotel was not exactly a synagogue but suggested he would invite all the Jews he knew of in the area to come along, and I could run a service!

I instantly agreed, and he managed to rustle up ten to fifteen Jews from the town and surrounding villages. After the service Mike said: 'I've laid on a lovely kiddush and I've even got some delicious, chopped liver.' We did not enquire where the liver pate came from but appreciated the gesture in such a remote location. I am pleased to say that I helped Montgomery become a self-sustaining community for a short while. A year later I noted that their kiddush was perfectly in order, with the simple expedient that they avoided meat altogether.

Several years later Mike Michaels sold his hotel, and while he himself maintained a home in the village, the Montgomery Jewish Community fell into abeyance. Parmiter's Welsh Field Centre had also closed, therefore I had no longer a need to visit the area for that reason. These days, if the Jews of Montgomery want to attend a service, they have to travel 70 miles East to the Liberal community in Birmingham or 79 miles north to an orthodox one Liverpool.

Lo and behold, in 2006 Mike Michaels called me and invited me to be his Chaplain when he became Mayor of Montgomery.

Others near Montgomery, Wales
(190 miles northwest of London)

A Community of one: Eli Kahan

I was told about a very observant Jewish man named Eli Kahan, who lived up a narrow lane in the Welsh Mountains near Montgomery. The next time I was in the area, I decided to contact Eli. His homestead was isolated amongst sheep farms and often his remote farmhouse would be snowed under for months. It proved more difficult to reach than I was led to believe, but the effort was worth it!

Eli Kahan was a remarkable character. He was a former lecturer in physics at Imperial College, London and a talented painter. He was also passionate about playing the bagpipes. He was, above all, a really committed Jew, steeped in the study of the six major tracts of the *Talmud*. I have heard that he used to invite visitors to join him studying Jewish texts for up to six hours at a time! I enjoyed deep religious discussions with Eli Kahan.

Eli's nearest Jewish neighbours were 25 miles away in Montgomery, but they were not the kind of people who were interested in *Talmud* study. Whenever I went to Montgomery, I would try to make the tortuous 20-mile detour down the country roads, and then three or four miles up the unmade lane to his home. The trip must have caused havoc to my car's suspension. I once had a puncture on the journey to the Kahan farmstead. Luckily, Eli was a dab hand at mechanics. He did a lot of his own repairs and home maintenance. He managed to pump up the flat tyre and made sure it had enough traction to reach the nearest garage for a full tyre change. In a sense Eli constituted a one-man community; therefore, by default, my smallest!

Newport, South Wales (140 miles West of London)

Not quite as tiny as Eli's single-representative outpost, or Bangor's erstwhile synagogue on a church porch, was the community of Newport, South Wales, across the Bristol Channel and 12 miles northeast of Cardiff. An Ashkenazi synagogue was opened in Francis Street in 1869, consecrated by Chief Rabbi Dr Herman Adler in 1871, and in 1934 moved location to 45 St. Marks Crescent.

My personal involvement in Newport dates to 1980. I was called upon when the community was struggling to maintain itself and its minister had to leave as they could no longer afford to pay him. The synagogue closed in 1997, and the congregation moved to the Prayer House at the Jewish

Burial Ground on Risca Road. I visited and spoke when I could. I received a warm letter of thanks from Mr Nathan for my presence in 1999. He said, 'Amongst the attendees were descendants of some of the earliest members of the community.' He continued, 'There is the wish to keep the symbol of Judaism alive as long as there is someone to open the doors. To have visitors, a minyan and an address becomes the highlight of the year and for that we are grateful to you.' Alas that was not to be for long.

Swansea and South Wales

South Wales' first Jewish community was established in Swansea in the eighteenth century, with a plot of land allocated for a Jewish cemetery in 1768. The Industrial Revolution attracted workers from Russia and other areas of Eastern Europe. By the late nineteenth century there were also thriving communities in Merthyr Tydfil, Brynmawr, Aberdare and Pontypridd. Jewish businesses in Pontypridd became so successful that the town's high street was colloquially known as 'Jewish Street'. Yet by 1999, Merthyr Tydfil's once 400-strong community had disappeared altogether. The end was marked when George Black, known as 'The Last Jew in Merthyr', died aged 82. The old Merthyr Tydfil synagogue (pictured) that

22. Merthyr Tydfil Synagogue, South Wales

closed in 1983 has been empty for decades. There are tentative plans I hear that it will be restored one day. There is only so much one can do to stop the inevitable.

Around the UK – Northern Ireland

I have been invited to Belfast a few times mainly on Council of Christians and Jews missions or to give a talk. However, the community is self-sufficient so did not need my attention.

Around the UK – Scotland

I have visited the city of Edinburgh often, as my mother's family came from there and at one time half the community were somehow related to her. On occasions, I have been invited to give a talk or attend a CCJ event, but Edinburgh was a large and self-sufficient community, not in need of my services.

There had been seven viable Jewish country communities scattered around Scotland in the early twentieth century stretching from the borders to the highlands. They were Aberdeen, Ayr, Dundee, Dunfermline, Falkirk, Greenock, and Inverness. By the time I came on the scene, there was just one remaining in the far north, in Aberdeen. As they had no resident rabbi, they requested my services. I would make the thousand-mile round trip by car, as often as I could. I am still in close touch with the members in Aberdeen which I am glad to say remains a viable community.

One of the first reliable mentions of Jews in Aberdeen, is of sixteen who graduated in medicine in between 1739 and 1829, becoming the first Jews in the English-speaking world to do so. Unlike English universities, Jews were allowed to study medicine in Scotland.

Aberdeen
A new lease of life from oil

The first Aberdeen synagogue was opened in 1893. Promptly the Minister/*Shochet* of the new community, and its President were prosecuted by the local branch of the Society for the Prevention of Cruelty to Animals. Fortunately, the case was won with the judgement given that the Jewish ritual slaughter had been expertly carried out.

Between the wars the Jewish families became more bourgeois, and set up a Jewish Literary Society, a WIZO group, and Hebrew classes. Ernest

Bromberg launched a dance hall and opened Aberdeen's first cinema in 1936. As the community became wealthier and outgrew their rented rooms, the present building at 74 Dee Street was bought and converted into a synagogue which was inaugurated in June 1945. It is still in use.

Since the 1970s the economic boom triggered by the massive oil finds in the North Sea, saw the population increase dramatically and the prosperity of the city soar. This clearly has had an impact on the Jewish community, which endeavours to support all Jews in the Aberdeen area, regardless of which type of Judaism they follow. The boom attracted Jewish families with young children from America and Israel as well as from all over the United Kingdom to work in the oil industry and at the universities. The staff and the student Jewish Societies at the two Aberdeen Universities have a close relationship with the local community and enjoy joint activities.

In 2008, a successful joint programme over Purim and the following *Shabbat*, began with reading the *Megillah* (Book of Esther) at Aberdeen University Library using a 200-year-old scroll from the University's extensive Judaica collections. This was organised by Chris Fynsk, who is a member of the community and a Professor of Philosophy and Literature at the University. The Megillah was read expertly by Ephraim Borowski, director of the Scottish Council of Jewish Communities to a large, appreciative and noisy gathering of the Aberdeen Jewish community which included many children. (It is the custom to drown out each mention of the name 'Haman' by stamping, shaking rattles, and generally making a noise.)

This was followed on Friday by supper at the synagogue in Dee Street for thirty participants followed *Minchah, Kabbalat Shabbat* and *Maariv* services, led by Ephraim, the first time there had been a minyan for evening services in Aberdeen outside the High Holy Days for many years. Visitors are always welcome to the shul and indeed on many occasions visitors have helped them make up a *minyan*.

In 2017 there was a serious flood in the synagogue which almost brought an end to the Aberdeen community. Fortunately helped by donations and practical help from local people and from around the UK and from as far afield as USA, Canada, Israel, and Hong Kong, the synagogue was quickly up and running again.

Renovations included new *bimah* furnishings and *torah* scroll covers, new flooring, repainted woodwork in the hallway, new chairs both in the synagogue and in the community hall, window repairs, and a brand new and hugely improved modern kitchen area.

I went up to Aberdeen in June 2018 to rededicate the building. It was a joyous celebratory weekend. I led the Friday night and *Shabbat* morning services.

The president, Mrs Taylor, said:

Rev Weisman knows the congregation well from his days of visiting us as the small communities minister. This was the first time the Sifrei Torah had been in the building since the flood.

On the Sunday the community held an open day to thank some of the many non-Jews who had offered financial and practical support after the flood. Many local VIPs attended as well as a group from a church which had donated a dozen new chairs. Visitors were able to enjoy some kosher cuisine as guests from Glasgow had brought provisions from Mark's Deli, the only kosher deli in Scotland. Having got through the flood, the community now has the task of maintaining a B-listed building in a conservation area. Fortunately, there is the possibility of finding a long-term tenant for the

23. Chief Rabbi Ephraim Mirvis visiting Aberdeen Synagogue renovated after the serious flood in 2017.

basement flat in the building which would bring them some financial security.

Geographical 'Quests'
Bringing small communities together

As part of my activities for small communities I created some very large events to which I invited all the communities for miles around. I called them 'Quests'. I saw this as a way of stimulating a number of small communities in one go, helping them to meet others with the same problems, and giving the mainstream community an opportunity to interact with and to offer support to small outlying groups of people wanting to lead a Jewish life.

Southeast Quest

The largest of these events was my Southeast Quest in 1990. For this I took over part of the Alconbury American Air base, near Huntingdon in Cambridgeshire. This had been opened in 1938 for the use of RAF Bomber Command and from 1942 was used by the United States Army Air Force. King George VI had visited the site and seen the Boeing B-17 Flying Fortresses there. It has remained a US base. In 2015 The Pentagon announced its closure by 2020 – however the unrest in Crimea in 2017 made them think again. I wonder what their plan is now in 2022.

We were able to use some empty barracks on the site, for a more peaceful (I hoped) activity to help my isolated groups. I invited every imaginable Anglo-Jewish organisation that had something to offer a small a community, to set up a stall. These included the Jewish Welfare Board, youth movements, old age organisations, carers and caterers, kosher food suppliers, and many charities. I invited the United Synagogue to send a team to advertise what they could offer small communities. Going across the board, I also invited leaders of the Reform and Liberal movements to participate as some of my people are a bit more inclined to the liberal approach and I did not want to cut them out. We had representatives of the Jewish National Fund, the Zionist Federation, and even Israeli travel agents.

In addition to having a stall, I arranged for VIPs and personalities from these different organisations, to give a talk to the gathering. Starting at 10.00am till about 6.00pm we had lectures running all day. This really gave people a chance to hear what was available to help them. There were also talks on aspects of Jewish history and culture that proved very popular.

I remember standing at the main gates of Alconbury at 8.30 in the morning, marvelling, as the cars just kept rolling in. Without any sense of direction (and given no directions) they parked wherever they found a space. The airmen came rushing to me, very perturbed, when their aeroplanes could not take off as cars were parked on the actual runways!

We had included lunch and tea and kept the prices low. We had no trouble getting takers. I had asked each community to say how many people were coming, but some forgot to tell me. We had food laid on for about 600 people but in reality, more than 1200 turned up! Some groups even arrived by the coachload. We soon ran out of the salt beef sandwiches, fish balls and other Jewish delicacies. Some people were of course very upset by this. I had to work hard to placate them. I was almost destroyed by the success of this event.

West Quest

I had started organising these combined events in 1986 with a 'West Quest' near Bristol for all the communities in the West Country and Wales. That day of intense social and cultural activity was so popular that they requested it be repeated the following year. The West Quests were supported in a rare collaboration between both the Orthodox and Progressive communities of Bristol.

The next year in 1987, West Quest took place at the large country mansion of Julius Silman in Corsham, Wiltshire, thanks to his generous support and hospitality. The programme included a talk by Geoffrey Paul, who was the editor of the Jewish Chronicle, and there were also several workshops and discussion sessions. I was assisted again by Rev Jonathan Gorsky who was the director of Yakar Jewish Adult Education centre in Hendon at the time. His seminar on Jewish history at the previous year's West Quest had been very popular.

The Yakar Educational Foundation was the brainchild of Rabbi Michael Rosen, known as Mickey, who had the burning desire to make the glories of Judaism accessible to the broadest possible spectrum of British Jewry. In 1978 with the backing of Jewish academics and philanthropists he established Yakar as an innovative religious, cultural, and adult educational study centre 'to reawaken Jewish consciousness'. Its popularity took it from its first home in Stanmore to Hendon in 1983, drawing in even more people. It had its own synagogue, independent of any denominational organisation, of which Michael Rosen was the rabbi. The name Yakar (meaning 'precious' or 'worthy' in Hebrew) is an acronym the initials of Michael Rosen's late father, Yaakov Kopel Rosen. I got to know Kopel Rosen who was highly regarded in Anglo-Jewry. He was considered by some to be a candidate to become the next Chief Rabbi. He favoured being open to the best that the secular world has to offer, while remaining passionately committed to Jewish religious life. This is a philosophy that chimes very much with my own.

After holding pulpits in Manchester, Glasgow and becoming principal rabbi of the Federation of Synagogues, and other posts, Kopul Rosen left the rabbinate in 1948 to concentrate on education. He founded Carmel College, the only independent Jewish boarding school in the UK, in Wallingford, Oxfordshire, serving as its headmaster until his death in 1962. In this venture, he sought to combine Jewish Orthodoxy with the discipline of the English public school. The college eventually closed in 1997 overtaken by developments in Jewish day school education. Mickey Rosen and his older and younger brothers Jeremy and David were all first educated at Carmel College and influenced by their father, before attending *yeshivot* around the world. They all became distinguished and innovative rabbis and educators. My son Brian attended Carmel College for a while.

Unsurprisingly, because of his open approach, Michael Rosen was involved in the launch of Limmud, the experimental cross-community educational seminar, at Carmel College in December 1980. Yakar also served as a platform for the late Rabbi Shlomo Carlebach's unique and very popular hippie style of outreach. In 1993 Michael Rosen, made Aliyah to found and develop Yakar in Jerusalem and then Tel Aviv. He continued to visit Yakar in London for some time. The Yakar centre and synagogue in Hendon closed in 2002. The efforts of the Foundation are now mainly directed towards supporting its two centres in Israel. Mickey Rosen died in 2008 in Jerusalem aged 63. His brother Rabbi Jeremy Rosen said of him that 'The most important thing about him was that he stood for passionate commitment to Judaism with social responsibility and an open mind. That's incredibly rare in the world today.' So it is!

My West Quests, in which Yakar collaborated, became an annual event by popular demand. The basic structure and programme were now well established and the details, of finding and hiring a venue, the speakers to be invited and the catering were organised by members of the communities. A particular driving force was John Adler of the Bristol Hebrew Congregation. They felt a great thirst for joining up for social and cultural activities and sharing experiences. The enthusiasm and dedication to achieve a meaningful Jewish life that we witnessed in these small outposts, stands out against some of the apathy one might find in a large city congregation.

Apart from the concentrated social and cultural input at the Quests, a really valuable part of these events was the informal discussions that took place over coffee and lunch, talking together about how they cope with various issues. It was wonderful for me to witness the mood of determination amongst the delegates to keep their communities going. The lasting benefits of these West Quests were the creation of joined-up events between the communities in the west and the establishment of a newsletter covering the whole area.

In 1988 another successful West Quest took place in Wales in conjunction with the Swansea Community and in 1996, West Quest celebrated its tenth anniversary, with another meeting at Julius Silman's country house in Wiltshire. There were enthusiastic representatives there from thirteen communities: Bath, Bristol, Cheltenham, Exeter, Newbury, Newport, Plymouth, Reading, Stroud, Swansea, Swindon, Torquay and Winchester. Their backgrounds covered a wide spectrum of communal allegiance from progressive to mainstream orthodoxy. The programme of this event included historian Alexander Rosenzweig talking on Sephardi Jewry and Alexander Knapp, then the Joe Loss Lecturer in Jewish Music at City University London, talking about the origins and development of Jewish music, plus live Jewish music from a new Bristol choir.

East Quest

Our inaugural East Quest took place in the beautiful Chatham Memorial Synagogue in Kent in 1990. It was packed to capacity with several hundred people attending from a wide area of Kent and Sussex. In 1995 Norwich Synagogue and community hosted an 'East Quest' for communities particularly in East Anglia. They felt proud that they had the capacity for running an event for a large number of attendees.

South Quest

In 1997 we ran our first South Quest at Canterbury. I was delighted to see over a hundred people representing communities in Chatham, Chelmsford Cheltenham, Eastbourne, East Grinstead, Guildford, Hastings, Luton, Margate, Portsmouth, St Albans, Southampton and Worthing. This demonstrated the vitality of Jewish life that prevailed in these regional centres.

Northeast Quest

The last Quest that I organised was the Northeast Quest in April 2002. It was hosted by the small Harrogate community that I enjoyed looking after when they had no minister. There are many scattered small groups of Jews around Yorkshire who were pleased to attend such a gathering and meet co-religionists that they did not know existed. An addition, when they heard about it, people from the larger centres of Leeds, Newcastle and the orthodox enclave of Gateshead clamoured to come. Some of my community members even came across the Pennines from Lancaster. The place was packed to capacity with a couple of hundred people present.

Looking back, each Quest had been a mammoth task and had taken months to organise. I had guided the communities, goaded the mainstream movements to support them and helped to raise the considerable funds needed to run them. It was certainly worth all that effort to provide these rich resources and meeting opportunities. It was noticeable how this experience strengthened the resolve of small community leaders to work even harder to sustain their small groups.

What was clear, was that more people like me were needed to serve this large, eager and widespread Jewish population, who yearned to retain their Jewish heritage and were eager to learn more about and embrace it. More visits were required to more of these provincial communities on a more regular basis. I could not tear myself into any more pieces or fit any more visits in my working week. We needed more manpower. I suggested all sorts of solutions to the powers that be. At one stage we had arranged to have a young Israeli emissary to be based in regional communities. He would conduct services, organise events and assist in youth and adult education. Sadly, the funds were not forthcoming to create this ideal programme. I also tried to convince Jews' College, the rabbinic training school, to send rabbinic students to spend some time in outlying areas. I felt it would be a useful part of their training and also it would surely enhance the communities enormously. But the scheme was not taken up. In the early twenty-first century, I still had the responsibility, almost on my own, of keeping up the schedule of visits and support that I had started in the early 1960s.

11

Jersey, Malta and the Commonwealth Jewish Council

Jersey – An English home from home

Just fourteen miles from the coast of France and a hundred miles from the coast of England, the Bailiwick of Jersey is still unmistakably English. But being quite distant from the mainland, in the matter of *Minhag Anglia* (Anglo-Jewish custom) the Jersey Jewish Community has its fair share of local innovation. One such novelty, however, was purely accidental. It was touching and funny, even though it involved a funeral.

When the cortege arrived at the burial ground, they found that they could not open at the cemetery gate. The keys did not fit the rusty lock. The funeral officials said they could not wait as they had to deal with another internment elsewhere. Thinking fast, the party decided to put up ladders; then the funeral directors lugged the coffin over the weather-beaten four-foot wall. They also helped all the mourners to follow on the ladders over the cemetery wall.

Now, half the attendees were non-Jewish friends of the deceased who had never been to a Jewish funeral before. I wondered what they were thinking, but then came the feedback. Apparently, they were greatly moved, and particularly loved the symbolism of climbing over the wall. They saw it as a Jewish tradition signalling reluctance to let a dear one depart for the hereafter!

The History of Jews in Jersey

Jews are recorded as living in Jersey in the 1790s. In 1843 the Old Jersey Jewish Congregation was officially founded, but numbers whittled away, and that synagogue closed around 1870. Yet some Jersey-born Jews were still around when the Nazis captured Jersey together with the other Channel Islands in 1940. This was the only part of the British Empire to be occupied by Nazi Germany during the war.

The Jews were ordered to 'identify themselves' according to an edict of October 1940 and were subjected to antisemitic legislation. There were Jews from Jersey among the 700 who died in Nazi concentration and forced labour camps on Alderney. Some were sent to other slave labour and concentration camps in Germany. There were three Jews from Guernsey who died in Auschwitz. Miraculously, most survived; and both Jersey and Guernsey and the other Channel Island were liberated on 9 May 1945. Those events however, cast a pall over the Jewish history of the Islands.

I attended a moving memorial ceremony for those Jews who were interned and who had died on Alderney. In attendance were French Jews who had survived. They were transported to the event on Alderney on a French Navy ship. The monument in Jersey commemorating the wartime occupation includes, an explicit mention of the Jews from Guernsey who were murdered by the Nazis. (One of the Jersey Jewish Community's former leaders, Frederick Cohen, wrote about these matters in his booklet 'The Jews in the Channel Islands During the German Occupation 1940–1945'.)

After the war, Jews from London and elsewhere on the mainland began to join the tiny number of Jersey-born and ex-Continental Jewish returnees. Middle-class Jews came to the Channel Islands during the 1960s and 70s to service this now booming offshore tax haven. They were a pragmatic group of professionals, accountants, doctors and lawyers. Estimates place the peak Jewish population in the 1980s at between 80 and 120 members within a general population of the island of a little less than 100,000 people.

A new British orthodox community in the 1960s

I began visiting Jersey together with Rosalie and our young family in 1963, about three years after the community had re-established itself. Jersey is truly dear to my heart. It was the venerable financier Sebag Cohen, a much-admired and very learned man, born in Sunderland, who was the driving force for establishing the 'new' community in 1960. His collaborators were the newly arrived Doris Bloom with her 17-year-old daughter Anita and Alf Regal (father of David and Stephen) who had come to Jersey to set up a construction firm.

In August 1961 they formed a provisional committee. Sebag advertised in the Jewish Chronicle for 'A *Sefer Torah* and also silver and other ritual requirements for newly organised services in Jersey'. He must have been successful as the paper announced on 24 November that year, that for the first time in this century organised religious services were being held regularly by the Jersey Jewish Congregation.

On Friday evenings services were held at the houses of various members of the tiny community (about 25 families) and efforts were being made to hold regular Sabbath morning services. At first, these were conducted in a wooden shed in Sebag's beautiful garden. In March 1963 it was announced in the newspaper that, as the Minister to Small Communities, I was to lead 'Full services for Passover'. The Regals had been members of the orthodox Hendon United Synagogue. They confidently imported a sense of northwest London synagogue organisation and ritual practice to their new home on the Island – despite opposition from some long-time Jewish residents. From its inception in 1960, the president of the congregation was Wilfred Harold Krichefski. He was born in St Helier, the capital of the Island, where his grandfather had established a clothing business. He was brought up in London where he had also attended the Hendon United Synagogue for which his grandfather had laid the foundation stone.

Wilfred was the only one of five siblings, to return to Jersey after the Second World War, to work in the family business. After serving in the British Army in the Pay Corps, he arrived in Jersey in 1945. He was elected a Deputy to Parliament serving until 1951 when he became the youngest elected Senator of the Island. He held many official Government posts. He was awarded the OBE in 1958. At times, as Senior Senator, he was able to preside over the States Assembly when the Bailiff (or Speaker) was not available.

My long relationship with Jersey

When I first came for *Pesach* in 1963, Jewish Islanders were in the process of re-establishing their community. They were using a small hall at Saint Brelade's Church, located in the elegant suburb of that name, just east of the capital, Saint Helier. Most of Jersey's Jews live there. Our Passover services were packed to capacity. The Majority of Jewish people in Jersey had come from the prevailing orthodox 'United Synagogue' background and expected an orthodox service. It felt like one was in a smaller version of a mainland 'United Synagogue' *shul*. No one was inclined to question conventions. Congregants dressed for the occasion, men in suits and hats, and women wore their finest attire.

First Jewish Wedding in 100 years!

Anita Bloom and David Regal soon paired up and in 1966, I was called upon, along with Reverend Leslie Hardman from Hendon, to celebrate the first Jewish marriage on the island for over a century. This couple, Anita and David Regal, were to become pivotal members of the community. Anita worked tirelessly, managing the community and teaching Hebrew and Jewish topics to successive generations of Jewish children on the island. Her late husband David was the president for many years followed by her brother-in-law Stephen Regal who is still currently the president.

Sebag Cohen was the stalwart of the services in the synagogue. He attended every week and was our regular *baal koreh* (reader of the *Sefer Torah*). He *leyend* each *sedra* (chanted the weekly Torah portion) perfectly, according to the ancient traditions, so I was released from this duty.

The community acquires its own synagogue building.

In 1972, with the assistance of the Jersey Government, the community was able to buy the former Wesleyan Methodist schoolroom at La Petit Route des Mielles in St. Brelade, for use as a synagogue. The building has a lovely meeting hall, a *sukkah* in the garden for the festival of *Sukkot* (Tabernacles). There is a flat upstairs with a sea view, that was always put at our disposal whenever Rosalie and I, and our sons, visited. It became our happily anticipated destination for Pesach, Rosh Hashanah and Yom Kippur and festivals in between for decades. Alas, the Covid-19 lockdown stopped us travelling to Jersey.

24. The Jersey Synagogue at St Brelade. The flat upstairs was where we stayed.

11. Jersey, Malta and the Commonwealth Jewish Council 163

25. Chief Rabbi Immanuel Jacobovits is with me and the Jersey community president Wilfred Krichefsky, together with subsequent president David Regal in the hallway, prior to consecrating the Synagogue building.

There were approximately fifty Jewish families in the early 70s, though at the inaugural service that I conducted in the new synagogue building in September 1972, more non-Jews than Jews were present. There were nuns and representatives of all the local churches, as well as members of the States Assembly, the local pan-islandic Parliament. A month later, in October 1972, Chief Rabbi Jakobovits came to Jersey, joining me in consecrating the new Synagogue. Senator Wilfred Krichefski, who had held this position since the establishment of the community in 1960 was still the president at the time of the opening of the *shul*. Krichefski was a political heavyweight, being a senior member of the Channel Island's Government. On this occasion he welcomed many civic dignitaries to the synagogue including Lady Davies, the wife of the Lieutenant-Governor of Jersey, the Bailiff (the Civic Head) of Jersey and the Dean of Jersey.

In 1978, I also had the honour of consecrating a new cemetery and prayer hall. The existing cemetery at Westmount had been in use since the nineteenth century but was almost full. This new one was the third Jewish burial ground in Jersey on land donated by the municipality of St Helier.

When Sebag Cohen passed away in 1980, his son Freddie Cohen took over many of his late father's synagogue activities. Sebag's family commissioned a new *Sefer Torah* which they donated to the synagogue in his memory. Celebrating its arrival in April 1981 was another memorable occasion in Jersey, at which I officiated for the community. Guests included Rabbi S Zahn, Principal of Sunderland Yeshiva, who had helped to procure the *Sefer Torah*. Sebag's nephew, Rabbi Benjamin Cohen of the Israeli Defence Force explained the significance of the ceremony.

Civic achievements and philanthropy

Though a small community, Jersey Jews have filled many civic and political roles with distinction. Their philanthropy has also benefitted many young people. Sebag Cohen was a generous sponsor of *yeshivot* in England and Israel; Hundreds of students benefited from the Sebag Cohen and William Leech Foundation.

Wilfred Krichefski's family set up a Memorial Scholarship Fund at Tel Aviv University, after his untimely death at 58 in a car crash, having suffered a heart attack. The departure hall at Jersey Airport has been named the Krichefski Hall, as a tribute to him. He had served on the Harbours and Airport Committee for 24 years, was vice-president from 1948-1960 and thereafter to 1969 was president. A memorial plaque was unveiled there by his widow Dolly and son Bernard, who is a member of the Board of Deputies of British Jews, representing Jersey.

Bergerac – our moment of fame

In 1988 congregants achieved brief national and artistic fame – as I suppose I did myself – when an episode of the popular television detective series *Bergerac* entitled *The Sin of Forgiveness* featured a scene in the synagogue. I was asked to lead a mock-up service complete with congregants in smart suits and hats (quite unlike it normally was by that time). There was much singing and chanting, and Jersey's Jews were soon in full swing, enjoying themselves immensely.

We got to know the actor John Nettles, who plays Detective Sergeant Jim Bergerac, quite well. In this scene at the synagogue, Bergerac is working with a Nazi hunter (played by the late Jewish actor John Bennett) to track down a man living in Jersey, who used to be a Nazi. The two actors confer at the door from the hall into the synagogue, to discuss how to track him down while I am busy conducting the service inside.

One problem followed another while filming was in progress. First was noise from an ancient and leaky water-pipe. Then there was a creaking floorboard and sounds from the attached kitchen. Finally, at the height of dramatic tension, a motorbike roared by and spoilt the scene. Somehow it was all sorted out in the editing process. After filming, on and off for a month, there we were in all our glory, for just a few moments on screen.

In gratitude for our participation in the Bergerac episode and our patience, the film company arranged a sumptuous lunch for us. They placed before me a huge grilled steak emblazoned with a *Magen David* (Star of David)! This stamp, however good the intentions, unfortunately did not confer on it a kosher status, so I politely declined, and it was distributed amongst the film crew. The episode is still watched 'on repeat' by thousands. We did not realise it at the time, but we have preserved on film, a tiny snapshot of Jewish life in Jersey – albeit in heavy disguise. Sadly, almost all the 'actors' for the film, who were part of that congregation in 1988, are no longer alive.

A troubling incident

Jersey's Jews have, by and large, been received with warmth and sometimes benign curiosity by the general public on the island. However, on one occasion in the 1990s, swastikas were daubed on the synagogue's front door. Almost immediately two residents from down the road came along with a steam cleaner and volunteered to remove the offending paint. Jersey's chief of police swiftly attended the scene of the crime. The synagogue received hundreds of letters from people, many with generous donations to help clear up the mess. Since then, there has not been any incident of this kind.

My relationship with the dwindling Jersey Community

For decades I was pleased to preside over the High Holydays and other festival services for the community in Jersey. Rosalie and I enjoyed the warmth, both of the community and of a late summer holiday on this beautiful island. Our sons, Brian and Daniel, regularly stayed with us in Jersey and supported the services. They helped to make up the *minyan*. We were given accommodation in the little flat above the synagogue that became a second home for us.

On *Rosh Hashana* (Jewish New Year) before the 2020 lockdown, we would still get a good crowd. I ran a short service starting at 10.30am and ending at 12.45pm. (On the mainland, in United Synagogues, it could last from 9.00am to 1.00pm). We use the standard Routledge orthodox *machzor*

26. An early High Holydays service in Jersey.

(High Holy Days prayer book) but skip *piyyutim* (special poems). Of course, people can read them to themselves, but I did not read them out loud.

The Routledge High Holydays prayer books were first published in 1906 and long held sway in the British and Commonwealth orthodox synagogue without any real competition, at least until the arrival of *Art Scroll* editions from America in 1995 and more recently in 2011 by a new *Machzor* compiled by Chief Rabbi Jonathan Sacks.

Nowadays, Jersey is a small community and getting much smaller. It has an aging population mostly retirees aged 70 to 90. Numbers dropped from 120 in 2003, to 85 in 2015. Today it may be less than half that number. Being tiny, presents problems for Orthodox Jews who require a *minyan*, a quorum of ten adult Jewish males in order to be able to bring out the scroll and read directly from the *Sefer Torah* on Sabbaths and festivals. On the first Saturday of the month, the community tries its best to get the required quorum with a three-line whip. With luck, they would manage to do so. There are two or three members of the community who, with my earlier encouragement and instruction, are now able to lead the service. Should there be a learned guest or visitor in the building, they are invited to participate in the service leading too.

If the community cannot manage a *minyan*, Anita Regal used to seat those attending in a circle for a 'reflective *Shabbat*'. Instead of reading the portion of the week directly from the scroll, they would read it from the prayer book, and talk about it. And by not actually calling people up to the *bimah*, one can do away with *brachot* (blessings) which normally need a *minyan*. If women wanted to participate, this approach made this much easier. In this way everybody feels included. It is impressive to notice how these adapted services mean so much more to participants than a conventional orthodox service. In any case, many congregants now come from a Reform background and are at ease with informal and mixed worship. We always try to make sure that all the people who have come to the synagogue on a Sabbath morning feel they have had a satisfying, spiritual, Jewish experience.

Commenting on the dwindling numbers in Jersey, my good friend Anita Regal said in 2020: 'Even my own children have left. It is amazing that we are still going to be honest. We stagger on as best we can. 'The pandemic and lockdown of 2020 and 21, prevented Rosalie and I from visiting Jersey for the High Holydays. Very sadly, their stalwart synagogue leader, Freddie Cohen, passed away in early 2021, which left a palpable gap in Jersey's Jewish life. The wonderful Anita Regal herself, also died in 2021. Without her warm and engaging presence, her constant enthusiasm for imparting her knowledge to fresh minds and the feeling of continuity she brought, I wondered how the community would cope in years to come.

Her brother-in-law Stephen Regal, the president and others, were cognisant of the fact that there were few left in Jersey who could read Hebrew fluently. Though naturally concerned about the future, Stephen is an optimist by nature. His optimism has been rewarded by the arrival, in the last couple of years, of energetic and capable new settlers who are running services and carrying the community forward. So, despite the concerns of Stephen, Anita and myself a few years back, Jersey's future now seems more secure.

I am pleased to know that my contribution to the Jersey Jewish Community is appreciated. Stephen Regal who has been the president for the last 22 years, has said of me: 'Reverend Weisman is the "glue" that adheres the community and we would have been lost without him. His ability to welcome all strands of the Jewish faith from both left and right, constitutes one of his greatest personal attributes. He was always there for all members of the community, from britot, bar and bat mitzvah to funerals; and is still always at the end of a telephone when required.'

Tombstone mix-ups

We started this Jersey section with a funeral – let's end it with stone settings. In a small community, things are always unpredictable. A community member needed some special wording on a tombstone in Jersey. An elder of the Spanish and Portuguese community in London, then living in Jersey, said he would help, claiming to be an expert in Hebrew. A year later, when we came to unveil the tombstone for the deceased, I could not read one word of the Hebrew on it! It was all gobbledygook. I do not know at what stage of the process the problem arose, but clearly nobody had checked the inscription. Well, as most people at the ceremony could not read Hebrew anyway, I got away with it. I conducted the service to everyone's satisfaction, and we made sure to correct the writing on the stone afterwards.

At another Jersey stone setting, there was an even worse situation. Once again, a cemetery key was the cause of strife. In the first instance, the key didn't work, this time it could not be found at all. The community president, at the time, David Regal, urgently sent one of his men to try to find the cemetery caretaker. The ceremony was due to start at 11.30 and time was running out. Suddenly someone burst breathlessly through the door... 'Good news and bad news', he announced. 'I have found the key, but the bad news is that the tombstone is on the wrong grave!' When I saw how frantic the widow was because of the delay in entering the cemetery, I decided that we should just carry on anyway, reckoning the poor woman was already so distressed. We duly swapped around the gravestone to the correct place later.

The Jersey Community invited me back again for the High Holydays in September 2022. It would have been a great honour for me to go there again. I have so many happy memories of being in Jersey with my family at this time of year. We so enjoyed being with and officiating for this dedicated and congenial community. But now, without my dear Rosalie and with the chaos of travel after Brexit and the Pandemic, it would not be the same.

The Jews of Malta
Sephardi and Mizrahi in character

Everyone versed in English literature has heard of Christopher Marlowe's play, *The Jew of Malta*. The full title is 'The Famous Tragedy of the Rich Jew of Malta'. He wrote it in 1590. Like Shakespeare's nearly contemporary *The Merchant of Venice*, it shares the curious feature of being written in England at a time when, officially at least, there were no Jews on English soil! The plot primarily revolves around a Maltese Jewish merchant named Barabas and combines religious conflict, intrigue, and revenge, set against a backdrop of the struggle for supremacy between Spain and the Ottoman Empire in

11. Jersey, Malta and the Commonwealth Jewish Council

27. The 'Admor' of Malta in his lavish robes, flowing hair, full beard and priestly headdress, holding his sceptre

the Mediterranean. There has been extensive debate about the play's portrayal of Jews and how Elizabethan audiences would have viewed it.

Far fewer people know about the real Jewish community of Malta today, and in particular, about the mysterious Jew of Malta who sometimes ministers to the community. He calls himself the '*Admor*'. The term is an acronym for '*Adonainu, Morainu, Rabbeinu*', meaning 'Our Lord, Our Teacher, Our Master'. That is quite some title for a man who, according to some, claims to lead the community of no more than fifty or so Jews. His name is Rav Dov Ber HaKohein, (pictured) though where he comes from, and what his history is, and even his role, seem to be unclear.

Since biblical times there has always been a small Jewish presence in Malta. It is one of those strategic Mediterranean islands, south of Sicily and north of Tripoli in Libya, that has changed hands according to the rise and fall of empires in Europe and the Middle East. Jews prospered under Arab and Norman rule. They were expelled under the Spanish in 1492.

Points of special Jewish heritage interest in Malta include old landmarks and street signs. In the walled city of Mdina, where the Jews made up almost one third of the population, there is a 'Jewish Silk Market' and a 'Jews' Gate'; and in Valletta, Malta's capital there is a sign 'Jews Sally Port'. Even the Island of Comino, almost uninhabited today but famous for the Blue Lagoon, has Jewish roots.

In 1792, Napoleon banished from Malta the Knights of St John, who had kept Jews captive against ransom, and free Jews began to settle on the island. When Napoleon and his army were in turn driven out by the British, more Jewish settlers arrived from Gibraltar, England, North Africa, Portugal and Turkey. A community could only re-establish itself after 1798 under British rule.

In 1846, the Maltese Jewish Community had grown large enough to invite Rabbi Josef Tajar from Tripoli in nearby Libya, to become the island's first official rabbi since the days of the Inquisition. The 1848 revolutions in Hungary, France and Germany brought an influx of poor Jewish refugees to Malta. Rabbi Josef and his congregation were unable to meet the needs of the enlarged Jewish population and appealed for funds from the Rabbinate of London. Sir Joseph Sebag-Montefiore (1822-1903) British banker, stockbroker and politician and a nephew-in-law – and heir – of Sir Moses Montefiore came to the rescue. He was effectively the leader of the British Jewish Community at the time. He visited Malta with his wife Judith and began to support the island community.

It is useful to know about the long and effective life of Sir Moses Montefiore (1784 – 1885) born into a Sephardi Jewish family from Livorno in Italy, based in London. He was an important figure in British business life and in Jewish history. Montefiore invested in the supply of piped gas for street lighting to European cities. He became a business partner with his brother-in-law Nathan Mayer Rothschild. A Government loan raised by the Rothschilds and Montefiore in 1835 enabled the British Government to compensate plantation owners under the slavery abolition act of 1833, and thereby abolish slavery in the Empire. In Jewish life he was president of the Board of Deputies of British Jews from 1835 to 1874, a period of 39 years, the longest tenure ever. He was a member of Bevis Marks Synagogue. He was a pivotal activist in the advancement to Jewish life abroad, especially in the Levant. He donated large sums of money to promote industry, business, economic development, education and health among the Jewish community in Palestine. His contributions are seen as pivotal to the development of proto-Zionism.

Back to Malta: In the 19th and 20th century, the Jewish community in Malta welcomed refugees from Italy and Central Europe, escaping Nazi rule. There was no rabbi or synagogue from the beginning of the twentieth century. They used a succession of rented properties, for example flats in apartment buildings. In the 1920s and 30s, when the Jewish population rarely exceeded fifty members, a minister would be brought in from Sicily for special occasions such as the High Holidays and Bar Mitzvahs.

I have had the honour of dedicating a couple of these temporary rented synagogues in Malta. The first time I visited the island I was on an RAF flight in 1959 en-route to Singapore. As I usually did, I made contact with the local Jewish community. Once they realised that a person was present amongst them with ministerial authority, the community exhorted me to consecrate the premises that they were using as a synagogue. They subsequently lost that place of worship when the old apartment building in Valletta was demolished in 1979. On a later trip to Malta in 1982, the community wanted me to check on the state of their current synagogue, and to dedicate that one too.

In the twenty-first century, a small community remains well established on the islands. By the middle of 1999 they had raised sufficient funds to purchase a large apartment, and to convert it into a Jewish Centre and Synagogue in time for the High Holyday services that year. They invited me to come to Malta once again to consecrate this new premises in January of 2000. This was the first property actually to be owned by a Jewish Community in Malta for over 500 years. About half of the community at that stage consisted of English, Australian, South African and Israeli expats. They then formed 'The Jewish Foundation of Malta', a legal entity, with a friend of mine, Robert Eder as its first president.

On the occasion of this visit in 2000, I finally got to meet the Admor. He seemed a fixture in the land and claimed to run everything in the community. However, exactly who he is, and what position he actually holds within the community is still something of a mystery. He makes a strong impression in his lavish robes, white gloves, flowing hair, full beard and priestly headdress, holding his sceptre. He brings to mind some medieval character or something out of Game of Thrones. He once ran his own website – 'admormalta.org' – though this is currently defunct. The non-Jewish Maltese people seemed to pay him more respect than did Maltese Jews.

The Admor appears to have access to an enormous amount of money and would spend a great deal of it on the community. He used to arrange Passover *Seders* in Malta, attended by many of the English emigres there whom I knew. In 2015, for instance, he hired one of the island's big five-star hotels. He paid for the whole community to attend and ran the services from the building.

So all embracing was the Admor, with his munificent activities for the community, that even the *Hassidic Chabad* movement was held at bay until 2012 – and we know how enthusiastic and zealous they can be in populating and stimulating pockets of Judaism all over the world! Maybe they were satisfied with his work, or daunted by his title, after all, it is bestowed only on the most respected of *Hasidic rebbes*.

Today there are about 100 core members, but it is believed many more Jews, including several Israelis, are living in Malta. The Admor can be seen on YouTube, officiating in 2012 at a Chanukah ceremony in Valetta organised by the newly arrived Chabad Rabbi, Reuven Ohayon, who has revitalised the Maltese Jewish Community (JCM) since then. Jewish religious life is Sephardic-oriented, though an Ashkenazi prayer book is used. Full services are offered on *Shabbat* and major Jewish holidays. In the Chanukah video, the Admor is celebrating alongside Rabbi Ohayon and also Malta's Minister of Culture and the Mayor of Valetta. On this occasion he spoke in English, acclaiming the miracle of the lights and the longed-for advent of peace. His provenance is still somewhat of a mystery to many.

The Commonwealth Jewish Council

When I was visiting Malta in 2000, to consecrate their new synagogue, Greville Janner (Lord Janner of Braunstone) who was the founder president of the Commonwealth Jewish Council (CJC) asked me to represent the Council on my visit. Greville said he would arrange a programme for us. He certainly laid on some high-powered events. Rosalie and I were feted and entertained by the highest civic and religious dignitaries on the Island. We met the President, the Prime Minister and the Archbishop of Malta, in addition to my Jewish connections, who were the people I had actually come to meet.

Greville was the prime mover in creating the Commonwealth Jewish Council in 1982. It facilitates the meeting of Commonwealth Jewish leaders with the leaders of their own countries. It also facilitates commonwealth Jewish Community leaders meeting each other and sharing experiences. Many small communities could be vulnerable, operating in dangerous and hostile environments. The aim of the CJC is to enhance the Jewish life of its constituent members and enabling them to live in safety and respect, and to support their efforts to contribute to the wider society in which they live.

Greville, knowing of my experience and interest in dealing with small communities, and my worldwide contacts through my military chaplaincy activities, immediately sought my participation in this venture and made me a CJC Ambassador. I have travelled with Greville and the Council to many Commonwealth countries meeting their Jewish communities for special events and CJC conferences. I am glad to have retained very friendly ties with Jews throughout the English-speaking world through my work and travels with the Commonwealth Jewish Council.

Greville Janner was a remarkably effective Jewish communal leader. Born in Cardiff in 1928 he followed his father Sir Barnett Janner in becoming Labour Member of Parliament for Leicester West. Much of his other time was spent in founding, directing, supporting and raising funds for Jewish organisations. He was president of the Board of Deputies of British Jews from 1979 to 1982. He was a prominent campaigner for the freedom of Soviet Jewry and for reparations for Holocaust victims and the creation of the Holocaust Memorial Trust. He was a firm supporter of the State of Israel and a vocal opponent of antisemitism in the Labour Party. For the Jewish Music Institute, of which I was a Trustee, Greville, a fluent Yiddish speaker, became the vice president of our International Yiddish Forum, which he launched in the Members Dining Room of the House of Commons. He loved the idea that the sweet voices of the choir singing the Yiddish lullaby *Rozinkes mit Mandlen* (Raisins and Almonds) could waft out of the windows of the 'Mother of Parliaments'.

While recounting the good works of Greville Janner, I should also mention that his latter years were profoundly affected by serious allegations concerning his personal life. By then suffering from dementia, the claims were vigorously denied by his family. He died in December 2015.

The Commonwealth Jewish Council committee would meet regularly in Greville's parliamentary office. It was a privilege for me to walk through the corridors of the Palace of Westminster, meeting old friends along the way. The Council also held regular dinners in private rooms there. Guest speakers included the politician and novelist Jeffrey Archer and Betty Boothroyd, Speaker of the House of Commons. Sometimes the guest of honour would be a visiting Israeli politician or a prominent Jewish Commonwealth personality, such as Irwin Cotler, who had been a Minister of Justice and Attorney General of Canada, as well as being a visiting professor at Harvard Law School and past president of the Canadian Jewish Congress.

The Commonwealth Jewish Council which he created and presided over from 1982, remains vigorous and effective under the direction of Clive Lawton, and I am still proud to be a CJC Ambassador, though I have not been able to travel anywhere for the last two years of Lockdowns.

12

The Long Haul – Journeys East

My work as a Royal Air Force Jewish chaplain took me to the furthest reaches of the British Commonwealth. It started in the late 1950s at a time when it was still the British Empire. As a military chaplain my prime focus was on the Jewish men and women who served our country around the world. Yet when my tasks were done, I would always seek out, and try to make contact with any local Jews. Sometimes this had unexpected consequences.

Bullets flying in Cyprus

The long-haul trips were always an adventure; though perhaps none were as potentially hazardous as the two places I visited in the late 1950s, Cyprus and Libya. As the RAF Chaplain from 1957, I used to visit our British military base on Cyprus to conduct high holiday services for Jewish personnel stationed there. There was, what was called a 'Church House', on our base in Kyrenia, which could accommodate 100 people. It was available to all religions to use for sacred purposes. We took over this venue each year for about a week in the spring and the autumn. This was where we brought all Jewish servicemen – and where I officiated for the Jewish High Holy Days of Rosh Hashanah and Yom Kippur in September (and my colleague Alex Goldberg did the same in April for Passover). We swopped roles on our base in Germany, where I conducted the Passover programme and he did the High Holydays.

Not only did we have to conduct all the services, but we also had to keep the servicemen and women busy during the whole period. After running a prayer service each morning, we then gave five or six lectures each day. We also had to organise social activities for the evenings, such as sports competitions, games, or a film show. It was a very intense and wonderful experience for me and for the servicemen too.

In those days of compulsory national service, we would regularly have at least a hundred Jewish servicemen and women for these events on Cyprus. I would travel to this large island in the eastern Mediterranean a few days early, to supervise that everything was 'Kosher' and that the appropriate foodstuffs were on hand.

The problem was that these visits in the late 1950s coincided with major unrest on the island. The population was mainly Greek Cypriot with a sizable minority of people of Turkish origin. The island had changed hands many times over the centuries. Two millennia ago, it was ruled by the Romans, then the Venetians. The Turks wrested in from the Venetians in the 16th century.

The British then occupied the island 1878, as a strategic asset in the eastern Mediterranean. In November 1914, Britain formally annexed Cyprus from the Ottomans, and it became a British Crown Colony. The Turks were not at all pleased that Cyprus had become part of the British Empire. Cypriot Greeks were initially pleased to have thrown off the Ottoman yoke, but by 1950 they wanted to be free from the British as well, and to be connected with mainland Greece.

By 1955 the charismatic Greek Archbishop Makarios had joined up with the radical generals of EOKA – Greek Cypriot nationalist paramilitary organisation fighting a campaign for the end of British Rule in Cyprus. They had started targeting public buildings and assassinating British military personnel. Two years later I arrived on the island. If I had expected an easy ride in my new role as military chaplain, I found myself instead confronted with what can only be described as a baptism of fire!

As a chaplain, I did not carry a weapon. You can imagine my surprise, even alarm, when I saw all participants at our High Holydays services praying with guns slung over their prayer shawls. Everywhere I went in Cyprus, north and south, I had to travel in an Army Land Rover with a cohort of soldiers, carbines at the ready to guard my safety. It was all pretty stressful, and my first experience of a 'live fire' environment. Despite Germany being the fulcrum of the Cold War between the Western and Communist worlds, at least when I went there to conduct the services for Passover, there were no bullets flying around, as was the case in Cyprus.

As for forming relations with local Jews in Cyprus, I found little trace of any Jewish inhabitants, which was surprising as I know that there had been a history of Jewish communities, smaller or larger, on the island from the second century BCE onwards.

After the rise of Nazism in 1933 however, hundreds, then thousands of Jews fleeing danger in Europe and hoping to reach the Holy Land, ended up being detained by the British on Cyprus. During the Second World War and after the liberation of the European concentration camps, the British, who held a mandate over the land, still severely restricted immigration to Palestine. Instead, they established detention camps on Cyprus for survivors who were caught 'illegally' attempting to enter British-ruled Palestine. Over 50,000 European Jewish refugees and survivors were held in detention camps on the island. Only once the State of Israel was created in May 1948, were they able at last to reach the Promised Land.

I remember meeting one Israeli who ran a small hotel in Nicosia. He used to join our military services until he decided to return to Israel. The Israeli Consul General used to invite me to dinner on Friday nights… though instead of *benching* (reciting the traditional prayers after eating) he used to play a Beethoven symphony!

By the time tensions re-erupted again in Cyprus in 1963, I was a long way away, tending to other outposts of Jewish life under the British military umbrella.

An Israeli Spy in Libya?

Even more terrifying was my first visit in 1960, to minister to British Jewish troops in Libya. We had an RAF base at El-Adem, a few miles from the capital, Tripoli. It was all very congenial at first. I remember how we played cricket on a makeshift pitch set up on the desert sands.

Problems started, however, when I decided that I would like to visit the Jewish community of Tripoli which by then was already quite small. The military kindly provided me with a Land Rover and driver, but he had difficulty locating the synagogue and was driving back and forth in erratic patterns. This aroused the suspicion of the Libyan security forces. Soon we were being followed. Eventually I arrived and joined the community at the prayer service and got back to base safely.

The next day the Libyan police informed the British authorities that they were going to arrest me! They suspected me of being an Israeli spy, masquerading as an RAF officer. Why else, they said, would a foreigner be driving up and down seeking out local Jews?

The RAF decided to evacuate me forthwith. I had an armed escort to the airport, and another two weaponised Land Rovers making up the convoy. Waiting for us at the airbase were Arab armed police who were bent on my capture. Luckily no shots were fired, and I boarded the aeroplane which flew me to safety in Cyprus. I later discovered that the police had arrested the whole Jewish community that I had visited in their synagogue! They had to endure two or three days of interrogation before thankfully, being released.

Libya had been home to a Jewish community for thousands of years. They had lived and thrived under Greek, Roman, Ottoman, Italian, British, and Arab rule, living mainly in the cities of Tripoli and Benghazi. When Libya became an Italian colony in 1911 there were about 21,000 Jews in the country (4% of the total population of 550,000). In the late 1930s there were 30,000 Jews in Libya. Tripoli's population remained 25% Jewish with 44 active synagogues. But by the end of the Second World War, the good days for Jews were over.

The beginning of the end for the Jews of Libya was the institution of harsh, discriminatory legislation by Italy against its own Jews in 1938. The war reached Libya in the autumn of 1940, when Italy attacked British-influenced Egypt from bases in Libya. This campaign was a disastrous defeat for Italy, at the hands of the Allies, who entered Libya. But Rommel arrived with a German army, and we know how fierce the war in the wWestern Desert was. Libyan ports such as Tobruk changed hands several times between December 1940 and January 1943. Tripoli and its Jewish quarter came in for massive bombing by the British and French.

Each time the British army had entered Libya, the Jews showed enthusiastic support for them, because, during their conquests, the discriminatory race laws were not applied. But each time Libya was recaptured by the Italians, the Jews were punished severely for their so-called 'collaboration' with the enemy. In 1942 the Italians, who had already determined to adopt a more radical racial policy against the Jews, used the Jewish community's enthusiastic welcome of the Allied soldiers as a pretext to punish the Jews of Libya for their betrayal. Mussolini deported the Libyan Jews to concentration camps in Italy, Germany, Algeria and Tunisia.

The final straw came in September 1969 when a band of twelve colonels led by a young Muammar Gaddafi toppled King Idris (who had previously asked the British for protection). The British and other foreigners including the remaining Jews were ordered to leave. The RAF closed and evacuated El-Adem in 1970. Another chapter in British military history came to an abrupt end. Alas, Libya's once-thriving Jewish community exists no more.

Many decades later I was in my local Brondesbury synagogue, when some unfamiliar faces approached me. They revealed themselves as a Jewish family from Tripoli, and said they remembered me from my ill-fated visit to their synagogue so many years before.

The long road to Singapore

My very first long-haul RAF flight was in 1959 and was full of incident. On the trip was a cohort of about sixty fellow military personnel. I was one of only two Jews on board, the other being a Corporal Goldberg.

We took off from a small private air base near the A3 in Kent. In those days this was our usual point of departure for all flights to the Far East. Our ultimate destination was Singapore. We flew on a medium-sized Hermes four-engine propeller transport carrier which the RAF had ordered to replace the old Halifax. Only 29 were built, all in Radlett Aerodrome, Hertfordshire, but it served us well.

The problem was that the aeroplane needed frequent refuelling. As a result, it took what seemed like a few weeks for us to reach Singapore. We had several shorter or longer stopovers on the way. The last Hermes flew in 1969. These days jet airliners can fly from London to Singapore non-stop in under 13 hours; not so in 1959!

Our first touchdown was at Nice on the French Riviera. Sadly, we were not allowed off the aeroplane to promenade along the Avenue des Anglais. Next, we refuelled on Malta. Here I contacted the Jewish Community who promptly whisked me off to dedicate their place of worship – a rented flat in an apartment building! I was also to dedicate two more of their apartment synagogues on subsequent visits to Malta.

Then it was on to Benghazi in Libya and Khartoum in Sudan. Time was limited during my overnight stopover in Khartoum, but at least I managed to track down the phone number of the secretary of the local Jewish community. I made contact with him and a few others. As it was in the middle of the night, they seemed not too pleased to hear from me at first. We eventually had a good long chat on the telephone. I promised to meet in person when I was next there. Sadly, that never happened. From there our next stop was Aden in South Yemen.

Aden and Yemen

The British occupation of Aden on the southwest tip of the Arabian Peninsula in 1839 was also a strategic rather than commercial undertaking, guarding the lines of communication with India, just like the later seizures of Cyprus in 1878 and of Egypt in 1882.

This desert region received a major boost after the Suez Canal opened in 1869 and Aden then became an important and lucrative coaling station for steam ships travelling east to Asia. Following Britain's humiliation in the Suez Crisis of 1956, she granted independence in February 1959 to the Federation of South Arabia, which was formed from the Aden colony and the surrounding protectorates. Nevertheless, Britain maintained a big army base in the area reinforcing its global presence. That is what we visited in 1959.

The Jews of Aden in South Yemen were a separate group, quite different in background and lifestyle to the more rural and numerous northern Yemenite Jews. They enjoyed close ties with British authorities and local Arab officials. This remarkable community kindly invited me to take a service, and, knowing no other, I led them in the first Ashkenazi service they had ever witnessed. I must say, they were most welcoming to me and happy with my – unusual to them – performance. Their usual services followed the Sephardi tradition.

During my few days in Aden the headmaster of Aden's Jewish school asked me if I would like to join him in a visit to the border of North Yemen. His school was run by the Anglo-Jewish Yemenite Association, which illustrates the strong bonds between Adenites and the British. I realised that he wanted me to witness first-hand the flight of Yemenite Jews from troubles in North Yemen across the border into Aden. When I met the refugees, I do not know who was more surprised – them or me. They were dark in appearance, like other Yemenis, and wore flowing traditional Arab garments. The only feature that distinguished the men from Muslims was their hairstyle showing their prominent Jewish *peyyot* or sidelocks.

These Yemenites in turn had never seen a white European Jew before. Being sceptical, they wanted me to prove that I really was Jewish. I recited a *bracha*, a blessing, in Hebrew of course; and I showed them my *tsitsit* (sacred tassels worn under one's shirt). Fortunately, that seemed to convince them.

On subsequent journeys, whenever our old short-range RAF transport aircraft had to refuel, I stayed with the community for shorter periods, sometimes just overnight, near our RAF base at Aden. British Forces Aden lasted until 1967. After that, there was no opportunity for me to visit again. As for the Jews of Yemen and Aden, almost all have left.

Most Jews from Yemen made it to Israel, both before and shortly after the State of Israel was declared in 1948. By far the largest Yemenite Jewish population in the world, nearly half a million, live in Israel. A sizeable group went to the USA and a smaller band came to Britain. A few Yemenite Jews have settled in Willesden, northwest London, not far from where I live and a small, but lively Adenite community lives and prays to this day among the strictly Orthodox groups of Hackney in northeast London. I have often enjoyed the pleasure of being invited to attend their services and other festive occasions.

Karachi, Pakistan

Our next stop on our way to Singapore was Karachi in Pakistan. When we reached the city, I managed to speak to senior members of the *Maghain Shalome* synagogue. The name means 'Shield of Peace'. The synagogue had been built in 1893 when Karachi was still part of India. The local Jewish community of only about fifteen to twenty members, spoke good English and many had family living in Britain and Israel. They were slightly better off than most others in the city. In 1947, following Partition, when Pakistan had separated from India, Karachi became part of a Muslim state. After the State of Israel was declared, in 1948, conditions for Jews in Karachi had deteriorated.

When I contacted the Karachi Bene Israel Community in 1959, they immediately offered to 'look after' me. They gave me a tour of their synagogue. They treated me royally, showed me around their homes and made sure I had nothing but delicious homemade kosher food to eat.

28. Karachi synagogue entrance.

I took some photographs of the synagogue and nearby property which included images of starving and ill people lying on the pavements. I took them to a local chemist shop to be developed. When I went to collect the prints, the manager claimed they were all bad. I think that they destroyed the disturbing pictures, maybe on police orders.

By the time we set off again – most of our passengers were suffering from stomach upsets. I seemed to be the only one who was quite alright. I was grateful for the excellent kosher food I had shared with the community during my stay. I had invited Corporal Goldberg to join me, but he had declined. He suffered the same digestive consequences as our non-Jewish fellow travellers.

I hoped to revisit Karachi someday, but as our aeroplanes got better, with the Comet replacing the Hermes, journeys needed fewer stopovers along the way. The synagogue was demolished by the government in 1988 and a shopping plaza put in its place.

Singapore at last

Soon after we finally landed in Singapore, the local RAF chaplain announced that all Jewish personnel were warmly invited to have Friday night dinner with Mrs Mozelle Nissim. Mozelle was the eldest daughter of the famed magnate and philanthropist Sir Manasseh Meyer (left) who had been the mainstay of the Jewish community in Singapore for many years.

Sir Manasseh Meyer was born in Baghdad in 1846 and educated in Calcutta. After travelling all around the far east, he settled in Singapore in 1873. With his brother Reuben, he founded Meyer Brothers, a very successful import-export business, involved in the opium trade. The Firm grew to dominate all trade between Singapore and India which was secured and managed by the flourishing Baghdadi Jewish communities of Singapore and Calcutta. His partner was Raphael Sassoon, born in Aleppo. Meyer also operated in the property market, building, and owning several of the most iconic hotels and other buildings in Singapore. He became a naturalised British subject.

Having made his millions, he turned to philanthropy. He gave generously to charity within and outside his Jewish community, particularly supporting higher education. With others, he donated land for the Jewish cemetery and funds for the main synagogue which opened in 1878 in Waterloo Road. It was called *Maghain Aboth*. The name means 'Shield of the Patriarchs'. The Iraqi Jews had brought silver encased *torah* scrolls from Baghdad and ran a strictly orthodox *Sephardic* style service.

12. The Long Haul – *Journeys East*   183

Over the years, the community grew considerably with many new immigrants from Europe as well as from Asia. Newer arrivals inevitably clashed with the descendants of the mostly Baghdadi Jews who had first settled on the peninsula from the 1850s over customs and rituals.

By 1902, there was a need for another synagogue. Manasseh Meyer resolved the issue by building a synagogue at his own expense in the grounds of his home in Oxley Rise for the use of his family and other Baghdadi Jewish families who had moved to the area. The new synagogue was completed in 1905 and was named *Chesed-El* which means 'Grace of God'.

I have come across several synagogues in sheds or out-houses in my travels to small communities, but this was hardly what one would imagine a private synagogue in a garden to be! This one is a huge opulent Victorian structure, designed in Renaissance style by Singapore's finest architects, Swan and McLaren. It is quite as large as London's New West End Synagogue in Bayswater.

Meyer also became an ardent Zionist, and supported Herzl. He travelled to Jerusalem with his daughters to 'inculcate them with a love of Zion'. In 1922 Meyer became the founding president of the Singapore Zionist

29. Exterior Chesed El Synagogue in Mrs Nissim's private garden, Singapore.

30. Interior of El Chesed Synagogue. I was often called upon to lead services there, whenever I happened to be in Singapore.

Organization. His home was known as a 'beehive' of Zionist activity in Asia. In 1922 he hosted Albert Einstein who was travelling through the Baghdadi Jewish communities of Asia seeking financial support for the Hebrew University. Sir Manasseh Meyer became a major donor to the Institution.

Manasseh Meyer was knighted by George V in 1929 'in recognition of his public services and benevolence.' He died on 1 July 1930 in Singapore, leaving his home and a great fortune to his daughter Mozelle, and also made generous provision for his other three daughters and three sons. Mozelle then became the recognised leader of the Jewish Community.

When I first met her in 1959, Mrs Mozelle Nissim was a widow in her eighties. At that time there was quite a large community of about 500 or 600 Jews in Singapore where she was highly regarded. Albert Einstein had encountered her on visits to her father to raise funds for the Hebrew University in Jerusalem. He had referred to her as 'one of the finest Jewish women I have ever met'.

Mozelle held court on Friday nights in her magnificent family mansion on Oxley Rise, to which she invited the many guests who were visiting the city-state. In particular, she welcomed all the Jewish military personnel. I soon learned that besides her wealth, good taste and generosity, Mozelle was also an Orthodox and very observant Jewess.

She insisted on a *minyan* for prayers every morning in her synagogue. To facilitate this, she sent a special bus round the city to pick up the '*Minyan Men*'. Her large Friday night dinners were legendary. When they heard, I was going to Singapore, previous visitors had already told me that I had to go to Mrs Nissim on Friday night. Accordingly, on arrival, I contacted Mrs Nissim, who duly invited me saying: 'You, must come to have dinner on Friday night and furthermore, you must come to my synagogue which is at the bottom of my garden on *Shabbat* morning'.

Since Oxley Rise was a long way from Changi RAF base where I was stationed, I booked myself an overnight stay at the Cockpit Hotel, a few doors away from the Nissim mansion. As she did not have a permanent minster in her synagogue, she was very pleased to make my acquaintance. From that first Friday evening, I knew that whenever I was in Singapore, this would be a regular rendezvous for me. We kept in touch for several years until she passed away in July 1975, just a month after turning 92.

On one occasion, having just flown in from England, I tumbled up the steps, late, just before the Sabbath started. When I got into my seat at the long and beautifully laid table for thirty or forty people, who do I see there, sitting at the far end, but the two airmen who had told me, months before when I met them at my base in London, that they were not interested in Judaism and did not want to get involved at all. They had said, 'Look, it's very kind for you to talk to us, but we don't believe in anything, so please do not bother to make contact with us. We do not deny we are Jewish, but we are simply not interested'. We had parted good friends. At least I admired their candour!

Seeing them at Mrs Mozelle Nissim's dinner table, I thought, this is really a bit of a *chutzpah*. Obviously, there's a really good meal here on a Friday night, and they are in it for some free food. I will have a word with them. I could not get near them because I was placed about twenty seats down at the other end of the table. When it came to the *benching* – the long grace after meals, which is chanted in Hebrew – Mrs Nissim called out to one of these fellows, whom I took to be atheists, and asked 'Oh, would you like to do it?' And he did!

Then afterwards she said, 'Let us retire to the other room for coffee, and we are going to have a short thought on the *sidra* (weekly portion of the *Torah*) and Mr X is going to give it'. Well, that was the *other* one of the 'godless duo'. I thought, what on earth is going on here? They are really working hard to get a free meal – they have learnt how to bench, and now they are even giving us a rabbinical *Torah* homily!

I went up to them afterwards and said, 'I don't understand – when I last saw you, you said you were not at all interested in anything Jewish'. They said, 'Ah, when we came to Singapore, we heard about this wonderful lady, and we went to see her. And she did not criticise us for our lack of any Jewish observance or any belief. When we saw you, we thought you would say 'You should do this, and you should not do that' whereas Mrs Nissim inspired us by her example'. This was a very important lesson for me at the outset of my career as a chaplain. She had clearly done a much better job than I had.

They were absolutely right. You cannot just tell people what to do. Mozelle Nissim and these young men taught me a lesson that was crucial to my future life on the road to military, university, and other small communities. It is a lesson that I have never forgotten. Often the trouble with ministers who come to small communities is that they start to dictate the way things have to be done. People shy away and say, 'Blow you, we don't want to do it at all'. Those two young Anglo-Jewish servicemen were inspired to explore their Judaism by Mrs Nissim's approach – her devotion and her tolerance, her lack of judgement and her quiet encouragement. I learnt a lot that night.

There is still a large Jewish Community in Singapore and the bonds between London and Singapore remain strong. The island is also famously close to Israel, militarily and politically, which is quite a rarity in the region.

In 1998 the Singapore government recognised *Chesed-El* Synagogue as a national treasure. Nineteen years later British funds helped renovate the synagogue. In 2018 the Liverpool-born Elaine Robinson, former head of Jewish Studies at the interdenominational Jewish Community Secondary School in North London (JCoSS) became the principal of Singapore's only Jewish school. I hear she has succeeded greatly in making the school a blend of local and global excellence, as well as teaching Hebrew and Jewish studies to a high standard.

A surprise trip to Vietnam

One time, when I was in Singapore on duty in the early 60s, some RAF colleagues told me that they were flying to Saigon the next day. Would I like to join them? There was a spare place aboard the aeroplane. I could not pass up this exciting offer.

I was not party to the reason for the visit. The plan was to stay just one night in Vietnam. As it turned out however, two of the airplane's four engines failed in mid-air halfway to our destination. I kept thinking: 'Please don't crash!' Luckily, we arrived intact, but our visit was extended to a full week to give the ground crew time to repair the aircraft.

This provided me with a great opportunity to explore Saigon and its surroundings. The city has magnificent French boulevards, and if you ignored the extreme heat and humidity, you could easily think you were in Paris. I was also taken outside the city perimeter to explore the dense untamed jungle.

On this occasion I found no Jews at all. Nor did I see any British military involvement, at least not overtly. I did notice several Americans amongst the local Vietnamese, and there was talk of Vietcong activity to the north. For that reason, we were encouraged not to stray too far from Saigon, the capital of what was still South Vietnam. This was a brief hiatus, a moment of calm after the French had been ousted from Indochina in 1956, and before the Vietnam War erupted. North and South Vietnam would soon be embroiled in a ferocious, deadly and costly conflict – the north supported by the Soviet Union and the South by America.

A guardian angel must have been watching over me, because on the way back to Singapore our supposedly repaired aeroplane, suffered yet more engine trouble over the Malayan jungle!

A Family Wedding in Thailand

Not all my trips abroad were for work alone. On more than one occasion I would holiday in Singapore with Rosalie, as we felt a great deal of affection for this place. Once, while we were there, we chose to visit nearby Thailand. After calling relatives in Bangkok, we learned that a distant cousin, a member of my mother's Litvak Ashkenazi family, was just about to get married to a Sephardi Jewish girl there, and they invited us to join the family celebrations.

I knew the young man already. He had been a pupil at Carmel College in Oxfordshire, an international Anglo-Jewish boarding school that operated from 1948 until 1997. We had also enjoyed meeting the family earlier at a *bar mitzvah*. On arrival in Bangkok the young man immediately whisked us off to his synagogue for the *aufruf*. This is a traditional Jewish ceremony on the Sabbath prior to the wedding, where the groom (or in Progressive communities the couple) is called up to the *Torah* to recite a blessing. When the blessing is completed, often the entire congregation wishes them luck and happiness by throwing soft sweets at them. The wedding service which took place the day afterwards was conducted in a completely Sephardi ritual. It was a happy and lavish affair that we were able to enjoy with the extended, and also some new family.

End of Empire

In the early 20th century, nearly a third of the globe was 'painted pink'. Huge tracts of foreign lands were ruled by Britain to some degree. By the time I entered active service as a British military chaplain, one by one, with increasing rapidity, the colonies and former protectorates on every continent claimed and won their independence. For a while, a skeletal British military presence remained in some places, hence still requiring my visits. Yet even in such places, more assertive local leaders would later demand that the Union Jack be lowered for the last time.

I was a part of history in the making: the final years of Empire. My later long-haul military journeys would be on duties around the world as a chaplain to NATO and also on behalf of the Commonwealth Jewish Council which I have described in another chapter.

13

Meetings with Royalty and Concerts in St Paul's Cathedral, Canterbury Cathedral and Westminster Abbey

In the course of my many Jewish and secular activities here and abroad, I have had many opportunities to meet heads of state and senior international figures both on a formal and also on a social basis.

A number of these personalities were especially impressive like President Nelson Mandela of South Africa and also the President of Malta. In earlier years I had got to know various members of the Italian Royal Family.

I had a genuinely meaningful relationship with many senior politicians around the world, especially in Germany and parts of Eastern Europe. However, my most memorable meetings of heads of state have been with our own late Queen Elizabeth II and the Duke of Edinburgh.

The most auspicious meeting with the Queen was when she officially opened a synagogue and was present when I completed its consecration. This was the first (and probably only) time a reigning monarch has formally opened a synagogue and attended a consecration ceremony. The date was 2 May 1969, and the synagogue was part of a large Multifaith Chaplaincy Centre on the campus of Lancaster University that she had come to open.

Lancaster was one of a wave of shiny new 'Plate-glass' Universities established in the 1960s. I was appointed by the Hillel Foundation to be the Jewish spiritual advisor to all of them. In that role I was able to guide the University of Lancaster on the creation of the Multifaith Chaplaincy Centre and explain the requirements for the Jewish students, such as that the synagogue should have a Holy Ark for storing the Scrolls of the Law and a *bimah*, the reading desk from which Jews read the *Torah*. Next door to the synagogue there is a kosher kitchen and a big socialising room. Similar facilities are provided for other faiths.

The Multifaith Chaplaincy Centre at Lancaster was a ground-breaking innovation. It is housed in a specially designed building with soaring spires.

31. I was honoured to greet the Queen when she came to Lancaster University to open the Multifaith Chaplaincy Centre in May 1969.

As well as the synagogue and Jewish lounge and kitchen, it housed an Anglican and Free Church Chapel, a Roman Catholic Chapel and also a 'Quiet Room' and a large central lounge that can be used by all students. Later it was to include a Buddhist Meditation Room and Islamic Prayer Rooms.

The Queen dedicated the building 'for the worship of God and the service of man, for refreshment and informal meeting, for acquiring fresh knowledge, and a place where counsel and help could be given'. For the consecration, of the synagogue, I brought out a mini-*Sefer Torah*, which I placed on the *bimah* and I read the traditional dedicatory prayers. Her Majesty spent quite a long time with us, asking me many questions about how a synagogue operates and, what we hoped to achieve with the Multifaith Centre. It was not just a routine, conversation. Everything she said on seeing the synagogue scrolls and architecture was pertinent and appropriate, such as 'How is it written' and 'What's the significance' of this or that. I remember thinking: 'She has really done her homework'. I came to realise that her sensitive and surprisingly easy-going approach reflected

13. Meetings with Royalty and Concerts in Cathedrals

an attitude of genuine curiosity and empathy, which benefited this country immensely over the many decades of her reign.

The Allied Air Forces Chiefs of Chaplains Committee, of which I was the Secretary General usually met for about a week once year in a different country. This gave the fifteen or so senior chaplains, the opportunity of meeting European heads of state and even royalty. When in Copenhagen, as part of our programme we were invited to tea with the King and Queen of Denmark. When the group met in London, as Senior Jewish Chaplain to the British Forces, I organised an invitation to tea with the Queen and Duke of Edinburgh at Buckingham Palace.

I recall the Queen and the Duke entering, prompting the waiters to serve us all with tea and sandwiches. I was sitting in a corner when the Queen came over to where I was with her cup of tea. She sat down next to me and started chatting. It was 1997, just after John Major's Conservative government had lost the General Election to Tony Blair's Labour Party. There had been a wipe-out of the Conservative Party. The papers were full of stories about Members of Parliament and Cabinet Ministers going to Buckingham Palace to hand in their Seals of Office. This topic prompted an unusual semi-political discussion initiated by the Monarch herself. She told me that she was a bit concerned about what these people were going to do. Not merely had their party lost the election, but some of them had also lost their seats. She wondered how they were going to make a living. 'Ma'am,' I replied, 'I don't think you should worry too much about it. They will be alright.' Then our talk turned to a general discussion of other matters. Again, our conversation, just one-to-one, lasted a considerable time.

The Queen and the Duke, as one would imagine, are very good at meeting and talking individually to a large number of people in a short time. At our Council of Christians and Jews 60th anniversary reception at St James's Palace in 2002, the attendees were grouped together in clusters of ten: with about ten clusters on one side of the hall which was laid out with refreshment tables in the middle. There were another ten groups on the other side. The Royal couple worked as a perfect team: she went to one side, while he took on the other. It was luck of the draw whom you would meet.

One of each cluster was deputed to be the leader, with a list of names, and when the Queen or Duke came to his or her group, they would introduce the other nine quickly. They would spend a few seconds with each person. It was a very well-managed procedure. What struck me every time I had the honour of meeting Her Majesty is that she really does connect with people. She makes direct eye contact and relevant remarks and shakes one's hand. Prince Philip was equally adept at making brief conversation with all sorts of visitors. He showed similar qualities of empathy and engagement and good humour.

I first came to know the Duke of Edinburgh in his role as Visitor to my Oxford college, St Catherine's. Every now and then I was invited to lunch or dinner with the Master. On one such occasion, of the six invitees to his private home in London, one was the Duke of Edinburgh. On another occasion I went up to Oxford to dedicate a stone or memorial plaque, and there he was again. I got to know Prince Philip quite well, so much so, that he started asking: 'Oh my goodness, you're here again – which hat are you wearing this time?' I replied, depending on the location or the event in question: If at St Catherine's I would say 'I am here as a member of the College'. If it was at Oxford or another University, 'I am here in my capacity as the Jewish Chaplain to the University'; or, at Sandhurst, 'I am a Chaplain to the Forces'. Another time, when he saw me at St James's Palace, I had to explain that I was there as a Trustee of the Council of Christians and Jews. On yet another occasion, I appeared representing the Commonwealth Jewish Council. I kept on popping up and before long Prince Philip got to know my name and exclaim, 'Oh good Lord, it's you again, Mr Weisman, is it?'

The Sovereign is the pinnacle of a large (though now considerably smaller) cohort of active royals. I got to know Princess Alexandra very well. She is the cousin to the Queen and sister of the Duke of Kent. She was the first Chancellor of the University of Lancaster from its inception in 1964 and remained so for forty years until 2004. For my part, as the Jewish chaplain to the university and subsequently as one of the planning committee of the Multifaith Chaplaincy Centre and eventually as an Honorary Fellow of the University, I got to meet her very often. When we had our annual Fellows dinner, Rosalie and I would stay in the same hotel as the Chancellor. On many occasions Princess Alexandra would sit in the lounge after the dinner, and we would join her for coffee and a relaxed chat. At the last Fellows Dinner at Lancaster University, after the meal she said: 'Ah, I've been waiting to see you; I wondered whether you were here.'

Sir Chris Bonington, the famous British mountaineer, took over as Chancellor when she retired. His career had included nineteen expeditions to the Himalayas, including four to Mount Everest. On one occasion the university planned a big reception dinner in honour of the Fellows; unfortunately, it fell during *Chol HaMoed Pesach* – the intermediate days of Passover – so, as I was officiating for the RAF Jewish personnel, in

13. Meetings with Royalty and Concerts in Cathedrals

32. On 16 April 2006, I was made an Honorary Fellow of Lancaster University, for my contribution to Jewish Life, to Chaplaincy and to students. In this picture, taken after the formal dinner, are from left, a cleric of Lancaster, my wife Rosalie, me clutching my citation, Sir Chris Bonington, who was the Chancellor of Lancaster University at that time, and our eldest son, Brian.

Germany I could not be there. The Vice Chancellor said 'Well, this is not good enough, when are you free?', and I gave him a date, 'We will host a special dinner, a black-tie affair with a number of VIP's, including the Chancellor. And so he did. It was a very convivial evening for Rosalie and me with about twenty-five guests for dinner at the university, including our son Brian who came up to Lancaster specially. Brian was a great admirer of Sir Chris whom he had met some years earlier.

A big surprise for me, and an actual honour, was being nominated to receive an OBE, the Order of the British Empire. The impressive investiture, where I was accompanied by my wife Rosalie and our two sons took place in 1997 at Buckingham Palace, with His Royal Highness Prince Charles, the Prince of Wales (now King Charles III) officiating. As is my wont – I was very happy to drive my family down the Mall, into the Palace. Brian said, *We were all so proud of my father, receiving the OBE. What impressed me most though, was that when we drove out afterwards there were hundreds of people at the gates waving to us and all the other recipients, which included a number of celebrities. It made us feel so important. It was just a wonderful experience full of emotion.*

In another capacity, I represented the Chief Rabbi for the Golden Wedding celebration of the late Queen and Duke of Edinburgh in November 1997.

On another occasion, wearing gown and honours, I had attended a service in the chapel at the Wellington Barracks in Birdcage Walk around the corner from the Palace and had taken the salute from the Jewish Lads and Girls Brigade, who had been invited to parade there on that occasion.

33. My family in the courtyard of Buckingham Palace on the occasion of my receiving the OBE. Our sons, Daniel on the left, and Brian on the right.

34. Receiving OBE from the then Prince of Wales in 1997

The Duke of Edinburgh attends a Jewish concert at St Paul's Cathedral

Another occasion when I spent time with the Duke of Edinburgh was when I assisted at one of Geraldine Auerbach's Jewish Music Heritage Trust concerts presented in a cathedral. This time it was at St Paul's in November 1995. As the religious advisor to the project, I had approached the Dean of the Cathedral, Canon Christopher Hill, to see if he would be interested in hosting the performance. He readily agreed. With his backing as well as mine and that of Sir Sigmund Sternberg, the request made by the Jewish Music Heritage Trust's Judy Obrart, to HRH Prince Philip to attend, was also granted. I had the honour of guiding the Duke of Edinburgh around the cathedral, introducing him to as many people as possible.

Having produced Ernest Bloch's *Sacred Service* in York Minster in 1990, Geraldine knew that Yehudi Menuhin was keen to conduct this work in London. Yehudi had first heard the music as a teenager from the composer's own lips at Bloch's home in San Francisco, where Bloch had, as Yehudi said, 'barked it out' to him at the piano.

Malcolm Singer (who had conducted the work in York) had subsequently become the Music Director of the Yehudi Menuhin School and Yehudi himself had become the President of the 'Jewish Music Heritage Trust', of which I was a Trustee, and which was later to become the 'Jewish Music Institute' and to be based at SOAS University of London.

Yehudi became a colossus on the world's musical stage. He was always interested in a wide range of music of the world. He formed lifelong friendships with performers such as Indian sitar player Ravi Shankar and jazz violinist Stephane Grapelli. It was poignantly fitting that Yehudi, in his last public appearance in London before he sadly died, had welcomed Jewish music to academia in 1999. This was when he officially inaugurated the Jewish Music Institute into a department devoted to world music at the School of Oriental and African Studies, University of London. At this prestigious event, the Director of the University, Sir Tim Lankester, hosted a dinner in his honour, Yehudi's friend Professor Israel Adler from Jerusalem gave a key lecture on newly found archives of Yiddish music in Russia and played a recording of the voice of the great Yiddish writer Sholom Aleichem.

I again saw to it that this concert of a Hebrew Sacred Service at St Pauls, was a collaboration between the Jewish Music Heritage Trust and the Council of Christians and Jews. It became the culmination and highlight of a ten-day interfaith festival that Geraldine created around it called 'Sacred Music of Two Traditions' running from 6 and 16 November 1995, with events taking place in churches and synagogues all in the City of London, exploring and celebrating the diversity and kinship of Jewish and Christian musical traditions – from ancient biblical chants to contemporary settings.

The festival opened with a concert of Gregorian Chant in the 11th Century Church of St Bartholomew the Great. There followed a concert of Jewish liturgical music by Cantor David Apfel and the male choir from Leeds at the oldest Ashkenazi synagogue in the City of London, in Sandys Row. Dr Malcolm Miller gave a talk on the 'Trumpets of Ancient Jericho' illustrated with *shofarot* (ram's horn trumpets).

A study-day of Jewish and Christian sacred music took place at City University in Islington, chaired by Alexander Knapp, holder of the Joe Loss Lectureship in Jewish Music. This interfaith festival concluded at St Giles Church in Cripplegate, opposite the Barbican Centre, with a Celebration of Psalms in English, Hebrew, Latin and German sung by Jewish and Christian choirs.

For the flagship concert at St Paul's Cathedral, the interior of the building was magically transformed by John Hill whom Geraldine had commissioned to illuminate the rich mosaic ceilings. Following a pre-concert reception in the crypt, and once the audience of 2500 were seated in the darkened nave and transepts, lit with what seemed like fairy lights,

13. Meetings with Royalty and Concerts in Cathedrals 197

35. Collage of St Paul's Cathedral

we heard the ethereal sounds of the St Paul's Cathedral children's choir wafting in from the great West Doors. It was thrilling.

In the bottom centre of a collage showing multiple images of the great and good at the event, Geraldine is handing Prince Philip a bound book of Jewish Music Festival programmes. Behind the Prince at the bottom, is the Precentor of St Paul's Cathedral, Canon Christopher Hill. Going upwards on the right-hand side are Sir Sigmund Sternberg and Judy Obrart (who, with her husband Roger. took most of the pictures). You can see me just northwest of the Duke's head.

Canterbury Cathedral 1986

This concert at St Paul's Cathedral in 1995 was actually the third in a trio of major interfaith cathedral concerts in which I, as a senior executive of the Council of Christians and Jews, collaborated with Geraldine Auerbach, then the Director of the Bnai Brith Jewish Music Festival. We have already mentioned the amazing interfaith long weekend she created in York in 1990. Four years earlier than that, in 1986, we had our first interfaith event at Canterbury Cathedral – no less.

Geraldine had been offered a new oratorio for cantor, choir, children's choir and orchestra by the British Jewish composer Ronald Senator. It was called *Kaddish for Terezin*. It was written in memory of Ronald's first wife who had been a camp survivor. The libretto was written by Rabbi Albert Friedlander, based on biblical texts and children's poems from Terezin (also known as Theresienstadt).

Terezin, while not an extermination camp itself, was a small garrison fortress town northwest of Prague, originally built to hold 6,000 soldiers. The Nazis crammed 60,000 Jews from Czechoslovakia and all over Europe into this small town, where living conditions were desperate. Many died in the camp of disease and malnutrition. When not working as slave labourers the cultured and talented prisoners, however, were permitted to organise entertainments for the inmates. Despite tremendous hardships, an incredible creative cultural programme emanated, which included lectures, composition and performances of theatre, cabaret, music and opera. Meanwhile 'selections' were constantly being drawn up and trains leaving daily with victims for the gas chambers of Auschwitz.

Geraldine told me that the '*Kaddish for Terezin*' needed a special and meaningful setting – not just a concert hall. With my CCJ hat on, I approached the CCJ Executive Director at the time, Reverend Marcus Braybrooke, (of whom we have spoken before). Marcus remembered that the previous year, he, together with the then Dean of Canterbury, had visited Neve Shalom, a centre in Israel for reconciliation and peace. The Dean had told Marcus that he was thinking there should be a memorial at Canterbury Cathedral to the victims of the Holocaust. He told me that the Deanery at Canterbury had actually been a refuge for Jews escaping Nazi Europe. When Marcus approached the Dean about hosting this oratorio, the Dean and Cathedral authorities were delighted, feeling that this would be a very fitting memorial. They were not keen on yet another stone plaque.

Geraldine began planning for a whole day in Canterbury as part of the 1986 Bnai Brith Jewish Music Festival. The day would commemorate the music, musicians and victims of that infamous concentration camp at Theresienstadt. Professor Dr David Bloch of Tel Aviv University now entered the picture. He was booked to perform Israeli music at the Bnai Brith Festival with his 'Group for new Music'. Once he heard about *Kaddish for Terezin*, he immediately offered to perform an additional concert of chamber music composed there. David had just been alerted to the extraordinary musical life in the camp from reading a recently published book about this. He also introduced us to two musician survivors, that we invited to join us in Canterbury and perform together for the first time since they had been incarcerated together in the camp. They were the pianist Edith Kraus, who was then living in Israel, and the bass singer Karel Berman, who had returned to Prague after the war and re-joined the Prague Opera Company.

We therefore needed to look for a suitable recital room for this concert. Lo and behold, we discovered that the Kings School's little concert hall, offered to us was in fact, fittingly, the old synagogue of Canterbury. It was designed and built in 1846, in Egyptian style with a pair of impressive lotus capped columns flanking the doorway. This was just perfect!

As the narrator for the oratorio in the Cathedral, we invited the charismatic and much-loved Rabbi Hugo Gryn of the West London Synagogue of British Jews near Marble Arch. Hugo was a nationally well-known figure through his appearances on the BBC's *Thought for the Day* and *The Moral Maze*. This was very meaningful to Hugo who had himself been incarcerated in Terezin during the war. It was a special moment for everyone to hear Rabbi Hugo Gryn blow the *shofar* in those hallowed halls.

BBC Radio London cleared its airways and the whole concert was broadcast live, with interviews and testimonies of survivors, broadcast in the interval of the live event. Marcus Braybrooke wrote in the programme note:

Canterbury Cathedral, chosen for the world premiere of Kaddish for Terezin has deep significance. It is the heart of the Church of England and the Anglican communion. Here Christians are acknowledging their share of responsibility for the sufferings of the Jewish people.... Having the premiere here is a sign of what has been achieved by CCJ and a pledge that Jews and Christians stand together in their determination that such atrocities should never be repeated.

After this auspicious premiere, *Kaddish for Terezin* went on in the following years to be performed in New York at the Avery Fisher Hall, at the Vatican, in Moscow, in Israel and in Terezin itself. David Bloch, inspired by these events went on to establish the Terezin Music Memorial Project at Tel Aviv University, and his Group for New Music presented the music by composers in Terezin widely, through concerts, lectures and recordings in the USA, Europe, South America and Australia.

David Bloch, who sadly passed away in 2016, sent his archives to the United States National Holocaust Museum. He told us:

The power of music to reveal a truth beyond words and to heal, he hoped was able to give a sense of solace and dignity to the victims of Terezin. The music created there is not only a testament to the memory of the Holocaust but is music of the highest quality that deserves to be known throughout the world.

Commemorations of Kristallnacht at Westminster Abbey

I also played a small part in the 75th anniversary commemoration of Kristallnacht held at Westminster Abbey. Such a commemoration had been suggested to the Dean of Westminster by a member of his own congregation, but it was not until the Dean spoke to Dame Julia Neuberger, the Senior Rabbi of the prestigious, Reform, West London Synagogue in Upper Berkeley Street, and she showed interest, that the event became a reality.

Again, working with Geraldine Auerbach now the founder and Director of the Jewish Music Institute, I visited West London Synagogue with her and joined the planning committee. We were glad to ensure that Cantor Paul Heller and choir Director Benjamin Wolf and the choir of Belsize Square Synagogue (founded by German speaking Holocaust refugees in 1939) was invited to participate in this moving event, together with the choir of West London Synagogue conducted by Christopher Bowers Broadbent.

'Kristallnacht', a euphemism for something much darker and more terrible, was a series of coordinated attacks on Jews and Jewish property carried out by paramilitaries and civilians throughout Nazi Germany and parts of Austria on the night of 9 November 1938. This was the beginning of the realisation of what the Nazis really had in store for the Jews, and what was to become known as the Holocaust. Many Jews were killed that night, and their properties looted. Synagogues all over the country were burned to the ground. It was known as the 'Night of Broken Glass' because the attacks left the streets covered with shards of glass from the windows of Jewish-owned stores, buildings, and synagogues.

The Dean of Westminster, the Very Reverend John Hall, welcomed a congregation of 1,600 (many of them Jews) to Westminster Abbey on Sunday 10th November 2013 and spoke about the atrocities. In this moving event in the Abbey, there was a reading by actress Ruth Rosen from Martin Gilbert's book, *Kristallnacht, Prelude to Destruction*. Rabbi Stuart Altshuler from Belsize Square Synagogue lit one of the six candles (one for each million Jews who were murdered) on the Belsize Square Synagogue Holocaust Memorial Candelabra. Rabbi Dame Julia Neuberger gave the address. There were personal testimonies from those who had experienced the wreckage on 9 November including journalist John Izbicki whose voice never recovered from his screams as an eight-year-old, seeing his parents beaten and their shop looted and destroyed.

13. Meetings with Royalty and Concerts in Cathedrals

Five years later in 2018, Westminster Abbey once more created a similar interfaith event commemorating the 80th anniversary of *Kristallnacht*. The service was once more conducted by the Dean of Westminster, the Very Reverend Dr John Hall, who said in his Bidding:

Here in this holy place at the centre of our national life, we shall pray together as we worship the one God sharing a common experience. We shall pray for a growth in mutual respect and understanding between the children of Abraham: Jews, Christians, and Muslims. We shall pray for trust in the God who makes and loves his people. Our prayer together will itself be a sign of hope.

It was a great moment of reflection for the Christian community, but in a way I felt a bit sad that most of the audience who flocked there were Jews – whereas it is the Christian congregation that needed to be there.

The very moving address this time was given by Jonathan Wittenberg, the son of Holocaust survivors and senior Rabbi to Masorti Judaism and of the New North London Synagogue in Finchley. Rabbi Stuart Altshuler, of Belsize Square Synagogue read a Psalm and the Reverend Anthony Ball, Canon in Residence, and Co-Chair of The Council of Christians and Jews (Central London Branch) read St Matthew 5: 1-10. Rabbi Baroness Neuberger DBE, Senior Rabbi, West London Synagogue, read a Reflection; and Testimonies were read by survivors who endured terrible Holocaust ordeals, Bea Green, Freddie Knoller, and Leslie Brent.

I am pleased that I, as a senior executive member of the Council of Christians and Jews, was able to play a significant part in making these activities happen, with their lasting ramifications.

14

My Wife Rosalie and her family, the Spiros

This book has been many years in gestation. We started to work on it in 2015 when I was still in full swing, travelling around the country and the world. In all my working years Rosalie was by my side, travelling with me wherever possible, encouraging me, quietly seeing to all my needs, and always making my busy life easy for me. Even though she was first diagnosed with cancer back in the 1960s, I felt that she was a cat with nine lives – immortal. Each time a crisis came along she surmounted it. She was so strong and resilient and never let on if she had any fears or worries. When she could not walk easily, she used walking aids. When she could no longer manage the stairs up to our flat – we installed a stair lift, and we carried on together. I could never envisage a life without Rosalie. But sadly, that has now come to pass. My dear Rosalie could not survive the latest episode of her illness. She passed away on Friday 6th May 2022 at about 4:00pm in the Royal Free Hospital.

Just reading the numerous condolence letters and notes that I have received from all over the world has made me aware of how much Rosalie has been appreciated both for herself and also as a part of my career. So many people from all aspects of my life have written to me expressing their fond memories of our part in their lives. They highlight the wonderful helpmate that Rosalie was. They expressly mention her calmness and kindness. Not only have these letters come from small communities across the country such as Oxford, Cambridge, Aberdeen and Jersey, but they have also come from my legal colleagues, from Admirals and Generals at NATO headquarters where I am a life member of the Chaplains Committee. I even had a letter from an officer at the Pentagon, commenting on our long and fruitful association.

I met Rosalie Spiro in the late 1950s. We were both part of a Study Group that I ran attached to the New West End Synagogue in Bayswater. The group met regularly in each other's homes under the patronage of the remarkable Rabbi Louis Jacobs. Rosalie's family, the Spiros, were members of his synagogue.

We were married at the New West End Synagogue in January 1958. Unusually we had three rabbis officiating at the service! As well as Louis

14. My Wife Rosalie and her family, the Spiros 203

36. Rosalie Spiro and I marry in January 1958 at the New West End Synagogue, Bayswater

Jacobs, there was Dr Isaac Levy, a fellow though then very senior army chaplain, plus the revered Rabbi Dr Solomon Schonfeld of the strictly orthodox Adas Yisroel Synagogue, who had been a friend and powerful influence on my religious upbringing. Actually, you could say there were four clerics if you include Cantor Raphael Levy.

For the first few years of our marriage, we lived in a flat in St John's Wood Court. Rosalie who would have preferred to study medicine if not for the war became a radiographer and worked at the Westminster Hospital. We then found our house in Brondesbury Park, Willesden. We turned it into two flats and have lived in the top flat for the last 60 years. Our sons Brian and Daniel grew up in Willesden and I have lived here ever since. I would often drop the boys off at school, Brian at JFS and Daniel at City of London on my way to Chambers.

It is not easy for me to talk about Rosalie – but here is what her cousin-in-law Nitza Spiro wrote about her:

Nobody has ever left a meeting with Malcolm and his beloved Rosalie without being no less impressed by her than by him. Their flat was a welcome haven for family and friends – even large numbers of them. The walls seemed to expand in those many gatherings. Rosalie would always smilingly offer delicious refreshments and create a most welcoming and happy atmosphere.

With her sharp mind and brilliant memory Rosalie was the reliable family oral encyclopaedia. She showed great warmth and genuine love for every member of the family, be it a child or an adult. She was always attentive to everybody's story and remembered these anecdotes years after they were told when even those concerned had forgotten all about them. When a grandchild of mine needed to create a genealogy study for a school project, Rosalie was the first and the last port of call.

When I, a foreigner from the Middle East married Robin and entered the Spiro family – a bastion of British Jewish middle-class aristocracy, both Malcolm and Rosalie in equal measure showered me with recognition and gave me the courage to spread my wings. This enabled me to find my way into an easy integration and gave me the self-confidence to dare to act and contribute. Rosalie and Malcolm stand at the top of our family's pantheon.

I am grateful to Nitza for writing about my dear Rosalie who was my staunch supporter and wonderful companion for 64 years until she passed away in May 2022. I would like at this time to express my profound gratitude to Rosalie for her supportive role.

37. A quiet moment with Rosalie at our Cotswold Cottage in 2000.

Our sons Brian and Daniel

I am also deeply appreciative of the lifetime of support given to us, by our two sons Brian and Daniel. Without Rosalie's encouragement and without Brian and Daniel's supportive role, I would never have been in a position to do so many of my away trips or my legal work.

When I was a Recorder, on circuit judging cases, it could mean that I had to stay away in Suffolk, or Cambridge or wherever, for up to three weeks at a time. Also, I could be away over a weekend in a small community taking services over *Shabbat*. I was always secure in the knowledge that Brian and or Daniel would stay overnight with their mother, or Rosalie would go to one of them for evening meals, or even to stay over for a while.

My elder son Brian tells me that in more recent times, even when Rosalie's health had deteriorated and she could no longer join me on my trips, she never wanted me to stop doing what I felt I needed to do and what I also enjoyed so much. Brian says:

Mum always said, 'The day dad stops is the day he drops! So, she never curbed his travelling and Daniel and I would spend time with mum to keep her company. It was always such a pleasure to do. Sometimes when dad would come home at 1:00am from visiting a small community, I would then leave mum and return home to bed!

Because of our father's amazing and interesting work, my brother Daniel and I have had countless trips and holidays in small communities. We have stayed with my parents in Jersey over the years too many times to count, for many festivals, especially for Pesach and Rosh Hashanah. Those were wonderful times.

Mum and dad also used to rent a cottage every summer in Elkstone, in the Cotswold's, so we spent many weekends there with them having a really relaxing Shabbat. Before that they used to rent a property in Lavenham, Suffolk and we enjoyed the same relaxing holidays there while he could tend to his flocks or legal duties in the area.

Also, I had many trips over a number of years to join dad at Amport House, for his regular Moral Leadership Courses, for Jewish serving military. I was just a bystander, but what an experience for me to eat and have a drink with men and woman from all three military services. We are so proud of everything our dear father has achieved, in all areas of his work. How lucky have we been and still are!

My younger son Daniel remembers that his dad was away a lot. He says:

I would say he was a bit unfocused when it came to home life, like the time he abandoned me as a child in Euston post office. But he was devoted to his larger family in his communities, universities and army charges. On the plus side, not many young people get a guided tour round a nuclear submarine because their dad knows someone. On the other hand, I remember spending an uncomfortable hour or so sat in the car outside the Verne Prison on Portland Bill, in the rain, while dad visited someone inside. We were on our way to a holiday, but he managed to sneak in some work anyway.

The Spiro Family

I first got to know her Spiro family when I got engaged to Rosalie Spiro in 1957. It was large and full of remarkable people. Rosalie's paternal grandfather, David Mendel Spiro, born in 1872, was one of nine children. They lived in Manchester where he founded one of the largest synagogues where he was the warden and a valued communal worker. When they moved to London, he founded the Cricklewood Synagogue, around the corner from where I now live, in Willesden Green. His brother Bernard represented the Manchester United Synagogue on the Board of Deputies in 1930.

David Spiro was a wealthy man through the family's firm, Spiro Linens which was based in London's Soho. The company also had branches in Belfast, Northern Ireland closer to the flax fields – the basis of linen. He became a great financial supporter of the famous Ponevezh Yeshiva (Talmudic College) in Lithuania, at which my mother's father, Bernard Lewis Segal, had studied. During the disruption of World War II and the Holocaust, the Ponevezh Yeshiva managed to re-establish itself in Bnei Brak in Palestine in 1944, even before the state of Israel was established in 1948.

David Spiro went to live in Palestine for a while in the 1930s. He purchased a house in Tel Aviv. Even after his return to live in Britain, he would go to his home in Tel Aviv every summer. He was the only man I know who, at that time, also had a home in Israel. It was unusual then. Over the years David Spiro became a great friend of Rabbi Abraham Isaac Kook, the first Ashkenazi Chief Rabbi of Mandatory Palestine. He also bought and ran an orange grove near Beer Sheva.

Grandfather David Mendel Spiro's wish was to be buried in the Holy Land, so when he realised that he was dying, in early 1940, he decided to spend his last days in Palestine (as it still was then). He suspected that with the Second World War raging, it would be difficult for his body to be transported there from Britain. So, he said goodbye to all his family, and Rosalie's father took him to the Holy Land, via the port of Marseilles from where boats were still going to Palestine. David passed away shortly after arriving in Tel Aviv. His wish was fulfilled, and he was buried right next to his old friend, Rabbi Kook on the Mount of Olives in Jerusalem.

Rosalie's father, Abraham Arthur Spiro was a very successful doctor. The other four brothers and many of their cousins ran their family textile business. The Spiro family were so established and well known in Soho that they had a regular table at the large Folman's Restaurant in Wardour Street. Occasionally, when I was in the West End and feeling hungry, I would pop over there, and see the four brothers sitting and enjoying their lunch. If they were in a good mood, they would allow me to join them. The proprietor, old man Folman, had something of a temper, and sometimes the waiter would warn us: 'Mr Folman is having a row with the chef in the kitchen… I would go somewhere else today if I were you'.

When Rosalie and I first went to Israel, the Spiro brothers – my uncles-in-law, encouraged me to visit Rabbi Yosef Shlomo Kahaneman, head of Ponevezh Yeshiva now in Bnei Brak. He was one of the most revered religious authorities in Israel's strictly Orthodox Haredi community. My goodness, he really put the red carpet out for us with the full VIP treatment – all because Rosalie's grandfather had been such a firm supporter of the institution.

In 1986 the Spiro family held a big reunion of all the children, grandchildren and great grandchildren to mark the 100th anniversary of their ancestors' arrival in the UK in 1886. The whole affair took place in the garden of Rosalie's cousin, Leon and Tricia Goldstone, near Elstree. As many as 120 people turned up. The event was covered by the Jewish Chronicle, with an extensive article spread across five columns.

Every now and then Rosalie's cousin Robin Spiro (who sadly died in 2021) the much-loved founder and promoter, with his wife Nitza, of adult Jewish education in Britain, used to organise follow-up reunions. In 2015 he held a party on a boat on the River Thames. Despite giving just three months' notice, that event attracted about 70 people, many of whom had flown over to be there from various places around the world.

Robin and Nitza Spiro

Robin's father, Rosalie's uncle Saul Spiro, was the pillar of the London family. He became a senior warden of St John's Wood Synagogue. He had great ambitions for Robin and his sister Judy. Robin was educated at Harrow where Winston Churchill had been a pupil. He played cricket for that historic public school, against its old rival Eton College. Robin went on to play cricket for the MCC (Marylebone Cricket Club) at Lords. His sister Judy was presented at Court, in one of the last Debutantes' Balls. The family was quite special.

Robin, then went to Pembroke College Oxford to study law. While there he played cricket for his college – as I had done for mine. He was also a talented painter. He became a Chartered Accountant. He married and had a son and daughters. Later his first wife sadly died at a young age.

In the 1960s, Robin lost interest in accountancy, and became a property developer. There's a very great property project, St Christophers Place, near the Wigmore Hall which he developed at that time. With demolition looming, Robin recognised the potential of reviving its charming period shops – once home to cheesemongers, drapers, lamp manufacturers and bookmakers. True visionary that he was, Robin transformed the backwater into what is today a hub for thriving businesses and restaurants which is a delight for tourists.

When Rosalie and I were first married we lived in a flat in St John's Wood Court, the same building in which Robin was living. This is opposite

Lord's Cricket ground, next to the Liberal Synagogue. Walking to synagogue together one Sabbath morning, Robin invited me to be his partner in some of the property developments he was involved in. I said, 'I'm not a businessman, I do not know anything about property' and I declined. Now, had I had taken up the offer, who knows, I might have been living in a mansion in the Bishop's Avenue, I don't know. But I have no regrets, it just did not interest me.

When Robin met Nitza, who was his Hebrew teacher on his first trip to Israel – a passion for Jewish life and culture developed which it was clear that they shared. Nitza is a brilliant and inspiring teacher and innovator. They formed a dynamic partnership. In due course, they married and brought up a large and loving family – some of his and some of hers and some of theirs.

After a long honeymoon in India, they decided to go back to Oxford, Robin to do a degree in Jewish history and culture at the Postgraduate Centre for Hebrew and Jewish Studies under Dr David Patterson and Nitza as a teacher of Hebrew literature at Oxford University. Rosalie and I visited them in their big house just outside Oxford one Chanukah. On every one of the eight nights of Chanukah, they had a huge wild party for the kids. Not just one party, but every single night of the holiday! We happened to turn up for one night. We joined quite a riotous party. It was certainly great fun, and the kids were loving it.

During their studies, Robin and Nitza began to realise that the story of Jewish survival though the millennia is an inspirational topic, both for Jews and for non-Jews. They started to think how they could spread the story of the Jewish contribution to civilisation. They felt that this could break down many prejudices amongst the general population and help to create better understanding of Jewish people and their history.

Robin first looked at what could be done for those Jewish children, quite numerous, who were in boarding schools, or public schools, like he himself had been. They were often compelled to attend chapel and so the very people who could become the leaders in Jewish society, were almost cut off from any form of Jewish education.

He then created a curriculum for a school qualification in Modern Jewish History at a senior level. Robin taught this himself at his old school Harrow and then at Eton and other public schools – to students who were Jewish and also to those who were not. This caused quite a sensation with many organisations and individuals clamoured to take these courses outside of these schools. At this stage Nitza decided to give up her university teaching position at Oxford and to join Robin in setting up classes and courses, not only for children and schools, but also for adults.

38. Robin and Nitza Spiro.

Together they revolutionised Jewish cultural life in London. Whereas before there was mainly religious education, based at synagogues, suddenly exciting classes in Jewish history and civilisation became available at several places of learning, taught by the charismatic Spiros themselves and then by teachers that they sought out and trained. Today such things are commonplace.

They introduced hitherto unknown educational and cultural ideas such as working with the Open University, preparing with them a course of Jewish history and culture. Audio recordings and films were broadcast on the Open University programs on BBC TV and radio for some fourteen years.

During the 1980s and 90s Robin and Nitza's offerings proliferated. As well as language, history and culture classes and courses, they created ground-breaking Jewish film festivals at the National Film Theatre on the South Bank and at the Institute for Contemporary Arts in the Mall. They produced Israeli film festivals at the Everyman Cinema in Hampstead. There were after-show discussions with directors and actors.

They organised concerts introducing Jewish music and songs from all corners of the world, performed by international artists and sung in many Jewish languages: Ladino, Hebrew, Judeo-Arabic and Yiddish. These took place years before the establishment of the current Jewish and Israeli Film Festivals, and before the Bnai Brith Jewish Music Festival and Jewish Music Institute were established. The Spiros are widely recognised as having been the role models for these later activities and Institutions.

Another Spiro innovation was to establish Jewish trails and tours to cities and towns in the UK and abroad that had rich Jewish histories. They sought out the best professors, teachers and tour guides to share their knowledge.

The popularity and success of their courses and events covering history, language, philosophy, science and culture soon grew into what they called 'The Spiro Institute'. This reached its zenith in the 1990s with active programmes morning, afternoon and evening based at the prestigious premises in Kidderpore Avenue Hampstead, at the old Westfield College Campus of London University. They also presented events around the country.

Sadly – and astonishingly – in 1999 the Spiro Institute was eliminated! In a dispute with their backers, Robin and Nitza left. Their resources, their programmes, premises, and even some of the Spiro Institute teachers were scooped up and turned into the 'London Jewish Cultural Centre'.

Having received this body blow, Robin and Nitza were nevertheless determined to embark on a new project bearing their name. They set up 'The Spiro Ark' to take their vision forward and carry on their innovative programmes. The name Ark had symbolic meaning for them – both as the Holy Ark of the Covenant and for physical survival from the flood.

Looking back, the very thought that it was Robin and Nitza Spiro's pioneering efforts that had become the first 'London Jewish Cultural Centre' is something they can surely be proud of. It is nevertheless shameful, that their personal ground-breaking endeavours and hard work were simply obliterated at the time and that that Robin and Nitza were not given due credit and acclaim.

Ironically, the London Jewish Cultural Centre itself was shortly afterwards subsumed into JW3 – the Jewish Community Centre in Finchley Road, funded by the Clore Foundation that opened in 2013. What many people do not know is that in the year prior to the opening of JW3, Nitza Spiro was asked to plan a creative language and related topics department and run it with teachers that she would train and supervise. This was to be JW3's flagship programme, based on Robin and Nitza's reputation and track record.

Nitza duly prepared this programme. But yet, again this was eradicated, because the former Spiro Institute then under the changed name of the

London Jewish Cultural Centre (LJCC) refused the planned merger with JW3 if Nitza was to be running her courses there. This was yet another injustice to Nitza and Robin Spiro. The key people at JW3 were also very upset.

To redress matters, and to give Robin and Nitza Spiro the respect and recognition they deserve, the JW3 management together with the Pears Family Foundation have established an annual regular major Spiro tribute event. This has always been packed with many disappointed people on a waiting list. In the opening words of the yearly tributes, the organizers, without fail acknowledge publicly that without Robin and Nitza's groundbreaking imaginative, creative and wide ranging educational and cultural vision, JW3 would not have had the bedrock on which to establish its programmes and receive wide support.

Last time I was at JW3, as I was walking towards the restaurant, I walked past a classroom, and somebody waved to me, and it was Nitza, running a class. I feel great satisfaction that the Spiros' legacy has come full circle and will always be recognised at this flagship Jewish cultural centre in London.

Rosalie's family really made a big contribution to society.

15

Conclusions: What now, and Would I do it all over again?

My congregation of thousands – in small groups

Over almost seven decades since the late 1950s, I have ministered to huge numbers of people who identified themselves as Jewish – army conscripts, students and congregants. I meet people all the time who say, 'You looked after me the 1960s or 70s or whenever, when I was here or there.' Of course, I can't remember them all – but they remember me as someone meaningful who helped them along their Jewish journeys. What a legacy that is for me to know that I have affected the lives of thousands of people, many at a young and impressionable age.

I have to thank the British Army for making it obligatory for anyone who said they were Jewish to see the Jewish chaplain. Otherwise, for some young Jews, the connection to their Jewish heritage may have been lost forever. Some of course, rejected this intrusion – but even then, it made them think about what their Jewish roots did, or did not, mean to them.

I am very grateful to all the servicemen, scholars, and isolated groups for the warm response they gave to my overtures and interventions. Mine was certainly a much larger cumulative congregation – and a vastly more diverse one than most, if not all other rabbis get to minister to. The many thousands of people in the groups around the country that I visited, saw me not just as a minister but as a teacher, a mentor, and above all as a friend. They knew that they could call on me for advice and support whenever they needed to. I would try to visit each place as many times as possible, sometimes eight or ten times a year, to maintain the continuity.

My role with the leaders of such groups, was to be their consistent and available lifeline and support. I strove to give them confidence in the Jewish travels they were undertaking and to equip them better for the responsibilities they took upon themselves for their communities. I would try to help them and their families and colleagues to lead a meaningful Jewish life.

What is the position now?
Students on Campus

In the early 1960s I was the first and only Jewish chaplain in British universities. I was employed by the Hillel Foundation to look after the dozen new universities that had sprung up around the country.

Through my visits, Hillel and the community in general, realised just how much support Jewish students needed on campus, and the issues of antisemitism and anti-Zionism they were facing. I was pleased to be at the heart of the development of not only Jewish chaplaincy but also of multi-faith chaplaincy centres, such as the one at Lancaster University, that I helped create. It was opened by the Queen in 1969 and has since been emulated in other new and also at older universities.

At these places of further education, I found small groups of young people from varied Jewish backgrounds thrown together because they had chosen a particular course at a particular location. Some of the students I met had never been inside a synagogue nor had they had any Jewish education, but they wanted to be involved.

The common denominator (as with all my work) is that many of these students are on the fringe of the Jewish community. I started by organising *Shabbat* events, helping to access kosher provisions and increasing the collaboration between these students and any existing Jewish societies. I found to my joy that there was a great demand from students for my time.

They really appreciated it when I ran a weekend programme for them, for instance like the one I did at Canterbury. This included a service at the old Canterbury Synagogue in the shadow of the city's famous cathedral – the first service to be held in the shul since it closed in 1931. Around twenty-five students participated, including a number from Gibraltar who had not previously attended Jewish events on campus. Some of the students subsequently joined the JSoc after two years of not taking part in any Jewish life at the university.

I did similar weekends around the country. At Lancaster University we attracted around thirty Jewish students to our services and other events. We were joined by members of Jewish communities in the Lake District as well as Muslim students from the campus. These kinds of events are an excellent way to promote interfaith relations on the campus, and also enhance connections between students and local Jews.

I have always advocated that more was needed to help students and that more people were required in the field to help. Successive Chief Rabbis have realised how important it is to support Jewish students on campus. Starting with Immanuel Jakobovits and particularly developed by Jonathan Sacks, there is now a properly constituted, managed and funded university chaplaincy organisation looking after the spiritual welfare of students in the UK. It operates from the Chief Rabbi's office and has properly trained and salaried rabbis and rabbinic couples (a rabbi and his wife also trained to inspire young people) working in twelve regions, serving nearly all universities in Britain. I rest assured that the Jewish spiritual needs of students are now properly cared for on campus.

The Army

39. This picture was taken at our Army Chiefs of Chaplains Conference, with a slightly more diverse set of chaplains.

What started out as three years of National Service as a Chaplain to the RAF became a life-long mission to all military services in this country and further afield. When I started, Judaism was the only other religion recognised by the British Army after the Church of England and

Catholicism. The fact that all servicemen who said they were Jewish had to see the Jewish Chaplain – provided another great opportunity to influence young people's Jewish feelings.

I lived to see and helped to expand this service in the military into Multifaith Chaplaincy Centres. Today there are chaplains for many of the faiths, in keeping with the changes in the demography of Britain.

I still rejoice in the long title of 'Life President of the Allied Air Forces Chiefs of Chaplains Consultative Committee', having served as the Secretary-General of that committee from 1993. I am also a Senior Chaplain on the NATO Armed Forces Chaplaincy Committee. In this capacity I am invited to attend NATO weekend chaplaincy conferences in different cities in the world. I enjoy meeting my international colleagues and I am moved by how well I am treated. The organisers used to go to great lengths to ensure that Rosalie and I could properly observe the Sabbath and that the food served was kosher.

Small communities

Provision for small communities is far more complex. Many of the groups I tended to would not have existed or would have folded by now if I had not been ready to call on them to have coffee and a chat to see what could be done to keep them together. Very often when I would visit a community over the Sabbath they would happily gather together from far and wide. We would get a good number of people for a service on the Friday night and again on the Saturday morning. However, even when I had trained members to run the services themselves, if I was not there, they sometimes did not get so many attendees and maybe did not even try to run a service. I have to recognise that there was something about my presence that made a difference.

I have enjoyed the firm backing and support of a succession of Chief Rabbis, starting with Israel Brodie (Chief Rabbi from 1948 to 1965) who originally appointed me his 'Chief Rabbi's Minister for Small Communities' and set me off on this journey. I had offered to do this, as I had noticed that nobody else was looking after these people.

Brodie was followed by Immanuel Jakobovits (1966 to 1991) whom I was able to introduce to many of my communities. I had a particularly warm relationship with the next Chief Rabbi, Jonathan Sacks (1991 to 2013). The current Chief, Ephraim Mirvis is also a great friend and supporter. The United Synagogue too is very supportive nowadays, and they do realise that country communities are not the same as city ones. Yet they have never seemed to have found suitable ways to help small communities.

It was perhaps fortuitous for all these people in faraway places that I was interested in them and able to undertake this task. It was fortunate that it fitted in so well along with my other commitments. I am glad to say that this work has also given me great personal satisfaction throughout my life.

Dealing with small communities is a finely tuned and specialist job needing flexibility, nurturing, and psychology. It is not just about sending a minster to run a service or providing sufficient prayer books. My 'training' for dealing with small groups of Jews of differing backgrounds, or none, was being a chaplain in the military and similarly being university chaplain to groups of Jewish students thrown together at a particular university. In these situations, my first task would be to find out what their Jewish connections and knowledge were. I would ask them to raise their hand if they had been inside a synagogue before – sometimes nobody would have. Then I would ask if they could read Hebrew – maybe one could. I was not judgemental. I tried to provide what they felt they could handle, some readings, a discussion, or a talk on a Jewish subject. Once we had developed into a group of people who liked being together as Jews, and who seemed to enjoy my company, we could build on this to engage in more ambitious activities.

Over the years there have been several attempts by the mainstream to take the small Jewish communities seriously. Sir Jonathan Sacks (at the time – later Lord) the penultimate of the Chief Rabbis under whom I served, tried to put a few more people and services in place to look after country communities. For instance, in 2008 instead of my just being the 'lone' Chief Rabbi's Minister for Small Communities, Sacks created a more substantial 'Office' for Small Jewish Communities' (OSC) and appointed a director. The first in this role was Mr Elkan Levy, a historian and past president of the United Synagogue who dealt with some of the day-to-day activities and shared some of the duties with me for a while, before going to live in Israel.

In 2008, Chief Rabbi Sacks honoured me with a special reception at his residence in Hamilton Terrace, where I was officially named the 'Emeritus Minister for Small Communities'. But I told them there and then that I had no intention of hanging up my keys, as long as communities still valued my attention.

The Jewish Chronicle reported on the 2008 event saying that 'A crowd of over fifty well-wishers travelled from as far afield as Norwich and Aberdeen to the London home of the Chief Rabbi to celebrate Reverend Malcolm Weisman becoming emeritus minister for small communities. Sir

Jonathan Sacks paid tribute to Rev Weisman's years of service since the inception of the idea of a Minister for Small Communities in the 1960s. He said, "Malcolm Weisman is a deeply respected and loved figure in Anglo Jewry, because he cares for everyone. No community is too small and no distance too great." In his response, Rev Weisman noted that he expects to continue to rack up the miles but is also considering writing his memoirs.'

By 2013, while I continued my activity as strongly as ever, the Office for Small Communities (OSC) was in trouble. Elkan Levy had left for Israel and Rabbi Reuben Livingstone, the subsequent director from 2012, was struggling. Funding from the Jewish Memorial Council had ceased, and the main community funding body the United Jewish an Israel Appeal (UJIA) became responsible, but it seemed that it was reluctant to provide what was required. Rabbi Livingstone reported that he was dealing with 46 Jewish 'clusters' around the country, ranging from barely a dozen to 80 families, amounting to around 3,000 Jews in all and he begged for a solution.

At that stage the Board of Deputies was preparing to launch a new cross communal scheme called the 'Community Partnership Project' to help the country's smallest communities. The Board's senior vice-president, Laura Marks, said it would cover communities 'that might have just a handful of members, as well as ones that are affiliated to the Board, some of which are growing and some of which are shrinking. The initiative would be about bringing the richness and resources of British Jewry to small communities, which contribute to the diversity of the Jewish community'. Good intentions maybe, but sadly, this never came to fruition.

The Jewish Small Communities Network

I am pleased to know that today there actually is some excellent support for small communities in isolated places. This is not a mainstream effort, but an initiative by another insightful individual who has recognised the needs of small communities and who has the motivation and time to provide support to them. That man is Mr Ed Horwich, and his initiative is called the 'Jewish Small Communities Network' (JSCN).

Ed's journey towards dealing with small communities has been different to mine, but his aims are very similar. He started his Small Communities Network voyage in 2003 when he was trying to support his own community in Southport on the Lancashire seaside. Many other small communities asked to join and thus his initiative has mushroomed. I am delighted to know that he now keeps in touch with nearly a hundred communities and congregations in seventy-two towns. His work for small communities has become his full-time, dedicated occupation.

With new technology, Ed has created a wonderful website with ideas and resources and the details of each of the communities. He keeps the leaders and members in isolated places connected with stimulating, and informative newsletters. Ed also creates meetings over the internet for their leadership and sets up talks and events for members. This is a great boon when distances between them are so great.

Not being a minister, Ed does not personally conduct synagogue services, like I did, but he works with rabbis and cultural organisations of all Jewish denominations to help enrich Jewish life, spiritually, socially and culturally.

Ed also arranges regional events, as I did in my 'Quests' where communities can physically meet each other and share ideas and projects making them feel less isolated. He too, as I did, deals with people across the whole spectrum of Jewish life and worship, as is necessary in dealing with small groups. It shows that it takes a dedicated, perhaps a maverick, individual to succeed in this role.

I was very pleased that Ed came to visit me at my home in August 22 He invited me to record a message for him to the small communities that Ed was going to broadcast alongside a message from the Chief Rabbi at his annual 'One *Shabbat*' event in September, where all smaller communities

40. Ed Horwich visiting me in August 2022

connect virtually as well as being stimulated to do their own thing in their individual communities.

I was very touched when Ed told me that:

Over the years, time and again someone would ask me 'Do you know Malcolm Weisman? Have you taken over from him?' As I speak with community leaders it is evident that you are dearly loved and held in great esteem by all those communities that you visited, not just once but time and again over the decades. Indeed, just before we were locked down in the pandemic I visited the Isle of Wight, and a couple of weeks later, you were there too!

You have made a difference, a big difference. Whether it was just turning up, or whether it was running a service or actually helping to build a synagogue. And let me tell you, all are equally important.

We both care, and we are both driven by an invisible force that won't let us stop. Your legacy is in the hearts of people you touched, and in the souls of communities you helped to build. The most powerful tribute is the simplest... Kol Hakavod.

I am grateful to Ed, for these kind words. I in turn am very pleased to know that Ed has created strong relationships and is doing such good work with nearly every small Jewish community. It gives me peace of mind to know that the communities that I nurtured and looked after for so long, and still do, now also have Ed's excellent and robust help. He believes, as I do, that through supporting local leadership, a rich Jewish life can be sustained around the country, for as long as communities wish to continue.

And what about me?

In my time I have conducted countless marriages, baby blessings, bar and batmitzvot, prayed and mourned with numerous families far and wide. These days I am more likely to be called to funerals, and I am asked to officiate at many tombstone settings. Families seem to want my presence because I am the person who knew the deceased and their family and worked with them throughout most of their lives. I am happy to fulfil their wishes for as long as I am able, as these are people whom I have known and loved for most of my life.

Even though I gained the title of 'Emeritus' in 2008, I said that I would carry on even if I had to pay my way myself. People may question my resolve, but I remain at the end of the telephone for all these people, and when they call, I like to help them if I can. I reckon that in 2012 alone, I travelled about 25,000 miles on visits. I find great satisfaction in bringing people to a greater appreciation of the value of their Jewish heritage. It's very much part of my life and I am not ready to stop.

I am immensely grateful to my late wife Rosalie and our sons Brian and Daniel who stoically bore the fact that several times a week I would be out until way after midnight. With their strong support and encouragement, I was able to hop into my car after the court hearings ended at 4.00pm and be off to Bangor or Bognor, Cheltenham or Chatham. If I was going as far as Lancaster, I would leave at about 11.00am get there by 4.00pm to meet the community leaders, run a service at the University, give them a talk and turn round and drive home the same evening. This would be a five-hundred-mile round trip, but I thought nothing of it.

The two years of lockdowns in 2020 and 2021 have prevented me from going anywhere. This has been very frustrating to me. I was still able to communicate with communities far and wide by telephone. In 2022, I was still regularly receiving invitations from my 'congregants' to come to spend a *Shabbat* with them or to minister to them for the High Holydays. I am still in continuing touch with about sixty communities around the world.

The Jersey Community the Jersey Community wants me to come back there again for Rosh Hashanah and Yom Kippur. Before the Covid-19 pandemic struck, Rosalie and I used to go to Jersey each year. We would arrive a few days before the High Holydays began and stay there for several weeks until after the festival of *Simchat Torah*. Often our sons Brian and Daniel would join us there. The community always gave us a warm welcome and made the charming flat above the synagogue in St Brelade available to us. The weather could be quite lovely there in September and October.

I also had a call from Hastings to ask that if I decide not to go to Jersey this year, would I come to Hastings to celebrate the High Holydays with the small community there. In fact, Aberdeen is also after me, as is Eastbourne. I even have an invitation to go to Christchurch in New Zealand and also the Cayman Islands. I will have to see what the transport possibilities are. At the moment trains and aeroplanes are in chaos with lack of staff and strikes – and Covid-19, although it has become a milder infection, is still rampant.

I prefer of course to drive, but both my previous cars are out of action. Just recently a friend from a village near Oxford called me up and offered to help me to buy a new car. My garage is sending me a catalogue. However, my children do not want me, at the age of 92, to drive anymore, and that is another problem. I feel perfectly capable of driving.

I am a still a vice president, or trustee, patron, or an ambassador of many organisations from NATO to the Commonwealth Jewish Council and the Faith and Belief Forum and the Jewish Music Institute. I receive many calls with invitations to meetings and functions that I really would like to attend.

During the 64 years of our happy marriage, Rosalie and I and our sons Brian and Daniel, had many enjoyable and interesting meetings with leaders of communities and heads of states. Together we enjoyed many uniquely special functions all over the United Kingdom and in many other parts of the world, because of my connections and associations in the military the law and the ministry.

My long life in all its dimensions has been exceptional, quite unlike that of any other person I know. If I were to have the chance to have my life over again – I would not change a thing.

Glossary

Hebrew (H)
Yiddish (Y)
Aramaic (A)
German (G)
Russian (R)
Ashkenazi pronunciation of Hebrew marked by (Ashk.)
Asterisk denotes reference to another word in the glossary

Adath Yisrael (H)	Assembly of Israel (Adas Yisroel, Ashk.); name of Orthodox congregation
Adon Olam (H)	Master of the Universe, hymn sung at *Shacharit
Alef Bet (H)	Hebrew alphabet, synonym for studying Hebrew; (alefbeis, Ashk.)
Aliyah (H)	lit. ascent; a call-up to the *bimah; also, immigration to Israel
Aron Kodesh (H)	holy ark holding *Sifrei Torah in synagogue
Ashkenazi (H)	Jews of central and eastern European origin
Aufruf (Y, G)	call-up to the *bimah; also means a pre-wedding *Shabbat service
Baal Chesed (H)	a righteous man
Baal Teshuvah (H)	a Jew who returns to faith; see *Teshuvah
Baba Metzia (A)	tractate from *Talmud meaning The Middle Gate
Bar Mitzvah (H, A)	ceremony for Jewish boy at 13 marking confirmation into the community
Bat Chayil (H)	ceremony for girls at 12, similr to *bat mitzvah
Bat Mitzvah (H)	female equivalent of *bar mitzvah
Beit Hamidrash (H)	prayer hall attached to larger *synagogue (Beis Hamedrish, Ashk.)
Benching (Y)	prayers after a meal (birkat ha-mazon in Hebrew); from Latin benedicere

Bet Din (H)	Jewish rabbinical court (Beis Din, Ashk.)
Bimah (H)	platform or lectern in synagogue where Jews read the *Sifrei Torah
Blitz (G)	German bombing raids on Britain in World War II
Bnai Brith (H)	an internatioanl Jewish service organisation, est. 1843
Bnei Akiva (H)	lit. Sons of [Rabbi] Akiva; religious Zionist Jewish youth group
Brachot (H)	blessings; bracha (sing.) or brocha/us (Ashk.)
Brit (H)	short for Brit Milah, covenant of circumcision; britot (pl.); bris (Ashk.)
Broiges (Y)	a fierce and apparently insoluble quarrel, usually within a family
Chabad (H)	acronym for 'wisdom, understanding, knowledge' [see *Lubavitch]
Challah (H)	special plaited bread eaten on *Shabbat; challot, pl.; chollah (Ashk.)
Chatunah (H)	Jewish wedding; also hatunah or chaseneh (Ashk.)
Chazan (H)	synagogue cantor
Cheder (H)	Jewish and Hebrew classes for younger children; also Heder,
Chevra Kadishah (H)	voluntary Jewish burial society
Chevra Tiferes Bachurim (H)	(lit) splendid fellowship of young men
Chol HaMoed (H)	intermediate days of *Passover
Cholent (Y)	slow-cooked meal served on *Shabbat
Chumash (H)	Five Books of Moses – first books of Hebrew Bible, Old Testament, *Torah
Chupah (H)	canopy under which a Jewish wedding is solemnised
Chutzpah (H, Y)	barefaced cheek, uncalled for candour, or bold initiative
Dati (H)	religiously observant – from Persian/ Aramaic for law
Daven (Y)	to pray; derived from Latin
Dayan (H)	Jewish religious judge; see *Bet Din
Drasha (H)	sermon, lesson or homily, usually by rabbi; drosha (Ashk.)

Etz Chayim (H)	Tree of life; name of a British *Yeshiva
Galut (H)	Diaspora; golus (Ashk.)
Gemara (A)	commentary on *Mishna; part of *Talmud
Haftorah (H)	second reading on Sabbaths, festivals, from prophets or writings
Halacha (H)	traditional Jewish rabbinical law – lit. the way or path; see also *Talmud
Halachic (H derived)	conforming to *Halacha
Hamantaschen (Y)	sweetmeats eaten on *Purim, meaning Haman's pockets
Hanukkah (H)	festival of lights marking Jews' defeat of Greco-Syrians (also Chanuka)
Haredi (H)	a strictly Orthodox Jew – see *Hasidism and *Mitnagedim - also chareidi
Hasidic, Hasidism (H)	spiritual revival movement of Orthodox Jews, starting in 18th century Poland
Hasidim (H)	plural for hasid– see * Hasidic (also Chasidim)
Haskalah (H)	Jewish enlightenment movement, esp. in 19th century; member is maskil
Heimische (Y)	Homely or comfortingly traditional atmosphere
Hora (H)	lively circle dance at a *simcha; Balkan, Greek, Turkish origin
Kabbalah (H)	Jewish mystical tradition
Kabbalat Shabbat (H)	small ceremony to welcome the *Shabbat as a "queen"
Kaddish (A)	traditional Jewish prayer for the dead, derived from H/ A for holy
Kashrut (H)	the practice or state of keeping *Kosher
Kahal (H)	a Jewish community, congregation; also kehillah, kohel (Ashk.)
Ketubah (A)	Jewish marriage document, often ornamental, written in Aramaic
Kfar Hanoar Hadati (H)	lit. religious youth village
Kibitzer (Y)	a gossip, nag or complainer
Kiddush (H, Y)	benediction over wine and bread, or communal meal after *Shabbat service
Kindertransport (G)	programme that brought Jewish child refugees to Britain from Nazi Germany
Kippah (H)	Jewish religious skullcap; kippot (pl.) – also called yarmulka

Klup (Y)	to hit someone
Kosher (H)	lit. clean (adj.) – meaning food that is acceptable according to *Halacha
Kristallnacht (G)	Night of Broken Glass – Nazi rampage against Jews, 8 November 1938
Landsleit (Y)	Jews from the same village or town in eastern Europe
Levaya (H)	Jewish funeral; also levoya (Ashk.)
Leyen (Y)	public chanting from the *Sifrei Torah* also leyening
Litvak (Y)	Jews of Lithuanian origin; also refers to anti-Hasidic Orthodox
Lubavitch (R)	large *Hasidic sect known for its Jewish outreach; equiv. to *Chabad
Machzor (H)	prayer book for *Yamim Nora'im, *Pesach, *Shavuot and *Sukkot
Ma'ariv (H)	lit. evening; meaning synagogue service at that time
Magen David (H)	shield (or star) of King David; symbol of Judaism; also Mogen Dovid (Ashk.)
Malbim (H)	Acronym for Rabbi Meir Leibush Wisser (1809-1879) and his writings
Maoz Tzur (H)	traditional *Hanukkah song meaning Rock of Strength or Rock of Ages
Maskil (H)	a member or follower of *Haskalah
Masorti (H)	lit. traditional; meaning a congregation between Orthodox and Reform
Matza (H)	special flat bread eaten over *Pesach
Matzeiva (H)	Stone-setting ceremony to mark Jewish grave within year of burial
Mazel Tov (H, Y)	congratulations, from Hebrew mazal, or luck
Mechitza (H)	A barrier to separate male from female worshipers in Orthodox synagogue
Megillah (H, Y)	lit. a tale, usually Megillat Esther, Book of Esther, read on *Purim
Mensch (Y)	lit. man; used as meaning reliable, upstanding person
Mezuza (H)	capsule containing *Shema placed on Jewish home's front door lintel

Glossary

Mikvah (H)	Ritual bath for Orthodox and women (also mikveh)
Midrash (H)	homilies behind the Bible stories; or moral lesson by a rabbi
Mincha (H)	afternoon synagogue service
Minhag (H)	a local Jewish custom or tradition
Minhag Anglia (H)	Anglo-Jewish style, law or mode of service
Minyan (H)	quorum of ten needed for reading of the *Torah
Mishna (H)	lit. study by repetition; opening section of *Talmud
Mitnagedim (H)	Orthodox opponents of *Hasidim (Misnagdim, Ashk.)
Mitzvah (H)	lit. commandment or law; also a good deed or honour; see *Bar Mitzvah
Mizrachi (H)	Jews of Middle East and North Africa origin; see also *Sephardi
Musaf (H)	Additional service for Jewish holidays
Ne'ilah (H)	concluding service for *Yom Kippur
Ner Tamid (H)	eternal light in synagogue
Nosh (Y)	food; in UK slang, a nosh-up is an impromptu feast
Parsha (H)	*Torah 'portion' read on *Shabbat, festivals; see *Chumash
Pereneh (Y)	eiderdown quilt that east European Jewish immigrants brought to Britain
Pesach (H)	Passover, festival about Israelites leaving Egypt and freedom from slavery
Peyyot (H)	sidelocks worn by some religious Jews; also peyyes (Ashk.)
Pogrom (R)	armed attack on Jews
Purim (H)	Joyous festival set in ancient Persia with reading from *Megillah of Esther
Purimspiel (Y)	community play using *Purim festival to satirise local issues
Rashi (H)	Acronym for Rabbi Shlomo Yitzhaki, noted medieval Talmudist
Reb (H)	honorific title for Mr
Rebbe (Y)	honorific title applied to a *Hasidic rabbi
Rosh Hashana (H)	lit. head of the year – Jewish New Year; see *Yamim Nora'im

Seder (H)	ritual meal and service at home marking festival of *Pesach
Sedra (H)	portion read from Torah; also sidra; see also *Parsha and *Haftorah
Sefer Torah (H)	scroll of the *Torah; in plural, *Sifrei Torah
Sephardi (H)	a Jew of Spanish or Portuguese origin; more broadly, Middle East Jews
Shabbat (H)	Sabbath – day of rest, Friday sunset to Saturday sunset (Shabbes, Ashk.)
Shabbos (Y)	See *Shabbat
Shacharit (H)	morning synagogue service (Shacharis, Ashk.)
Shas (H)	acronym for shishei sidre Mishna – six books of the *Mishna
Shavuot (H)	Festival of Weeks – giving of the Torah (Shavuos, Ashk.)
Shema, (the) (H)	lit. "hear [O Israel]"; basic affirmation of Jewish faith; fuller, Shema Yisrael
Shir (H)	singing, a song
Shiur (H)	lesson about *Torah portion of the week (shiurim, pl.)
Shoah (H)	Hebrew term for Holocaust, mass murder of Jews in World War II
Shochet (H)	ritual slaughterer – see *kosher
Shofar (H)	ram's horn blown on *Rosh Hashana
Shtetl (Y)	small village with Jewish population in old eastern Europe; plural shtetlach
Shtiebl (Y)	room in private home used as synagogue by Orthodox Jews
Shul (Y)	lit. school; invariably used for synagogue by *Ashkenazim
Sifrei Torah (H)	plural of *sefer torah
Simcha (H)	A happy occasion, a party, usually religious, a wedding
Smicha (H)	rabbinical ordination
Sukkah (H)	tabernacle, wooden booth with vegetative decoration for *Sukkot
Sukkot (H)	Festival of Tabernacles; sometimes Sukkos (Ashk.)
Tallit (H)	Jewish prayer shawl (tallis, Ashk.)

Talmud (H)	vast corpus of post-Biblical rabbinical writings and rulings; see *Shas
Talmid Chacham (H)	great Torah and Talmud scholar
Teshuvah (H)	lit. return, answer; used to mean religious repentance; see *Baal Teshuvah
Torah (H)	five books of Moses (*Chumash); more broadly, Hebrew Bible, Jewish law
Torah im derech Eretz (H)	*Torah in the way of the land – combining religious study and work
Tsitsit (H)	sacred tassels worn by men under shirt or at corners of *Tallit
Tzadik (H)	Lit. righteous person, usually refers to a charismatic Hassidic rabbis
Unsere Yidden (Y)	lit. our Jews; meaning "one of use"
Yahrzeit (Y)	commemoration of a loved one year after their death
Yamim Nora'im (H)	High Holy Days, meaning chiefly *Rosh Hashana and *Yom Kippur
Yarmulka (Y)	see *Kippah
Yekke (Y)	slang for Jews of German origin; metaphor for punctiliousness
Yeshiva (H)	rabbinical academy, equivalent to seminary or madrasa; yeshivot (pl.)
Yiddish (Y)	secular language based on German once spoken by *Ashkenazim
Yom Kippur (H)	Day of Atonement; see *Yamim Nora'im

Index

Entries in bold denote sub-headings and main references
Entries in italics denote images

Aberdeen, Scotland **151-53**, 26, 87, 91, 129, 201, 217, 221
Abrams, Prof Nathan 147
Adath Israel Synagogue (also Adas Yisroel Synagogue) **13-15**, 9, 16, 17, 204, 223
Aden, Yemen **179-181**, 39, 40, 42, 108,
Adjudicator, Parliamentary Boundaries Commission 50, 57-58
Adler, Chief Rabbi Nathan 83, 84, 100,
Adler, Dr Herman 14, 22, 84, 149
Adler, Israel 196
Adler, John 156
Alconbury, USAF base 130, 154, 155
Alderney, Channel Island 160
Alyth Choral Society, London 68, 78
Amport House 40, 206
Amsterdam, the Netherlands 40, 78
Andover, RAF base 40
Antwerp, Belgium 5
Arkush, Jonathan 95
Aronson, John 147
Ashkenazi Jews 149, 172, 108, 141, 149, 172, 180, 187, 196, 207, 223, 228, 229
Auerbach, Geraldine xii, 14, 67, 195, 197,
Auschwitz concentration camp 5, 75, 160, 198
Austria 15, 40, 41, 65, 72, 76, 84, 104, 200,
Baal Shem Tov 4
Badawi, Sheikh Zaki 77
Baghdadi Jews 182, 183, 184
Ball, Rev Anthony 201
Bangkok, Thailand 187-8
Bangor, North Wales **146-7**, 149, 221
Barschak, Fred 23

Bath, Somerset **118-9**, 140, 157
BBC (British Broadcasting Corporation) 5, 142-3, 199, 210
Belfast, Northern Ireland 72, 151, 207
Belgium 5, 35, 40, 44
Beloff, Michael 86
Belsize Square Synagogue, London 200-1
Ben Avraham, Dov Ber 3
Bendish, Rabbi 13
Bene Israel Community, Pakistan 181
Bergen-Belsen concentration camp 38
Bergerac (television series) 164
Berkman, Cantor Louis 68
Berlin, Germany 120
Berlin, Sir Isaiah 27
Berlinski, Herman 69
Berman, Karel 199
Beth Din 45, 46, 99, 224
Bethnal Green, London 10, 48
Bevis Marks Synagogue, London 2, 92, 170,
Bexhill, East Sussex 143, 144
Biala, Hassidic dynasty 3, 4, 5
Blackpool, Lancashire 140, 141
Bleehen, Prof Norman Montague 120
Bloch, Dr David 198, 199
Bloch, Ernest 68, 195
Blood Libel 66, 103, 106
Bloom, Doris and Anita 160, 161-2
Bnai Brith (organisation) 14, 17, 67, 197, 198, 211, 224
Bnei Akiva, youth movement 26, 92, 224
Bnei Brak, Israel 207
Bnei Yaakov Club 18

Index

Board of Deputies of British Jews 35, 50, 68, 95, 164, 170, 173, 207, 218,
Bognor Regis, West Sussex **141-2**, 60, 86, 88, 144, 221
Bonaparte, Napoleon 170
Bonington, Sir Chris 192, 193
Boothroyd, Betty 173
Borehamwood, Greater London 95
Borowski, Ephraim 152
Boston, Terry (later Lord Boston of Faversham) 52, 55
Bournemouth, Dorset 62, 85, 91, 94, 144
Braybrooke, Rev Marcus 73, 77, 198. 199,
Brent, Leslie 201
Bridgenorth, RAF base 17
Brighton, Sussex 91, 142, 145
Bristol, Avon 155, 156, 157, 102, 119, 139
British Army of the Rhine (BAOR) 44
British Forces Germany (BFG) 44
British Union of Fascists 71
Brittan, Leon 7
Broadbent, Christopher Bowers 200
Brodie, Chief Rabbi Sir Israel 13, 34, 35, 60, 80, 86, 216
Brondesbury Park, Willesden, London 178, 204
Brookes, Rev Reuben 37
Brotman, Honor 50
Brunel, Isambard Kingdom 121
Buckingham Palace, London 191, 193, 194
Calcutta, India 182
Cambridge, England **119-20**, 60, 118, 202, 205,
Camissar, Cantor Ian 68
Canada 44, 152, 173
Canterbury, Kent **197-99**, 11, 29, 74, 75, 79, 97, 143, 157, 214
Caplan, Rev Herschel 41
Cardiff, Wales 149, 182
Cardington, RAF base 37
Carey, Dr George, Archbishop of Canterbury 75
Carfax Tower, Oxford 26
Carlebach, Rabbi Shlomo 156
Carmel College 156, 187
Cass, Ronald 78

Cemeteries 27, 82, 103, 107, 122, 130, 132, 150, 159, 163, 168, 182
Ceylon (see Sri Lanka) 39
Chabad 4, 172, 224, 226
Changi, RAF base, Singapore 185
Channel Islands **160**, 87, 91, 126, 159, 164
Chanukah, Jewish festival 61, 101, 124, 126, 136, 142, 143, 144, 145, 172, 209, 225
Charles, Prince of Wales (see King Charles III) 193, *195*
Chatham Memorial Synagogue *122,* 157
Chatham, Kent **120-1**, 118, 157, 221,
Chelmsford, Essex **123-4**, 11, 88, 118, 125, 151,
Cheltenham, Gloucestershire **106-12**, 11, 24, 78, 84,92, 96, 97, *107*, 139, 157, 221,
Chesed-El Synagogue, Singapore 183, 183, 184, 186
Cholent Society, Oxford 22
Christian Council for Refugees 73
Church House, Kyrenia, Cyprus 175
Church of England, Anglican 2, 73, 115, 108, 190, 199, 215
Churchill, Winston 33, 71, 208
City of London 55, 60, 67, 196, 204
Cliffords Tower, York **66-70**, *67*
Clinton-Davis, Baron Stanley **57**, 10
Clissold Park, London 1, *1*, 2, 8, 9
Clore Foundation 211
Coggan, Donald, Archbishop of Canterbury **4**
Cohen, David vi
Cohen, Frederick 160
Cohen, Rabbi Benjamin 164
Cohen, Rabbi Cliff 122
Cohen, Sebag 160, 162, 163, 164
Colchester, Essex **124-7**, 118, 123
Commonwealth Jewish Council (CJC) **172-4**, 192, 222
Conservative Party, UK 7, 55, 191
Copenhagen, Denmark 191
Cornwall, English county 61, 97, 98, 126, 127
Cotswolds, English region 106, 205

Council of Christians and Jews (CCJ) **72-4**, 29, 67, 76, 77, 78, 79, 130, 134, 151, 152, 191, 192, 186, 197, 198, 199, 201
Covid-19 pandemic 81, 95, 102, 142, 143, 162, 221
Crest, Gerry and Sharon (Worthing) 145
Cricket 18, 19, 20, 32, 49, 177, 208-9,
Cricklewood Synagogue, London 206
Cromwell, Oliver 70, 99, 103
Crown Court 3, 52, 56, 60
Crusades 65, 68, 74, 96
Cyprus **175-7**, 35, 39, 41, 91, 179
Czech Republic (also Czechoslovakia) 43, 72, 84, 116, 198
Dakar (Israeli submarine) 41
Dalston Synagogue, London **13-15**, 18, 143
Daniels, Rabbi Mark 110. 112
Darlington, County Durham 141
Dartmoor, Devon 61, 101
Davis, Rev Moshe **38**, 35, 39
Denham, Buckinghamshire 62
Denmark 191
Devon, English county **97-8**, 9, 60-1, 63, 101, 102
Disraeli, Benjamin 2, 92
Dobson, Prof Christopher 120
Dorset, English county 98, 144
Dov Ber of Mezrich 3, 4
Drake, Sir Francis 99
Duke of Edinburgh (see Prince Philip)
Duke of Wellington 106
Dundee, Scotland 151
Dunston, John 29, 31
East Anglia, English county 86, 104, 129, 157
East Grinstead, West Sussex 100, 144, 157
Eastbourne, East Sussex **142-4**, xi, 221
Eder, Robert 171
Edinburgh, Scotland 6-7, 8, 10, 18, 72, 81, 151
Einstein, Albert 27, 184
El-Adem, British base, Libya 177, 178
Elstree, Hertfordshire 95, 208
Etz Chayyim Yeshiva, East End, London 13, 225
Exeter, Devon **97-102**, 90, 91, 96, 100, 140, 157

Faith and Belief Forum **76-7**, 222
Farnham, Surrey 46
Federation of Synagogues 156
Fidler, Brian 30
Fleming, Sir Lancelot 42
Folman's Restaurant, Soho 207
Football 19
Ford Prison, Eltham 61
Fox, Hilary 40
France 35, 40, 44, 66, 85, 159, 170
Frank, Fiona 119, 219
Franks, Raymond 128
French Indochina 187
Friedlander, Rabbi Albert 198
Fynsk, Chris 152
Gaddafi, Muamar 178
Gateshead, Tyne and Wear 85, 158
Gerber, Leonard 6, 51
Germany **35, 39**, 15, 38, 44, 72, 73, 76, 84, 91, 99, 100, 120, 159, 160, 170, 175, 176, 178, 189, 192-3, 200, 225
Gibraltar 40, 58, 126, 170, 214
Gifford, David 29
Gilbert, Martin 200
Ginsburg, Rev Alec 35, 39
Glasgow, Scotland 118, 133, 153, 156
Glass, Marcus Kenneth 136
Gloucester, Gloucestershire **78**, 97, 106
Goldberg, Rabbi Alex 117, 175
Goldstone, Leon 208
Gordon, Ian and Barbara 145
Gorsky, Rev Jonathan 155
Gottesman, John (Colchester) 125-6
Gray's Inn Square (Malcolm's Chambers) 50, 52, *52*, 55
Great Synagogue, Dukes Place, London 14
Green, Bea 201
Greener 135
Grimsby, North East Lincolnshire **81-84**, 95, *83, 94*
Gruneberg family, Yatesbury 138-9
Gryn, Rabbi Hugo 199
Guernsey, Channel Island 160
Guildford, Surrey 96, 97, 104, 112
Guildhall, London **112-17**, 95, 96, 104, *113, 115*, 140, 157
Guttmann, Prof Sir Ludwig 131

Index

Hackney Central, east London constituency 57
Hackney Downs School 10, 11
Hackney, London Borough of 2, 180-81
HaKohein, Rav Dov Ber 169, 169, 171-2
Hall, Very Rev John 200-1
Hampstead, London 210, 211
Hanley, Staffordshire 132, 133
Hardman, Rev Leslie 38, 161-2
Harman, Jack 42
Harrogate, North Yorkshire 7-8, 9, 21, 84, 157
Harvey, Barry 40
Hassidim 2, 3, 4, 5, 225, 229
Hast, Rev Marcus (cantor) 14
Hastings, East Sussex 86, 88, 143, 144, 157, 221
Hebrew University, Jerusalem 184
Heilbron, Dame Rose 52
Hendon. London 16, 155, 156, 161
Henig, Prof Stanley 127
Her Majesty's Armed Forces (HMAF) 2, 27, 42
Her Majesty's Forces Jewish Community 27, 42
Hertz, Chief Rabbi Joseph Herman 17, 74
Herzl, Theodore 183
Hess, Rudolf 120
Hill, Canon Christopher 195, 197
Hill, John 196
Hillel Foundation, Hillel House vi, 86-7, 88, 189, 214
Hinsley, Arthur (Roman Catholic Cardinal) 74
Hitler, Adolf 71, 73
HMS Dryad, Royal Navy vessel 41
Hoffbrand family 23
Holland 40, 99
Holocaust Memorial Day services **28**, 24, 111, 124,
Holocaust Memorial Trust 173
Hong Kong 39, 40, 152
House of Lords 31, 55, 57-8
Hull, Yorkshire 81. 82
Hungary 15, 43, 87, 170
Huntingdon, Huntingdonshire 154
Immigration Tribunal **58**, 57

Ipswich, Suffolk 125
Isaac of Southwark, medieval Jew 112-13
Isaacs, Jeremy 23
Isle of Wight 63, 220
Islington, London 5, 6, 13, 14, 15, 18, 196
Israel 6, 15, 23, 28, 34, 41-2, 43, 67, 75, 102, 129, 152, 154, 156, 158, 164, 173, 177, 180, 181, 186, 198, 199, 207, 209, 210, 216, 217, 218
Israelites, Ancient 97, 227
Italy, Italians 71, 99, 170, 171, 178, 189
Ivanhoe, novel by Sir Walter Scott 66
Izbicki, John 200
J Lyons & Co 51
Jackson, Rabbi Edward 114-15
Jacobs, Dr Elizabeth 110
Jacobs, Jack 142
Jacobs, Rabbi Louis 202, 204
Jakobovits, Chief Rabbi Sir Immanuel vi, 77, 104, 105, 123, 125, 130, 133, 133, 215, 216
Janner, Greville 172, 173
Janner, Sir Barnet 173
Jeffries, Leslie (born David Jaffa) 142
Jersey, Channel Island **159-68**, vii, 29, 31, 87, 91, 93, 119, *162, 163, 166*, 202, 206, 221,
Jerusalem 4, 33, 65, 111, 156, 183, 184, 196, 207
Jewish Association for Mental Health (JAMI) 63
Jewish Burial 45, 82, 163, 224
Jewish Chronicle 46, 84, 87, 98, 109, 155, 160, 208, 217
Jewish Lads and Girls Brigade 194
Jewish Memorial Council (JMC) vi, 63, 87, 88, 115, 218
Jewish Music Festival 67, 197, 198, 211
Jewish Music Heritage Trust 195-6
Jewish Music Institute 11, 14, 173, 195-6, 200, 210-11, 222
Jewish National Fund 154
Jewish Secondary Schools Movement 16, 186
Jews College, now London School for Jewish Studies 100, 114
Jolles, Dr Michael 129-30

Jones, Catherine Heller 78
Josce of Guildford, Medieval Jew 114
Joseph, Chief Rabbi of London under Normans 96
Josephs, John 130-31
JSoc, students' university Jewish society/ies 21, 22, 23, 127, 128, 129, 214
Jurnet of Norwich (medieval figure) 103
JW3, Jewish Community Centre, London 211-12
Kaddish for Terezin (oratario) **198-199**
Kahan, Eli **149**
Kahaneman, Rabbi Yosef Shlomo 207-8
Karachi, Pakistan 181-2, 35, *181*
Kaufmanns of London (handbag firm) Handbags 10
Keble College, Oxford **28**, 24
Kent, English county 86, 120-21, 125, 126, 157, 179
Khartoum, Sudan 35, 179
Kimberley, South Africa 100
Kindertransport 28, 72, 225
King Charles III 193
King Edward I 66, 114
King Edward VIII 71
King George II 108
King George V 184
King George VI 154
King Hassan II, Morocco 76
King Henry I, England 96
King Henry II 64, 65, 97
King Idris, Lbya 178
King Richard (the Lionheart) 65-6
King Stephen, England 97
Kings College London 49
Knapp, Dr Alexander 157, 196
Knight, William Hill, architect 107, 108
Knoller, Freddie 201
Kook, Rabbi Abraham Isaac 207
Kopelowitz, Dr Lionel 68, 95
Koussevitzky, Cantor Jacob 14, 18, 143
Kretinga, Lithuania 135
Krichefski, Wilfred Harod, and Dolly 161, 163, 163, 164
Kristallnacht (pogrom) **200-1**, 73, 226
Kyrenia, Cyprus 39, 175

Labour Party, UK 52, 55, 57, 127, 173, 191
Lancaster, Lancastershire **127-9,** 86, 118, 119, 158, 189
Lankester, Sir Tim 196
Latvia 2, 83
Lawton, Clive 174
Leeds, Yorkshire 67, 68, 80-1, 118, 158
Leicester West, parliamentary constituency 173
Levy, Elkan 217, 218
Levy, Lord Michael 10
Levy, Rabbi Abraham 46
Levy, Raphael 204
Levy, Rev Dr Isaac 39, 203-4
Lewes, Sussex 144
Liberal Jewish Synagogue, St John's Wood 73
Liberal Party, UK 49
Libya **177-8,** 39, 169, 170, 175, 179
Liebenberg, Lazar and Nina 144
Lincoln, Lincolnshire 97
Lithuania 2, 4-5, 6, 7, 17, 71, 81, 83, 135, 136, 207
Littlehampton, West Sussex 145
Litvak (Lithuanian and Latvian) Jews 134-5, 187, 226
Liverpool, Merseyside 14, 52, 81-2, 85, 148, 186,
Livingstone, Rabbi Reuven 218
London School of Economics (LSE) 20, 48
London Society for the Study of Religions, The 73
Lubavitch, Hassidic dynasty (also Chabad) 4, 224, 226
Lucas, Edwin 133
Luton, Bedfordshire 40, 157
Magnus family 120-22
Major, John 40
Makarios III, Archbishop ond President of Cyprus 176
Malaya 39
Malbim (Rabbi Meir Wisser) 34, 226
Malta Jewish community **168-72**, 126, 173, 179, 189,
Manchester Jewish Museum 147
Manchester, English city 4, 26, 69, 72, 81, 82, 85, 143, 156, 206-7

Index

Mandela, Nelson 189
Manor, Arnon 41-2
Marazion, Cornwall 97-8
Marble Arch, London 51, 199
Margate, East Kent 141, 157
Marlowe, Christopher 168
Masorti Jewish community 24, 90, 201, 226
Mendelssohn, Moses, Felix and Rev Meyer 100
Menuhin, Yehudi 76, 195
Merthyr Tydfil synagogue (photo) 150, *150*
Meyer, Sir Manasseh 182-3, 184
Mezrich, Poland 3, 4
Michaels, Mike 148
Middle Temple, Inns of Court 48, 50, 51
Middlesborough 141
Miliband, David 76
Military chaplaincy **33-47**, 13, 44, 60, 80, 88, 123, 173
Miller, Dr Malcolm 196
Ministry of Defence, UK 42
Mirvis, Chief Rabbi Ephraim vi, 130-1, 153, 216
Mirzoeff, Eddie 23
Mitnagdim 4, 5, 225, 227
Mocatta, Frederick David 84
Modern Jewish History, UK school subject 209
Moldova 2
Montague, Sir Samuel (later Lord Swaythling) 14
Montefiore Memorial Synagogue, Grimsby (photo) 83, 94, 95
Montefiore Society, Vienna 15
Montefiore, Rev Hugh 125
Montefiore, Sir Moses 84, 170
Montgomery, Mid Wales **148-9**
Moral Leadership Courses, RAF **39-40**, 44, 206
Morris, Sydney and Martin, MBE 132-4
Multifaith Chaplaincy Centres **127-8**, 128, 189-90, 190, 192, 214, 216
Muslim, Muslims 44, 45, 65, 76, 77, 180, 181, 190, 201, 214
Mussolini, Benito 178

Mysad, Lithuania 7
National Film Theatre, London 210
NATO (North Atlantic Treaty Organisation) **42-4**, 40, 43, 45, 79, 188, 202, 216, 222
Netherlands 44, 71
Nettles, John 164
Neuberger, Rabbi Dame Julia 200, 201
Neve Shalom, peace village, Israel 198
New West End Synagogue, Bayswater 14, 183, 202, 203
Newbury, Berkshire 157
Newcastle, Tyne and Wear 13, 72, 81, 134, 136, 158
Newcastle-under-Lyme, Staffordshire 132, 133
Newman, Rabbi Isaac 34, 35
Newport, Wales **149-50**, 140
Nissim, Mozelle **184-6**, 182
North Shields, Tyne and Wear 141
Northampton, Northamptonshire **129-30**, 65, 97, 118
Norwich, Norfolk **103-6**, 42, 72, 87, 96-7, *105*, 124, 126, 140, 152, 217
Obrart, Judy 195, 197
Office for Jewish Small Communities (OSC) 87, 217-18
Ohayon, Rabbi Reuven 172
Old Bailey, London court 58, 60
Open University 210
Orthodox Judaism **160-1**, 8, 11, 16, 34, 92, 94, 105, 136, 140, 141, 156
Ottoman Empire 168-9, 176, 178
Oxford Centre for Jewish Studies 31
Oxford JSoc 22, 23
Oxford Union 3, 21-3, 49, 58
Oxford, Oxfordshire **20-31**, 3, 10, 13, 33, 41, 48, 49, 58, 71, 80, 90, 120, 139, 192, 208-9
OxfordShir. Jewish community choir 20, 28
Pakistan **181-2**, 35
Pale of Settlement 2, 71, 80, 81
Palestine, British Mandate of 39, 170, 176-7, 207
Parkes Institute, Southampton University 73

Parliament, British 7, 66, 71, 72, 127, 173, 191
Parliamentary Boundaries Commission **57-8**
Parmiters School 10-11, 20, 48, 148,
Patna, India 55
Patterson, Dr David 209
Patterson, José 31-2
Paul, Geoffrey 155
Pears Family Foundation 212
Pentagon, USA 154, 202
Pentonville Prison, London 62
Peterborough, Cambridgeshire **131**, 118
Pevsner, Sir Nikolaus 108
Pinner, London 46-7
Plymouth, Devon 99, 157
Poland, Polish Jews **10**, 2, 3, 4, 5, 12, 17, 43, 71, 81, 83, 134
Pollecoff, Mr (Bangor) 147
Ponevezh Yeshiva 5, 6, 12, 207
Pontypridd, Wales 150
Pope Innocent III 66
Pope John Paul II 46, 75, 76
Pope Pius XI 74
Portsmouth, Hampshire **41**, 45-6, 141, 142, 144, 157
Prague, Czech Republic 198, 199
Prince Phillip **195**, 189, 191, 194
Princess Alexandra 192
Prison chaplaincy **60-3,** 206
Privy Counsel 54
Quaker 68, 104, 145
Queen Elizabeth I 21-22
Queen Elizabeth II **189-94**, 21-22, 42, 74-5, 76, 128, 128, 190, 214
Queen Victoria 108
Quests **154-8,** 125-6, 130, East 157, Northeast 157-8, South 157, Southeast 155-6, West 155-7
Radlett Aerodrome, Hertfordshire 179
Ramsgate, Kent 122 141
Rashi 34, 227
Regal, Alf 160
Regal, Anita 160-2, 166, 167
Regal, David 160-2, 163, 168
Regal, Stephen 160, 162, 167
Regent's Park Mosque 77

Reid, John (Defence Secretary) 44
Reigate, Surrey **132**, 118, 139
Rifkind family 7, 81
Rifkind, Sir Malcolm 7
Robinson, Elaine 186
Rochester, Kent **120-1,** 126
Rockman, Mr (religion teacher) 12-13
Romain, Rabbi Jonathan 69
Roman Catholic 45, 46, 73, 74, 96, 190, 215-16,
Rosen, Rabbi Jeremy 156
Rosen, Rabbi Michael "Micky" 155-6
Rosen. Rabbi Yaakov Kopel 155-6
Rosenthal, Daniel 106
Rosenzweig, Alexander 157
Rosh Hashana, Jewish festival 18, 39, 89, 101, 117, 135, 162, 165, 175, 206, 221, 224, 227, 228, 229,
Roth, Cecil 21
Rothschild, Nathan Mayer 170
Rothschild, Rabbi Walter 68, 69
Royal Air Force (RAF) xi, 33-4, 37, 49, 80, 86, 131, 138-9, 175
Royal Navy **120-1, 45-6,** 39, 41, 42,160,
Royle, Prof Edward 68-9
Rubin, Theo 114, 115
Russia, Russians **2-3,** 13, 44, 150, 51, 71, 81, 82, 108
Sacks, Chief Rabbi Lord Jonathan **217-18,** vi, 26, 75, 77, 111, 166, 215, 216,
Saigon, Vietnam 86-7
Saladin 65
Salmon, Cyril (Baron Salmon of Sandwich) and Montague 51
Samuels, Charles 100
Sandhurst, Berkshire 192
Sandler, Albert (Abraham) 142
Sassoon, Raphael 182
Schonfeld, Rabbi Dr Victor **16-17,** 8-9, 15-16
Schonfeld, Rabbi Solomon **17-19,** 204
School of Oriental and African Studies, University of London 14, 33, 196, 198
Scotland **151-4,** 7, 26, 85, 87, 126, 152
Scotland Yard 56
Scottish Council of Jewish Communities 152

Index

Sebag-Montefiore, Oliver 125
Sebag-Montefiore, Sir Joseph 170
Segal, Jeannie Pearl **6-9,** 8, 10, 17, 22, 151, 187, 207
Segal, Rev Bernard Lewis 5-7, 8, 9, 12, 207
Segal, Sarah 7, 9
Senator, Ronald 198
Sephardi Jews **168-70,** 2, 46, 70-1, 106, 157, 180, 187-8, 227, 228
Shabbat, Jewish sabbath **17-19,** 21, 23, 31, 37, 40, 46, 59, 62, 111, 124, 129, 130, 136, 224, 225, 228
Shankar, Ravi 196
Sheridan, Rabbi Sybil 69
Shipton, Sidney 77
Shirley, Dame Stephanie 28
Shomberg family, Colchester 124
Shoreditch 10
Sicily 65, 169, 171
Silman, H 104
Silman, Julius 155
Silver family (Oxford) 23
Silverston, Jennifer 111
Simmonds, Lionel 87
Simpson, WW (Methodist minister) 73-4
Singapore **182-6, 179,** 35, 38, 39, 40, 171, 181, *183, 184,* 187
Singer, Malcolm 68, 195-6
Singers Hill Synagogue, Birmingham 37
Skidelsky, Boris 13
Society of Jews and Christians 73
Soho, London 207
Solomon, Leo 95
Solomon, Rabbi Norman 68
South Africa 100, 171, 189
Southampton, Hampshire 73, 141, 157
Southend-on-Sea, Essex 85
Soviet Jewry, campaign for 173
Spanish and Portuguese Community (Sephardi), London 46, 167-8
Spiro Ark and Spiro Institute 211-12
Spiro family, Robin, Nitza and Saul **206-12,** 203, 203, 204, *210*
St Albans, Hertfordshire 42, 54, 157
St Brelade's, Jersey 162, 162, 221

St Catherine's College, Oxford 20, 32, 49, 192
St Christopher's Place, London 208
St Giles Church, Cripplegate 196
St Helier, Jersey 161, 163
St James's Palace, London 77, 181, 192
St John's Wood, London 23, 73, 78, 204, 208-9
St Paul's Cathedral, London **195-7,** 11, *197*
Staffordshire, English county **132-34**
Stamford Hill, London 2, 4, 8-9, 16, 146
Stamler, Sam, QC 50
Stern, Jack 106
Sternberg, Michael, QC 76
Sternberg, Sir Sigmund **74-6,** 75, 77, 79, 195, 197
Stoke Newington, London 1-2, 2, 8-9, 13, 15
Stoke-on-Trent, Staffordshire **132-4,** 118
Stone, Norma and Ruth 125
Stroud, Gloucestershire 157
Sudan 179
Suffolk, English county 62, 125, 205, 206,
Sunderland, Tyne and Wear **134-8,** 81, 88, 118, 137, 139, 160, 164
Sunkin, Prof Maurice (Colchester) 126
Surrey, English county 46, 61, 112-18, 132, 139
Susser, Rabbi Bernard 97
Sussex, English county 86, 141-2, 142-5, 145-6, 157
Swansea, Wales **150-1,** 157
Tajar, Rabbi Josef 170
Tarsis, Rabbi 18
Taub, Daniel 23, 28-9
Taylor family, Aberdeen 153
Taylor, Ronny and Linda (Eastbourne) 143, 144
Tel Aviv, Israel, and TA University 156, 164, 198, 199, 207
Temple, William, Archbishop of York 74
Templeton Prize 77
Terezin, Czechoslovakia (also Theresienstadt) **198-200**
Thailand 187
Thorpe, Jeremy 49
Three Faiths Forum 77

Tolstoy, Count Dmitri 51
Tolstoy, Nikolai 51
Trotter, Janet 110
Turner, Rev Reuben 14
Tzar Alexander II 3, 71
Union of Orthodox Hebrew
    Congregations 15, 16, 17
United States 21, 69, 71, 81-2, 152, 154, 166, 187, 199
United Synagogue 14, 46, 63, 85, 104-5, 110, 114. 131, 135, 145, 154, 161, 165, 206-7, 216, 217
University of Bath **118-19**, 140
University of Cambridge **119-20**, 60, 71, 202, 119
University of East Anglia 86, 104, 129
University of Essex 86, 123, 125, 126
University of Exeter 101-2
University of Oxford 20-32, 3, 10, 13, 33, 48-9, 58, 71, 80, 90, 119, 120, 139, 192, 208-9
University of Southampton 73
University of Surrey 116
University of York 67, 68-9, 86, 129
Uxbridge, RAF base 34, 35
Vatican 43, 75, 199
Vietnam **186-7**
Wales **146-51**, 85, 87, 139-40, 150, 157
Waley Cohen, Sir Robert 125
Walnes, Gillian 28
Walter, Rev William (chaplain) **65-6**
Warsaw Pact 43
Wartski, Isidore 147
Warwick, Warwickshire 86, 129
Webber, Michael 78, 111
Weisman, Brian, older son **205-6**, vi, xii, 29, 31, 40, 62-3, 109, 165, 193, *193*, 194, 204, 221, 222

Weisman, Daniel, younger son **205-6**, vi, xii, 40, 109, 163, 194, 204, 206, 221, 222
Weisman, Jacob (Reb Yankel), grandfather **5-6**, 12, 13, 15, 34
Weisman, Maurice, brother 8, *8*, 9
Weisman, Rosalie **202-5**, 40, 43, 75, 78, 102, 109, 111, 126-7, 143, 145, 160, 165, 168, 187, 192, 193, *203*, *205*, 207, 209, 216, 221-2
Weismn, David, father **3**, **8-10,** *8*, 12-13, 15
Wells, Willy 52
West London Synagogue, Reform 79, 121, 199, 200-201
Westminster Abbey **200-201**, 103
Weymouth, Dorset 93
Willesden, London 56, 180, 204, 206
William the Conqueror 64, 96, 97
Winchester, Hampshire **78-9**, 157
Wiseman, Group Captain Donald **33-4**
Wittenberg, Rabbi Jonathan 201
Wittering, RAF base 131
Woburn House, London 35, 40, 87-8
Worthing, West Sussex **145-6**, 143, 157
Yakar **155-6**
Yatesbury, Wiltshire **138-9,** 118
Yemen **179-81**
York Anglo-Israel Association 67
York, Yorkshire, and York Minster **66-70**, xi, 63, 67, 74, 86, 195, 199
Zack, Rev Chaim 143
Zahn, Rabbi S 164
Zanzibar 54
Zelah, Cornwall 87, 98
Zemel Choir 68, 69, 78
Zionist societies 22, 154, 183-4, 224